W9-AED-260

YOU ARE ABOUT TO GO ON A JOURNEY unlike any other you have ever taken. It is a survey of life on earth led by an archangel.

The tour begins with a pilgrimage to the place where Christ is born. Moving back and forth in time, scenes of history appear, some so old they have long been forgotten. Others which took place in a distant galaxy.

Soon you find yourself in the midst of a great drama, in fact a great battle of light and darkness, of good and evil, that began long, long ago.

You learn the unknown story behind the confrontations of Jesus and John the Baptist with the Pharisees and Sadducees, why there is terrorism, and about the hidden side of international power politics. You observe the connection between guerrilla warfare, pornography, and assassination. And discover the archangels' strategy for dealing with the problems of our time.

From the point of view of an archangel, you learn about karma and reincarnation. And what makes a Jim Jones tick. Or a Dan White. And discover Gabriel's opinion of the Supreme

Court. With new clarity you behold the inner workings of the cosmos, study diagrams charting the flow of energy from the Great Central Sun, and understand the unseen forces that shape your existence.

Archangel Gabriel takes you through the twists and turns of life evolving as the players return to the stage of earth. The curtain is going up on the final act. Some of the characters may seem strange at first. Others are familiar, perhaps too familiar. And one face, well . . . it is your own.

Throughout the journey the great mysteries of life unfold—unknown aspects of psychology, keys to self-discovery and self-fulfillment. And how the soul travels the path of the white light that leads from the twilight world of relative good and evil to the great God Self.

This is not a fantasy, an excursion down the yellow brick road. It is the quest for the Holy Grail—a journey that must be taken.

MYSTERIES OF THE HOLY GRAIL

THE QUEST FOR THE HOLY GRAIL

Be thou faithful unto death, and I will give thee a crown of life.

BP605
.S73 P76

ARCHANGEL GABRIEL

MYSTERIES OF THE HOLY GRAIL

RECORDED BY

author - ELIZABETH CLARE PROPHET

KANSAS SCHOOL OF RELIGION
UNIVERSITY OF KANSAS
1300 OREAD AVENUE
LAWRENCE, KANSAS 66044

SUMMIT UNIVERSITY PRESS®

spirit writings

ARCHANGEL GABRIEL
MYSTERIES OF THE HOLY GRAIL

Copyright © 1978, 1979, 1983, 1984 Summit University Press

All rights reserved. No part of this book may be reproduced in any form or by any electronic or mechanical means including information storage and retrieval systems without permission in writing from the publisher, except by a reviewer who may quote brief passages in a review. For information, address Summit University Press, Box A, Malibu, CA 90265 or Box A, Livingston, MT 59047.

Summit University Press and are registered trademarks of Church Universal and Triumphant, Inc. All rights to their use are reserved.

Library of Congress Catalog Card Number: 83-51154
International Standard Book Number: 0-916766-64-0

This book is set in 12 point Elegante with 2 points of lead
Printed in the United States of America
First Printing

SUMMIT UNIVERSITY PRESS®
LOS ANGELES

And it came to pass, when I, even I, Daniel, had seen the vision and sought for the meaning, then, behold, there stood before me as the appearance of a man.

And I heard a man's voice between the banks of Ulai, which called and said, Gabriel, make this man to understand the vision.

So he came near where I stood; and when he came, I was afraid and fell upon my face. But he said unto me, Understand, O son of man: for at the time of the end shall be the vision.

Now as he was speaking with me, I was in a deep sleep on my face toward the ground, but he touched me and set me upright.

And he said, Behold, I will make thee know what shall be in the last end of the indignation; for at the time appointed the end shall be. . . .

And the vision of the evening and the morning which was told is true; wherefore shut thou up the vision, for it shall be for many days.

And I, Daniel, fainted and was sick certain days. Afterward I rose up and did the king's business; and I was astonished at the vision, but none understood it.

Daniel 8

The Messenger Elizabeth Clare Prophet

TO THE CHILDREN OF THE SUN

I am Gabriel, that stand in the presence of God; and am sent to speak unto thee and to shew thee these glad tidings.

CONTENTS

Elizabeth Clare Prophet

on

Archangel Gabriel

And whiles I was speaking, and praying, and confessing my sin and the sin of my people Israel, and presenting my supplication before the LORD my God for the holy mountain of my God;

Yea, whiles I was speaking in prayer, even the man Gabriel, whom I had seen in the vision at the beginning, being caused to fly swiftly, touched me about the time of the evening oblation.

And he informed me, and talked with me, and said, O Daniel, I am now come forth to give thee skill and understanding.

At the beginning of thy supplications the commandment came forth, and I am come to shew thee; for thou art greatly beloved. Therefore, understand the matter, and consider the vision.

Daniel 9

I can truthfully say that the angel Gabriel is my friend. So blessed am I to know this emissary of heaven that I must share his love with all whom I meet and proclaim his fiery message.

In truth, Gabriel is the friend of many servants of God who do not identify his guidance as something apart from God or life or their own striving spirits. Though quite accustomed to his loving presence, his comfort and instruction, his courage to do battle with the Adversary in any and every form, they do not stop to think that these all-pervading attributes signal the presence of someone very special, or that they are entertaining the angel of the LORD "unawares." (Heb. 13:2)

So often we think that our inspiration and happiness simply well up from somewhere inside of ourselves, or that our compositions and inventions, hunches and hypotheses, sudden flashes of perception or bold new ideas are self-created out of the genes or genius of the mind or memory bank of the planet. While these occurrences may indeed be the products of man's spiritual and mental evolution, more often than not angelic servants of God sent by one of the archangels are standing by, magnetizing the higher intelligence to our auras, charging our personal energy fields with the light from far-off worlds or their own momentum of buoyant love in the service of the nature kingdom and the planetary evolutions.

These guardians convey the purity of Elohim who created not only angels, but elemental spirits of fire, air, water, and earth to be our gentle and powerful helpers as we seek to take dominion over our world, over time and space and the inner planes of being.

When one first begins to identify God's angels as companions and teachers who are a natural part of everyday life, one's heart leaps for joy to discover that the never-failing Presence of the Lord is often communicated to us by his hosts, God's messengers who bring us good tidings of great joy of the ever-new birth of the living Christ in our hearts.

Formidable as the Defender of the Woman and her seed, trusted Friend of the Most High, Gabriel has at least "ten thousand times ten thousand" legions in his command. He is known as the Archangel of the Fourth Ray—representative of the Light of the World Mother and bearer of the Holy Spirit's sacred fires by which every soul who is come from God is baptized into his kingdom.

Archangel Gabriel is the friend of God and man whom all lovers of the Light can claim as their special confidant and advisor. This blessed one has taught me much about the lawful communion of the saints dwelling in these lower octaves of earth with the saints moving in the higher octaves which we call heaven. An eyewitness of antediluvian epochs, he has also told me about the books of our father Enoch, vividly interpreting the battle of Light and Darkness. Archangel Gabriel has spoken about the mysteries of life and death, this world and the next, and the nature of an ages-old conspiracy to dominate the minds and souls and hearts of the lifewaves not only of planet Earth, but of this and other systems of worlds.

He has given me the Holy Spirit's instruction concerning the knowledge of relative good and evil, and how it was transmitted to our first earthly parents by fallen angels who conspired to tear the veil of innocence from Adam and Eve that they might no longer see the LORD God face to face—and their progeny be led astray for thousands of years.

Once the entire scenario of the temptation and the expulsion had taken place, it was the Archangels Gabriel, Michael, and Uriel who comforted our father and mother and sustained the holy contact between their souls and the planes of higher consciousness where they formerly had dwelt.

Thus the archangels became the chief guardians of the seed of the Ancient of Days and of the sons of light who went forth out of the ancient mystery schools to teach the children of men concerning the ways of the seed of the Wicked One and the snares of the Watchers—that breed of cursing fallen ones who corrupted the daughters of men. (Gen. 6:2, 4; Enoch 7:1–11)

Self-announced to the father of John the Baptist—"I am Gabriel that stand in the presence of God"—the archangel has diagramed Armageddon, introducing the most difficult concepts of Absolute Good and Absolute Evil. As I listened in wonder, this Man*(ifestation)* of God led me to the understanding of the one as God-Good and the other as an intergalactic force consisting of hierarchies of rebellious angels who fell from grace with Lucifer, Satan, Beelzebub, etc. By an ancient rite sealed with the blood of the holy innocents, these 'fallen ones' vowed to oppose—absolutely—that God-Good not only in heaven, but especially on earth in the hearts of His true sons and daughters.

Archangel Gabriel drew the curtain on the awful scene (showing me the actual records inscribed on the ethers) and pointed to that event as the origin of every conspiracy that has since been waged against the Freedom and the Enlightenment of the children of God.

He then showed me the record of our founding fathers signing the Declaration of Independence. He explained that at inner levels these sons of God were in fact inscribing in light their response to the ancient Luciferian declaration of war against the Christs—the sons of God dwelling among the people of earth as their true shepherds. At inner levels that document bears the heading Declaration of Independence of the Sons of God from the Tyranny of the Fallen Angels.

My beloved friend has taught me God's laws concerning the science of the spoken Word and the power of God's flame within the hearts of his own children to counteract the layers of illusion and the forces both subtle and fierce of the "cast down ones" (so named *Nephilim* after the war of the skies in which Archangel Michael cast the seed of the Wicked One out of heaven to take physical embodiment in the earth, Rev. 12:7 ff.) pitted against the reality of the soul and its destined reunion with the Almighty One.

Today there are millions of angels who never lost their first estate, never followed Lucifer and the rest in the Great Rebellion, who are yet serving under the archangels of the seven rays, ministering to the needs of the Adamic evolution, ever striving to restore them to the Edenic state of their higher consciousness.

In my volume entitled *Forbidden Mysteries of Enoch: The Untold Story of Men and Angels,* I have recorded some astounding insights on the above, given to me by the archangel of the annunciation. These will provide the reader with invaluable background on the cosmology of Evil and on the mysteries of the Holy Grail, which contain the keys to the soul's overcoming of the interplanetary force of anti-Good.

In another vein, one very precious encounter I had with beloved Gabriel which I would like to share—a mystery unveiled which, then, is no longer a mystery—reveals a beautiful facet of the angel that I pray you also will come to cherish:

As I was walking down the street in Santa Barbara one autumn day in 1974, I sensed a presence and found myself accompanied by none other than Gabriel himself! He graciously escorted me into a café; and as I sipped a cup of tea and wrote his words on a napkin, he dictated to me the program for a seminar he directed me to hold in San Francisco called "Portals of Purity."

Certainly not a title that would have occurred to me, but one that sounded awesome, much like the mind of an archangel! (When dealing with the angelic host, I am always impressed at their naturalness and daring, yet deeply aware of an inexhaustible strength and the power of the Godhead with them that moves with their garments as they move, unconcealable yet subdued out of their charity toward our lesser state.)

Well, I held that seminar in San Francisco as directed and many souls made firm contact with God and their own beloved I AM Presence through the aura of the archangel. The portals of purity Gabriel was talking about, I found out, are the seven spiritual centers in our bodies called chakras. His mission that weekend was to purify these centers in all who attended, to assist them in becoming portals of purity—the open door to God's light transferred through their chakras to help fill world need and alleviate world suffering.

The meditations for the purification of the chakras which he gave can be used again and again (via the electronic tape recording) by those just now renewing the acquaintance of the friend they've always had in Archangel Gabriel. Subsequently, the teachings of Serapis Bey on the ascension (also part of the path of the fourth ray) were transmitted to my heart by the tutoring of this most blessed archangel. These I have also carefully preserved for souls who are looking toward the New Day of their resurrection in Light.

One of the most memorable experiences of my life took place when the messenger of God descended from the heights of cosmic consciousness in answer to my call for his intercession in the healing of a sweet child of light, who, by some freak of darkness, had been shot at close range with a .30-06 rifle by the neighborhood bully. The single bullet entered his right side, went through part of his liver and spleen, and passed three-eighths of an inch from the heart, shattering his elbow and finally lodging in his wrist.

I saw with my own eyes the skill, the love, the infinite patience of Gabriel as he tended this child day by day for months until he was made whole. The doctors said the only reason he survived was his "will to live." He came to be known as the miracle child of Kootenai Hospital.

To see the heavens opened, to see an archangel whose daily duties take him to the Great Central Sun and across the galaxies so personally involved in the life of one child—one beautiful child—is enough to move my soul to eternal devotion and sacrifice, that the gifts of God so readily available through prayer and the dynamic decree might be placed directly in the hands of the loving servants of Christ on earth and all who can believe in the attendance of holy angels in their lives.

Many believers prayed for that child and not I alone. But I was the witness—in full waking consciousness, with my eyes open wide to the inner planes, I saw how the fire of my heart penetrated the veil and made the initial contact with Archangel Gabriel by the call of deep love that always compels love's answer.

To be sure, my call was reinforced in a prayer vigil of the hours held by classmates, family and friends for one small boy who had a right to live, whose heart had earned the attention of an archangel. Gabriel was *the* Friend who championed his cause like a Knight of cosmos, like the Good Physician, so that he could laugh and play and sing and grow with the wind and the stars to become a man and to fulfill his destiny—not alone on earth, but in the vast beyond that is still his to discover by the grace of the hosts of the LORD and one glorious archangel named Gabriel.

You can imagine my joy when this child, after months of operations, hospitalization, and convalescence, walked up to the altar a year later on Easter morning to receive the baptism of Jesus Christ. With tears blinding my eyes, I said to Stephen: "Are you whole?" He answered: "Yes, I am whole!" Praise the LORD and praise him in his servant Archangel Gabriel, our friend!

Yes, he is the same one who visited both Mary and Joseph, and Zacharias and Elisabeth, and the prophet Daniel and countless pure hearts throughout the centuries whose deep desire to serve God has magnetized those special favors and healings we all need in order to make our way Home.

Gabriel actually announces the birth of souls of light to sons and daughters of God who have drawn the circle of marriage and family as a holy thing, a life's offering of love and service on the altar of Alpha and Omega. But all do not see the angelic visitor, all do not identify the promptings of the heart, the salutation of the soul, or the first leaping of the child in the womb as a part of the intercession of Gabriel.

The holy aura of motherhood, the bliss of being with child, the comfort of the father's presence with the mother-to-be and with the soul swimming in that 'cosmic' womb—all these most precious, ethereal, intangible yet very real inner experiences of life are enhanced, protected, and monitored by many angels who serve in the legions of the archangels. The care our Father extends to us through his angels is incomparable. What would we do without the angels and the birds and the sunrise—and God's love—on this dark star!

Perhaps one of the most interesting and instructive experiences I have had with Archangel Gabriel as my teacher, repeated as if for emphasis on a number of occasions, has been in praying for the vision, the selflessness, and the discipleship of some who have come to me for consolation and wisdom on the Path. I have held the hand of souls greatly tormented by their confrontation with life's choices and the temptation to embody the unreal instead of the Real.

I have seen with my own eyes and I do bear witness before all the world that Archangel Gabriel has placed his mighty presence as an aura of light around such ones as these in the hour of their distress. I have seen the state of blessedness and joy return to their countenances, "just like the sun came out"—crestfallen faces elated with the instantaneous assurance of God's presence. I have seen Gabriel sustain his vigil, actually employing the power of the aura of an archangel to realign individual consciousness to its own Divine Self and Divine Plan.

And then I have watched as Gabriel, by cosmic law, would withdraw his aura from the one in need in order that that one might exercise free will and choose whether or not to continue to discipline himself, or herself, in the consciousness of God. For all must choose, all must elect to be the chalice of God's light. Each one must quest and find his own Holy Grail.

Thus there comes the moment when the archangel, having extended the very presence of the Godhead to a troubled soul, must withdraw and allow the individual to make his choice. How painful this must be to one who stands between two worlds ministering to life which cannot or will not see. The question that must be answered by the soul, then, is whether or not to remain in the harmony of God's love by entertaining angels' auras not "unawares" but voluntarily, by enlisting their aid; whether or not to summon the will to pursue the mastery of mind and heart through the contemplation of God-Good and His service to all life.

I have watched as one by one the devils of the mind would return as doubts and fears, an absence of self-worth, self-condemnation and self-pity; and the struggling soul, incapable or undesirous of retaining the vision so effortlessly gained, now just as easily would lose the contact through sheer absence of heart-power to hold on to the 'garment' (consciousness/aura) of so mighty an emissary whose identity the troubled one scarce took note of.

From witnessing the gap between heavenly and earthly auras, and realizing the responsibility of the individual to bridge that gap by free will, I learned to pray for the power of the Spirit to impart the vision of soul-freedom and the glories of the Endless Day that would kindle the spirit's native desire and will to be liberated from the addictions of astral (lower vibrating) unrealities.

The great lesson I learned in these experiences, in which Gabriel interceded by the sheer imploring of my prayer (as much to instruct me in the universal observance of free will as to help one whose desire for help was, in fact, not as great as my own desire for that one to receive the help!), was that individuals must walk by the law of their own karma (the causes and effects they have set in motion by word and deed in this and previous lives) and by their own ability to magnify the LORD through holy prayer and deep devotion. I learned why the archangels and ministering angels must, more often than not, stand back and let people's karma or individual free will or nonbelief seal them from the intercession of the Divine Helper.

I learned that people must want change with all their hearts if the transforming power of an archangel is to have any permanent effect in their lives; that they must not only want change, but be diligent in maintaining new levels of self-mastery gained by trial and error, striving and true discipleship on the Path—as well as by those extraordinary moments which may occur but once in centuries of embodiments: the direct transfusion of the energy of the Great Central Sun through the magnetic forcefield of an archangel.

I also gained wisdom in scientific prayer—

to ask what is lawful for the individual and to pray for the healing of the stubborn will and the froward heart, that by illumined obedience the portals of consciousness might open as petals of humble receptivity to God's ministering servants.

I learned that even the archangels themselves must obey cosmic law where the necessary ingredients are not present to allow their gracious intercession.

What are these ingredients? To list a few: the pure and undefiled love of God and of the divine spark in his children; the honorable maintenance of a relationship with God based on humility, good works done to his glory, and the pursuit of holiness; and participation in the hierarchical chain of one's own evolutionary being through the communion of saints, the intercession of the Holy Ghost, and the progressive revelation of the Spirit of the Ascended Master Jesus Christ through the personages of the heavenly hosts.

This oneness with God and with our brothers and sisters above and below includes not only angels, but also other ascended masters and beings of great light embracing God's consciousness in the ladder of life we are also mounting.

God's myriad manifestations of himself, created as we are for his Self-expression, are spiritual beings who people the universes with a love, an expertise, and an excellence readily available to us, which they do gladly and freely transfer to us in answer to our call. These are the graduates of earth and many planetary schoolrooms.

Yes, beloved, Life is grand and noble in its self-transcending purposes. There *is* meaning. There *is* more than meets the eye of earthlings. And some have found the Way, found the Grail, stepped through the portal and are in this very moment living the future we will one day enter as unfettered spirits at last free from the delusions of self.

The call to God for help, then, is a must if we are to receive that help. But the momentum of daily prayer or the recitation of Hindu mantras, the Our Father or the Hail Mary, Buddhist chants, Jewish liturgies or Moslem recitations of the Koran weaves an aura of receptivity and a halo of yellow fire that leads to the 'softening' and eventual 'opening' of the 'crown chakra' (the portal of wisdom, signifying the soul's *wise dominion,* marked by the soft spot on a baby's head) in the devotee and his establishment thereby of an extraordinary connection with the saints robed in white, described by John the Revelator. These with the "ten thousand times ten thousand" (Rev. 7:9; 5:11) comprise the heavenly order known as the Great White Brotherhood.

Loving the Lord thy God—the Great I AM—with all thy heart and soul and mind, and loving thy neighbor as thyself, keeping the commandments of God set forth by his prophets, living a clean life, maintaining cleanliness of heart, conversation, thought and feeling, refraining from gossip, complaining and back-biting and the spirit of condemnation (that hell-fire and damnation, ungodly fear and torment that characterizes the preachments of the false pastors)—all of these precepts, followed with sweetness and fragrant love, contribute to our daily contact with the ever-present angels.

However, as all who have ascended the holy mountain know, pursuing the great truths of any of the world's religions revealed by the prophets, avatars, and mystics of all ages—the *living* of true religion twenty-four hours a day—does result in that friendship with God and God's emissaries whose inevitable corollary is "enmity with the world." (James 4:4)

For those who treasure the heavenly contact more than "the things of this world"—more than the roads of success and the cults of personality and the morass of power struggles amongst the gods—I can assure you that, leaving behind these things which you will never miss and hardly remember, you *can* find the thread of contact with your own Divine Reality and a destiny beyond the stars that is yours to rediscover.

One of the best teachers I know to assist you in working out your destiny (salvation) is the unfailing, the Beloved, the Friend—Archangel Gabriel. May the teachings he has given to me, set forth in the following pages, unravel for you some of life's greatest mysteries and bring to you the understanding of your

True Self as the Holy Grail. May you accept your raison d'être to be a chalice for God's light even as you become that light. As one who has searched for many lifetimes and found the Friends of Light, I can witness in Truth to the fact that the glory of God is available to all who pursue it with honor.

Seated in the snow, alone on my holy mountain, I pen these words with profound and unspeakable gratitude for the privilege of recording the word of the LORD sent and signified to me by the angel Gabriel. May you read and run as a torchbearer of the stars whence you have descended "trailing clouds of glory"—and to which you may, if you so choose, one day return.

Elizabeth Clare Prophet

P.S. I hope by the time you finish reading this book you will say, "I too can say, Archangel Gabriel is my friend!"

November 20, 1983
Royal Teton Ranch
Montana, U.S.A.

I

Archangel Gabriel on the Mystery of the Christ

I

Children of the Light of the Mother,

I AM Gabriel archangel that stand in the presence of God.[1] I am sent by Alpha and Omega this day to stand in the presence of each and every son and daughter of God sojourning on earth. I salute thee, O child of the Most High God, in the name of the newborn Christ, the Christmas Child who even now, at the lateness of the hour, knocks at the door of thy heart.

Would you prepare him room? Would you receive the infant Messiah, helpless in his tiny form yet full of hope for the salvation of the world? The little Child, most fragile as he takes his first breath of the Holy Spirit, is yet a descending sacred fire, truly a gift from on high, that the people who have walked in darkness might see the great Light of His appearing.[2]

The appearing is that of the Lord God. Let us go together to see the place where He is born. Let us journey with the wise men as these three masters of the East come to commemorate the Word incarnate in Christ Jesus, the Son of God who declared his Sonship[3] so that you also might find your true self made in his image and after his likeness.[4] Truly it is out of the image of the only begotten Son of the Most High God that you were created, O beloved sons and daughters of God[5]—and that in the name of the Father, of the Son, and of the Holy Ghost!

The darkening hour of world chaos and confusion—the eruption of elemental life here and there as the blessed beings of air, fire, water, and earth seek to hold the balance for the coming of the Lord Christ into every heart—but signals the coming of the darkest night and in the midst thereof the Day Star of His appearing.[6]

It is the majestic light of the Holy of Holies that arcs across the sky and with measured descent, as shooting star, makes its abode in the devotee's upraised chalice in the very heart of God's children. Indeed they have confessed that he is LORD, that The Christ in the person of Jesus is come in the flesh![7]

Lo, I AM the messenger of the Almighty, and I have anointed my messenger on earth to sound the soundless sound of the light of God's coming into every temple swept clean by the purifying sacred fires of the Holy Spirit, invoked as the violet flame[8] from the sacred heart of Jesus, the immaculate heart of Mary, and the purple fiery heart of Saint Germain.

It is the message of salvation unto everyone that believeth[9] in the incarnate Word that I bear as my Christmas offering, concluding the year and dedicating winter solstice to the emerging light of Mother and Child within you, blessed ones.

The seven archangels[10] stand on the crest of Ascension Hill. Where is Ascension Hill?[11] It is the place marked by the cosmic cross of white fire—the sign of the convergence of the light of Alpha and Omega[12] where the Lord Christ is born, the Bethlehem Babe within you, and where that very same Lord Christ ascends to be reborn in heaven as in earth, in Spirit as in Matter.

Where is Ascension Hill? It is the place marked by that cross of white light, designated for your new birth first as Christ's child, then maturing on the path of initiation, following the disciplines of the Lord Christ—in Love, by Love, and for Love—until the newborn, reborn soul becomes the ascendant son and daughter—born to eternal Life because He lived, because He became flesh and blood, thereby sanctifying those who had descended into the planes of Matter, souls gone astray from the reality of everlasting Life.

Now the same Son of God, the Lord Christ, is come to be born within you, your own blessed Christ Self whom Jeremiah foreknew as The LORD Our Righteousness.[13] I bid you this eve of the Christ Mass, beloved sons and daughters of God, to celebrate with the Saviour Jesus Christ the coming of the Word incarnate within you as the Manchild.[14] For Alpha and Omega have sent me to announce to you the breaking of the bread of Life.[15]

This dispensation from the Great Central Sun is of a most extraordinary Presence of the Cosmic Christ overshadowing and blending with your own Christ Self, thereby increasing in a darkening world the light of Jesus Christ and the blessed servant-sons and daughters of God ascended.

The increase of light must come, my beloved, if the challenges of the coming year and the coming decade [the 1980s] are to be met. And so the seven archangels stand with the one hundred and forty and four thousand who are with the Lamb on Mount Sion.[16] We stand with all who have risen into that higher consciousness of the Lamb who is the Christ of Jesus and the Christ of the offspring of the Most High.

And the mountain is the holy mountain of God to which the prophets, messengers, and anointed ones have ascended to commune with the LORD God.[17] There, through his name I AM THAT I AM,[18] they have discovered the mystery of their very own life, the state of being God (i.e., the chalice for God's flame) in heaven and in earth—I AM WHO I AM—*the Holy Grail.*

The seven archangels summon all devotees

of Love both within and without the religious movements of the world. Traversing and transcending lines of doctrine and dogma, we summon the elect who have determined to stand in the place of the Holy of Holies to receive the Lord Christ, to become vessels for God and therefore to know that God through them will indeed save the earth in this age.

We summon the elect who will make their calling and election sure[19] through a studied and disciplined action of the Law, through an ingenious tapping of the inner resources of the great causal body of Life, through diligence and effort in the Holy Spirit, and finally through an understanding of the integration of the Word made flesh.

This Christmas Eve, as Christ is born within you to live to do the Father's work every day of the balance of your life, receive then the seven archangels into your midst.

Yes, God will multiply himself in earth as in heaven through the dedication of simple hearts, tender hearts, intelligent hearts who know unerringly the science of being: that only as God lives within them—as a sacred fire interpenetrating atoms, molecules, and cells of consciousness—can they live to know and see him as he is,[20] yea, to be in him simply the fullness of himself. For, as poets and apostles have confirmed, in him we live and move and have our being, for we are also his offspring.[21]

And it shall come to pass because he has

willed it so, O mortal. And because you have willed to make that will your own, I say, you are no more mortal but immortal!—yes, here and now in time and space. It is his mandate: For this corruptible *must* put on incorruption, and this mortal *must* put on immortality![22]

So, then, mount the mountain of adversity, of sin, disease, and death—of your sowings and your reapings[23] that are unreal. And let the Flame of Life, the rising caduceus of Alpha and Omega, burst from the fiery core of that Matter miscreation to consume by Trinity's light the mountain of karmic adversity.

Now raise up instead, with Christmas angels winging in and the Spirit of the Resurrection conflagration, a mountain of blessedness. That billowing, blazing, rainbow radiance will realign the energy of your being until you behold the mountain of adversity now become the Great Pyramid of Life. And that Great Pyramid, my beloved, is your very own Ascension Hill, the place you have prepared for the Word to incarnate in Matter and in Spirit.

It is upon *that* Ascension Hill that we stand this Christmastide. For some, it is in the etheric plane waiting to be made manifest by the good works of devotees of the will of God—by the geometry of their very own self-awareness in the star of the Christmas pageant. Others will see at Camelot a hill named Ascension Hill by devotees of the mysteries of the Holy Grail as the place to contemplate His word: "I go to prepare a place for you . . . that where I AM, there ye may be also,"[24] a place to renew the vow to the Ancient of Days[25] made by every son and daughter of God come to earth to bring peace, goodwill, enlightenment, and love:

"Lord God Almighty, I go forth in thy name to bring to thy children upon earth the message of the way back Home, the memory of Alpha and Omega, and the understanding of the ascent through thy Word incarnate in the white light of Mother. I will live again and again to rekindle hearts to the very love of thee, O my Lord."

Blessed ones, tarry with us this Christmas season. Meditate, contemplate, and activate the light of the Holy of Holies within you as we gather round to dedicate the Star of His Presence reborn within you, O ye blessed of the Most High.

I AM

GABRIEL

I ANNOUNCE TO YOU
THE POTENTIAL OF YOUR VICTORY
IN THE NAME OF
THE SAVIOUR CHRIST JESUS
AMEN

II

Archangel Gabriel on the Mystery of Salvation

II

O Man, O Woman of Earth,
Hearken to the Voice of God!

I AM Gabriel, messenger of the LORD. I stand in the earth midst the celebration of Advent. Yet scarcely do I find souls attuned to the reality of His coming, souls with the capacity to note the import of the Incarnation in Jesus Christ, the Saviour.

When I announced to Mary, "therefore also that holy thing which shall be born of thee shall be called the Son of God,"[1] I came with the message of salvation unto all people, that through him they might know the indwelling Light and through him rise to the full potential of the God Presence. In him was the hope of the world proclaimed by the hosts of the LORD singing glory to God in the highest.[2]

Yet, two thousand years after the birth of the Lord Christ, that hope has dwindled to the distorted specter of man nailed to a cross of materialism, of a death that is unreal and yet has torment because they know not the way of the resurrection. The earth is suspended upon a cross of time and space. And the sufferings of mankind are a self-made, synthetic crucifixion filled with torment as the ego-tyrant imprisons souls in a false path promising everlasting Life but leading in the ways of death to the suicide of the soul.

O my children, the Father desires that you should understand that there is a false crucifixion and a true crucifixion. Inasmuch as this initiation will come to all (because it is the hour of the crucifixion of the earth) as the most sublime translation from darkness to Light, from the limited to the unlimited expression of Good, we would make plain the eternal verities and alleviate the suffering often brought about by the false Christs but more often by the individual himself.

For except the children of light come down from the cross in the science of the resurrection flame, earth and her evolutions will not move on to the glories of the new heaven and the new earth foretold by the Lord Christ unto his servant John the Beloved in Revelation.[3]

There is a way which seemeth right unto a man, but the end thereof are the ways of death.[4] The way of seeking a Utopian society (whether through socialism or capitalism or communism) through a one-world superstate or a scientific humanism is all vanity and will lead to the death of the soul because it is not founded upon the rock of Christ,[5] the Real Self of the individual son and daughter of God.

Those who abandon the Mother as the Flame of Life, as the Woman clothed with the Sun who must rise in this age to give birth to the Manchild[6]—those who abandon the Father, the Son, and the Holy Spirit for the false gods, the anti-gods of the lesser self and the lesser personality—will find that their plans and their projects, however well intended, will come to naught.

We the archangels have beheld the great tragedy in Guyana,[7] and we have beheld the end from the beginning. Some have said, "Let us do evil, that good may come"—whose damnation is just,[8] and those who worship at the altar of the personality cult, when that personality is the human ego, have already been forewarned: "Thou shalt have no other gods before me!"[9]

Those leaders who lead the people—themselves in disobedience to the Ten Commandments, the Golden Rule, and the Great Command of Love, seeking self-gain while ignoring the admonishment "Feed my sheep"[10]—must be challenged in the name of Christ for their obvious exclusion of the Christ within these little ones.

But how the innocent sheep are led astray because they have not known them by their fruits![11] For there are many evildoers who come in the name of the Master, usurping his authority and the devotion of his followers by their proud and vain talking and even by their vain deeds.

Oh, for the gift of discernment of spirits,[12] that the children of God might know the Truth and not be led astray! "Blessed are the pure in heart: for they shall *see* God."[13] Yet purity in heart comes from the tutoring of the soul by the Mother flame and through invocation of the sacred fire for the cleansing of the mind and soul and for the purging of the temple of the demons of ignorance.[14]

The pure in heart may overlook the rough-hewn vessel of the Christed One and with compassion anoint his body with oil, but they must not overlook the sign of danger that always begins with the glorification of the self, the lies, and imitations of the Real.

The commune in Guyana was never a Christian community. It was founded by one who had abandoned the flame of Mother as America is intended to be, an avowed Marxist determined to destroy the Christ within the individual through the ultimate perversion of religion and the life of Christ and of the Word of God recorded in sacred scripture.

The evolution of Jim Jones is known by us: a fallen one, an archdeceiver who has appeared here and there with Lucifer's agents attempting to deceive, if it were possible, the very elect[15] by an anti-Christ philosophy, making himself a god unto himself as the fallen ones have done.

Denying the Law of the Logos, they have become a law unto themselves. And in the final hours of their incarnation, knowing that they have but a short time[16] before the final judgment before the Court of the Sacred Fire, they have sought to take with them the lightbearers—not in a mere suicide of the body, but in the suicide of the soul through the ultimate denial of Christ in a cult of anti-Life.

Again the LORD has warned, "Fear not them which kill the body but are not able to kill the soul: but rather fear him which is able to destroy both soul and body in hell."[17] This renegade had no power to destroy the souls of the innocent in hell. But he tried. While he stands before the Four and Twenty Elders,[18] they will live to see the light of day on earth, once again to challenge and be challenged by human tyrants masquerading as God.

The path of the masqueraders is the false crucifixion in which Marxists, Leninists, and Communists throughout the world have enslaved millions upon millions, replacing the glory of the risen Christ with the glory of a superstate that will surely come tumbling down even as the Tower of Babel[19] was destroyed through the judgment of Love.

The world wallows in the fear of the religious cult. Let them heed the warning of an archangel and read the handwriting on the wall: the deaths in Guyana of innocent men, women, and children were upon the altar of World Socialism to the glory of a godless society where the only gods are the fallen angels and the archdeceivers who have set themselves up in church and state for one purpose alone, and that to destroy the potential of the soul to realize the Real Self in and as the living Christ.

Make no mistake. The cult of death to be feared is the religion of hatred spawned by the fallen ones as World Communism, moving mercilessly through Africa and Asia and now into South America and the Caribbean. These forces would lure the children of God, promising the kingdom of heaven on earth through the enslavement of souls by the seed of the Wicked One instead of their liberation through the Lord Christ.

I AM Gabriel of the Sun. I stand in the blazing center of God-reality, and I stand in the very heart of hearts of the children of God on earth. I summon legions of light and sons and daughters of God in embodiment to enter now the battle of Armageddon[20] with the sword of righteousness and truth. Our strategy is one of enlightenment unto the people who are held in the bondage of a mass ignorance, the indoctrination and the brainwashing that promises the good life through money, science, education, and religion without God.

Let those who would be the true shepherds of the people come forward and understand that the false gods have invaded every area of human life. They cannot be eliminated by violent revolution or by the denial of freedom of religion, of the press, of assembly, or of speech. Let them speak, for by their words they shall be justified and by their words they shall be condemned.[21]

When there is the free, objective, and responsible communication to the people of the teachings of the ascended masters side by side with the philosophies of the fallen ones, Truth becomes crystal clear; and by the conversion of the Holy Spirit and *not* the hypnotism of the personality, the children of God will go free in this age.

All who lead the people in the way of their personality rather than in the way of the great Person of the Lord God, the Real Person of all, themselves walk in the way of death. And all who follow them must likewise experience the death of that ego which dies in vain because the soul has not followed the true way of the sacrifice of the self that leads to eternal Life in Christ.

O world, you have witnessed the false crucifixion of the blind leader of the blind.[22] This false crucifixion, this false suffering is wholly unnecessary. Let the way of death be shunned by the true seekers, and let them understand that the real crucifixion of the Christ is the consuming of personal and planetary sin (i.e., karma) on the cross of white fire of Alpha and Omega—the place where the soul is born to eternal Life through obedience to Love, the place where the soul through love of God nourishes a hungry humanity without ulterior motives.

This is the year for the slaying of the beast of World Socialism as the enemy of the true Christs and the true Prophets, as the enemy of thy soul on the true path of salvation through the Crucifixion, the Resurrection, and the Ascension.

"I AM the Way, the Truth, and the Life."[23]

I AM

GABRIEL

I ANNOUNCE TO YOU
THE POTENTIAL
OF YOUR VICTORY
ON THE PATH OF EVERLASTING LIFE

III

Archangel Gabriel on the Mystery of Consciousness

III

Children on the Path of the White Light,

When we contemplate the great mystery of the incarnation of the Word, we must understand how an all-loving and an all-wise Father-Mother God has provided for the gradual descent of the ineffable Light into the consciousness of the individual son of God.

We approach the great spheres of the memory body, the vast potential of the subconscious and the superconscious mind. Within these vehicles of self-expression—the Alpha, the superconscious, and the Omega, the subconscious—the soul maintains its thread of contact with eternal Life.

Continuity of being is seldom grasped let alone sustained by the evolutions of earth today. Mere broken fragments of experience are all that the personalities of the people can comprehend of that which is in reality a great moving stream of consciousness—the I AM THAT I AM that was and is and ever shall be that God who is the Real Self of all.

Thus the incarnation of the Word, of your very own Christ Self, begins with the soul's contact with the memory of Higher Consciousness. Within the superconscious Mind of God are the great solar rings of the causal body depicted on the Chart of Your Divine Self. (See p. 277.) As you contemplate these seven rainbow spheres of light, meditate more deeply upon the vast aeons of your experience in this womb of light, as your soul has both involuted and evoluted long before you ever took physical embodiment upon earth.

Here is the memory of a native innocence, sparkling as dewdrop glistening in the sun, of a childhood in eternity caressed by the presence of Alpha and Omega when you knew, O blessed heart, the arms of everlasting Love in the very lap of the similitude of the One.

With brothers and sisters of a common origin and lifewave, you frolicked in universes of etheric perfection of which the earth affords fragmentary glimpses, but reminders of an Edenic life once shared with angelic hosts and elemental beings of fire, air, water, and earth.

All of this experience preceding the challenges of time and space and of denser spheres provided for the laying of the foundation of the internal rhythm of Life which would one day be captured in the soundless sound pulsing in the centrosome of every living cell, in the rhythm of the tides of life, and in the breaking of the waves of light, cresting, dancing, foaming, intermingling with gull's delight upon the massive rocks of infinity.

And versions of sun and stars, billowing grasses, elysian fields, fruit-bearing trees, and the gentle wind of the Holy Spirit form the backdrop for the soul's assimilation of the Body and the Blood—the feminine and the masculine principles of the universal energy of the Cosmic Christ.

The encounter with the Person of God throughout this prenatal evolution of your soul was a most natural experience with the Great Ones who had already completed the evolution of the incarnate Word both in Spirit and in Matter—both within the great causal body and its spheres of light and in the pristine planes of earth which you now call the etheric octave.

These Enlightened Ones—the Lawgivers, Great Silent Watchers, World Teachers and members of angelic orders—were revered by all. They taught by example the logical order of spiritual/material evolution. The presence of their great majesty and magnanimity of heart was not considered exceptional but, in a most simple and obvious way, was understood to be the goal of each one's evolution Godward.

Within this great circle of oneness provided by the Almighty One for the gestation of the offspring of the Most High, there was no evil to resist the incarnate Word, no Antichrist[1] as such. Thus the urge to creativity was taught as the acceleration of the interaction of the forces of Alpha and Omega within the push/pull polarity of the plus and the minus of being. The very logical and necessary impetus to striving, to becoming, to putting on more and more of the infinite fire was all that was necessary for the increase of consciousness.

You see, my beloved, so great is God's endowment of his offspring with the desire to be more and more of himself that it is by love—this love and this love alone—and not in the midst of a battle of Light and Darkness and Good and Evil, that the soul learns the art and science of the sacred labor of working a work to the glory of that God Self that is the source of all good and all life. And always that work is unto the blessedness and the beatification of every part of life.

By and by, souls develop an immense momentum, a veritable whirling action of the sacred fire. It is an attainment of creativity in the ultimate sense of the Word, that creativity being the recognition of the destiny of sons and daughters of God to be co-creators with Alpha and Omega.

The sense of being the co-creator with God is the very driving force of cosmic consciousness. It is the will to do and to be each day the fullness of a potential that is more than one's own. It is the potential of expanding joy and happiness, a bubbling brook of light invigorating the mind unceasingly, restoring the soul and producing a laughter that both releases and increases the great tension of creativity.

O boundless becoming in the infinite fire, I, Gabriel, stand in the presence of God within the secret chamber of the hearts of the children of God. I come to restore the memory of the path of the white light, to establish the cosmic connection twixt the soul and a lost memory of other spheres and other cycles of freedom.

The freedom to be in God is the ultimate longing of the souls of earth. But alas, the descent into time and space and the subsequent misuse of free will and the misapplication of the crystal-clear energies of God flowing into the temple have resulted in a universal maya upon this planetary body, extending even throughout this solar system and other systems of worlds.

And thus the memory of experience in maya recorded in the subconscious mind has superseded and eclipsed the great central sun of being with the lesser luminaries of the astral plane. And thus an astral astrology was born as the action/reaction of forces unreal: rivalries and hatreds and vanities and jealousies—and misunderstandings heaped upon misunderstandings.

Now the resistance to the incarnation of the Word becomes the densification of the creations of the not-self. Now the incoming Christ must first push back the boulders of human pride and outwit the hostility of the modern Herods as they (the fallen angels incarnate) have purveyed a cult of anti-Life legitimized by the snobbery of a sophisticated science devoid of love and the blessed imagery of the humble manger scene.

The soul pursuing the path of initiation through the Word incoming, infilling its own sphere of self-awareness, must become worldly-wise to understand the preposterous diversions and dichotomies of humans who have not one thought to be divine. Now the restlessness of souls yearning for other years must become a whirling sacred fire that consumes within its pathway every resistance to the Truth aborning within the heart of the little Child.

Here on earth, the joy of creativity must be the knight in shining armor wielding sword to slay at once the dragons of social injustice, the abuses of the abundant life, and the interlopers who have stepped into the seats of government because the true sons and daughters of God have abdicated their authority to be bearers of the will of God in affairs both human and divine.

The defense of the incarnate Word, cycling from the great globe of the causal body into the dimensions of physical consciousness, is *the* great challenge of the period of transition between an age of darkness and an oncoming age of Light.

The tidal wave that is oncoming from out the Great Central Sun is the messenger of the new age of Aquarius. It is the energy of the Cosmic Christ that transmutes all in its cosmic pathway, buoying up the evolutions of light into a higher evolution, flushing them out of the murky waters of the astral plane and the mire of self-delusion.

We the archangels are seven in number representing the seven rays unto the evolutions of God, and we serve with our cohorts of valor to transmit our auric inclusion of light as a veritable transfusion to souls whose destiny it is to rise to those rainbow spheres of Higher Consciousness even while treading the veils of time and space. Ours is a most practical evaluation of the challenges of the path of the lightbearer as the evolutions of this earth approach a decade of initiation [the 1980s] under the eighth ray.

This ray is known as the ray of the Buddha and the Mother. The great symbol of the eight is the sign that portends the balance of the greater and the lesser self and the cosmic interchange between the higher sphere of selfhood, the Cosmic Christ, and the lower sphere that is the soul entering in day by day, increment by increment, to the house of the LORD.

We would fortify the children of God

with an understanding of the mysteries of the Holy Grail and with the vision lost of the paradise of being that is to be regained. This vision then becomes the lodestone of life, the beacon in the lighthouse fixed upon the rock, the true firmament of being.

With the vision of inner reality, you shall not be moved, my beloved. And the waves of astral condemnation of the little Child within you will be drawn into the whirlwind love-action of a heart aflame with the God-desire to balance life and set free every creature under the sun.

Now let the elements of adversity rush into the fountain of light in your heart—there to be transmuted by the violet-flame fiery circle that surrounds your soul, O devotee of freedom—as you give adoration to the violet all-transmuting flame within the center of being, the very essence of the God of Freedom, your own Real Self.

I AM Gabriel directing your attention now to the specific forms of resistance to the light of the Incarnation within the sons and daughters of God. By the Logos, I assess and I analyze the conditions of earth nation by nation, and I counsel the true shepherds of the people to direct the infinite fire into the cause and core of the diseases of mind and body now suffocating emergent souls because of their lack of surrender to the Law of the One—the Law of Love.

The celebration of the Christmas Child may remain a Santa Claus fantasy unless responsible Keepers of the Flame recognize that the guarding of the incarnate Word must become the supreme sacrifice and the ultimate affection of the disciple of Christ.

I AM

GABRIEL

I ANNOUNCE TO YOU
THE PURE REASON OF YOUR VICTORY
IN THE SON OF GOD

IV

ARCHANGEL GABRIEL ON THE MYSTERY OF ARMAGEDDON

IV

Children of the Diligent Heart of Mary,

The spirit of terrorism, anarchy, and assassination abroad in this world must not go unchecked, for it is the wedge which the fallen ones seek to drive between the soul and the ordered evolution of the incarnating Word.

As the Christ Child is born within you and matures, ripening the soul into the higher consciousness of selfhood, seedtime and harvest and the order of life must continue. Thus the seed of the wicked[1] come in the person of Antichrist, directing their venom against the little child before the child has become child-man—wary and aware of the real meaning of Light and Darkness.

The children of God are all too trusting, and theirs is often a misplaced trust given unto the ones who pose as angels of light.[2] They see not beyond the mask of a performed pleasantness the treachery of armed hordes, so jealous of the bliss of the innocent children of God who have never lost their innermost intimate communion with the Lord Christ and his Holy Spirit.

Now we see coming over the hillsides of the world not the vision of the hosts of the LORD but of a plague of locusts.[3] From the astral to the physical plane, there mounts a tide of astral armies pitted against the Defender of the Faith, Archangel Michael. One by one, the opponents of the seven archangels make their entrance upon the stage of life in the very hour when the Great Deliverer comes for the defense of the Woman and her seed.[4]

That seed, as sons and daughters of God in embodiment, must realize that all and everything for which the hosts of Archangel Michael stand—goodwill and faith, God-government, and the strength to be in God inviolate—is challenged by those who have already sworn their enmity not only with the World Mother but also with the Lord Christ to which she gives birth and the legions of angels that form the retinue of protection to the children of God.

Now we come to clear the way for the coming of Archangel Michael and his legions of blue flame! Some upon earth have formed the Blue Army[5] for the protection of the Mother and her children. They have sensed the vibration of the blue-flame angels in their midst, and their devotion is unto the Hail Mary as the great instrument to defeat World Communism in the battle of Armageddon.

Commendable indeed are the works of souls uplifted unto the vibration of the Virgin Mary, whose purity of heart has enabled them to see the extraordinary protection afforded by the science of the spoken Word in the giving of the adoration to the blessed Mother of Christ. Truly, entire legions of fallen ones, bent on the destruction of Christianity and the governments and economies of free nations, have been turned back by the blinding light invoked and sustained through the ritual of the Hail Mary.

Shunned by some prelates within the Roman Catholic Church and supported by others, this army of souls of light is truly the counterpart of the hosts of the LORD providing a most necessary reinforcement in the physical octave for the angels of the Mother and the contingents of the seven archangels, most particularly those of the first ray—the transmitters of the blue lightning of the Mind of God for the defense of the Word incarnate.

I speak to all who understand the necessity to defend Truth in the hour of maximum error and the utter hypocrisy of those who point the finger at the messengers of the LORD with irresponsible journalism and the abuse of freedom of the press.

Those who are the mouthpiece of "the accuser of the brethren"[6] in the fields of journalism and communication defend their right to investigate and to examine activities of Light and Darkness while taking such freedom as is accorded to all by God himself to abuse the privileges of Truth and Justice with sensationalism, sarcasm, and deceptions which they know will appeal to the self-deceived.

We see the standardbearers of the age, such as Solzhenitsyn and other proponents of Truth, mocked by those who have mocked the lightbearers since the very incarnation of the Word on Lemuria and Atlantis.

They were there in the hour of the judgment when the choice was given—Christ or Barabbas. And they cried, "Give us Barabbas!" because of the fomenting of lies and accusations unfounded in fact, circulated among the people by the henchmen of Caiaphas who saw not only to the crucifixion of Christ but to that of the enlightened Stephen, filled with the grace of the Holy Spirit.[7]

Children of God are not dismayed at falsehood or vilification leveled against the lightbearers.[8] They are the perceptive ones who understand the need to accelerate Truth as the printed word and as the flaming sword which turns every way to keep the way of the Tree of Life.[9]

As responsible watchmen on the wall of the LORD,[10] they correct the incorrect statements of the fallen ones both by dynamic decrees[11] and by the effective communication of the Word through the Holy Ghost. Character assassination side by side with the assassination of leaders to the right and the left of the political spectrum cannot be tolerated in the great forum of Truth and in a climate of Freedom which Saint Germain has implanted in the heart of America and her people.

The Lord of the World, Gautama Buddha, warns devotees of every faith that irresponsible action and the denunciation of friend or foe must not be cheered by either side. To applaud the assassination of one's enemies or even the enemies of Freedom is to invite the same upon one's own house. Moreover, it preempts the judgment of the LORD God who said, "Vengeance is mine; I will repay."[12]

Thus the defense of Justice and the standard of the Christ consciousness must be pursued on behalf of all, no matter what their position and irrespective of their alignment with cosmic law.

The fallen ones have projected their plan for terror, anarchy, and confusion in America based on doubt and fear and an overwhelming laxity in those necessary protective agencies—the armed forces, the police, the FBI, and the CIA. The protection of a nation, its people, and its freedom must be entrusted to individuals who will bear the sacred trust with honor, dignity, and love.

And while cruelty and brutality and high-handed methods must be shunned within these agencies created of the people for the people, the agencies themselves must not be put down, compromised, or weakened to the point where the strategies of the fallen ones are facilitated.

And what are these strategies? From the perspective of an archangel, they are very obvious:

To divide and conquer the children of light through rivalries of personality and the segmenting of the population along the line of relative truth and error and right- and left-wing positionings in politics, economics, and matters of faith and morals;

Then to engender hostilities in the mass mind through anxiety and an amazing absence of the awareness of the presence of God in the very midst of the fast paces of modern life;

Then to generate, through pent-up emotions and commercialized violence, a frenzied fanaticism outcropping in international terrorism of the Baader-Meinhof, Red Brigade, PLO variety with its uncontrolled hijacking and intimidation of innocent citizens[13]—or in the sudden crazed unleashing of subconscious hatred by one Dan White in the cold-blooded murder of Mayor George Moscone of San Francisco and fellow board of supervisors member Harvey Milk.[14]

From the inner planes, we the archangels see the danger and sound the warning. The strategy is one of anarchy. The original anarchist was Lucifer himself, who rebelled against the authority of the Lord Christ and the incarnate Word in the sons and daughters of God and therefore has, from the beginning, advocated the violent overthrow of the established order of the universe.

This philosophy, which has become dignified as a political theory declaring any form of government to be undesirable and unnecessary, comes sugarcoated with such euphemisms as "voluntary cooperation" and "the free association of individuals and groups."

Thus, to justify their relentless determination to destroy the order of hierarchy of Christ and his apostles and of an established path of initiation through levels of government spanning the Spirit/Matter cosmos and entrusted to enlightened sons and daughters of God, the fallen ones use a principle of freedom and free will to overthrow the very one, the LORD God himself, who is the giver of that gift of freedom and who, through his only begotten Son, the Christ in all, instructs his offspring in the responsible use of the gift of free will.

The counterpart of this strategy is to infiltrate the governments of the nations with irresponsible elements, the seed of the wicked themselves, and then to hold up the very corruption which their own members have created as the justifiable grounds for the overthrow of the entire system itself.

This circus of the fallen ones has been repeated again and again throughout the ages while self-centered and naïve children of God, who have failed to give their undying commitment to the Flame of Life within themselves and all people, have become susceptible to the ruses of Satan's spoiled children and even amenable to their demand for rights to the taxpayers' money to underwrite their guerrilla training.[15]

And a part of the conspiracy is to erase the connecting lines of the conspiracy in the physical plane. Hence no outer connection is evident between sudden assassination, kidnappings, murder outcropping in South America, Africa, Asia, or the streets of Rome, Paris, London, and New York.

The connection is one of a common vibration of individuals who have long ago rebelled against their own Real Self and the God-government of that Christ, who have thence fallen from grace, the state of oneness with the inner Christ through the World Saviour. Thus they are called the fallen ones, and their fall is from the Higher Consciousness of the God within, the I AM Presence whom they reject as their Lord and Master.

They have not the courage to stand alone in their rejection of the Almighty One, but they must go forth in their cowardice to overthrow the light of the Christ in the children of God and in the governments established by God to maintain a platform of evolution in the Matter plane. And their ultimate justification is the very imperfection of the children of God themselves who have been tempted by vice and greed to abuse the positions of public office entrusted to their care.

The solution of the archangels is not anarchy or the violent overthrow of established institutions but rather the tutoring of the souls of the children of God as to the nature of their own inner reality and a just application of the law of cause and effect.

We come to engender love in the souls of God's people, a love for God that leads to the sacrifice of the self for the many and for the community of the Holy Spirit which is indeed based upon the "free association of individuals and groups" but always under the authority of the enlightened ones who, by their character and their example, are most qualified to rule in the footstool kingdom.[16]

In the name of the LORD, we chasten those who have allowed their sacred duty and their very souls to be corrupted by the corrupt ones! It is the children of God gone astray who will bear the karma for allowing the wedges of darkness to penetrate civilization and threaten both the established order and the plan of God for the incoming golden age. It is you who will bear the karma of your neglect and your sins of commission and omission!

You do not have to give priority to the carnal mind[17] within yourself or to the carnal mind within the fallen angels embodied in your midst! Give instead priority to the Truth, and let the flaming sword of Truth be its own best defense. Through the silent witness of a good example and through a provocative vocalization of the Truth, you must exhort all evolutions of earth—both the laggards and the elect—by Holy Spirit-inspired orations.[18]

Yes, where are the orators of the Holy Spirit empowered by the spoken Word of the Christ Self within? We stand midst the congregation of the righteous, nation by nation, waiting to hear the challenging word of the sons and daughters of God that will set to naught the blasphemies of the wicked and the droning on of the self-made slaves of the welfare state. We are bored by their limited vocabularies, every other word a profanity and a mockery of the Mother.

We bear the insults and the offenses laid at the feet of the Virgin Mother of Christ by the jeering ones who in the name of God publish their pornography as they ridicule and despise the bodies of man, woman, and child, and the sacred exchange of the sacred fire that God has ordained between husband and wife in their aloneness, *all-oneness*—in the hallowed circle of life which it is not lawful to profane or to expose to the eyes of children.

This hatred of Mother Mary that comes as the ridicule and abuse of the bodies of her children also falls upon each child who comes in her name desirous of representing the Mother in the Aquarian age.

Thus from pornography to guerrilla

warfare to violence, kidnapping, assassination, and mechanized murder, the strategies of the fallen ones are connected by Satanic rite on the astral plane. And those who bear hatred for the beautiful Mother of Christ are jointly accountable for the slaughter of her children—whether by a suicide pact in Guyana or by the heinous crimes of the Khmer Rouge in Cambodia, the concentration camps of the Soviet Union or the insane dictator Idi Amin, a Hillside Strangler or a Skid Row Stabber.[19]

I, Gabriel, in clear awareness of the interconnection of the despisers of the Word incarnate in *all* messengers of Truth, summon Keepers of the Flame to a vigil of dynamic decrees and holy prayer in defense of Truth as the defense of the Christmas Child to be born in the hearts of the children of God in this oncoming year.

Let the decrees to Pallas Athena, great emissary of Truth, and to the Lords of Karma sound forth the note that legions of light on earth and in heaven stand with drawn swords, two-edged in their discrimination of righteousness, and that they have sworn upon the altar of God the hostility of the white light against every form of tyranny, church and state, that would encroach upon the freedom of the blessed children of every nation to know God and to see him as he is—the flame of eternal Life burning upon the altar of being.

Let the new-age rosary of Mother Mary

be accorded the place of honor in the homes of lightbearers that they would give to the Blessed Virgin herself. And let the Child's Rosary, a gift from Mother Mary to her children this Christmas, be both a devotional offering and the means of the edification of the little children in the sacred scriptures of the apostles of Christ.[20]

Let the little children and all advancing in the decades of Life's opportunity daily blend their voices nation by nation, chorusing with the angels of God who cry with one breath, "Ave, Ave, Ave Maria!" and themselves gather here and there to celebrate the Hail Mary as the adoration to Life as Mother, as God, as the soul suspended in the womb of time and space.

I AM

GABRIEL

I ANNOUNCE TO YOU
THE VIGIL OF TRUTH
AS THE POTENTIAL OF PROOF
THAT LIFE, ETERNAL LIFE,
IS THE VICTOR OVER DEATH AND HELL
WITHIN YOU

V

Archangel Gabriel on The Mystery of Being

V

Children of the Holy Ghost,

It is meet for thee to command the rebellious spirits within and without, abroad in the world, in the words of the Lord Christ: "Thou shalt worship the Lord thy God, and him only shalt thou serve!"[1] for this he said to Satan who did tempt him with the power and the glory of the kingdoms of this world.

Ambition and the pride of ambition have led even the children of God to stray from the straight and narrow path of initiation in the white light of the Mother. Always and always the treacherous deceptions of the carnal mind are based on its dissatisfactions with its position in time and space. Yet even the mendicant who is content with rough garment, begging bowl, and sandals must beware of ambition for spiritual power—and material power as well.

We see the positionings of the children of God side by side with the children of the devil.[2]

And often their outer appearance belies either the truth or the error of their state of consciousness, as the case may be. What was the difference between the offerings of Cain and Abel, whose material efforts and accomplishments were equal side by side?

One came with the offering unto the LORD God—the firstlings of his flock and the fat thereof—to glorify his name, I AM THAT I AM. For out of his love of the LORD, translated by the Holy Ghost into a sacred labor, his offering was endowed with a living flame.

The other came with his offering of the fruit of the ground, forged out of an efficiency and even a mechanical perfection born of a spiritual/material pride and the determination to exceed the humble offering of the son of God. And so the offering of Cain which lacked the living flame of love was rejected by the LORD because of the impure motive of his heart; for it was to the glory of the self, the lesser ego, instead of to the glory of the Great Ego, the Universal AUM.[3]

Likewise, the Tower of Babel was constructed for spiritual as well as material power. And when the sacred fires of God's all-consuming love descended, it confounded the speech of the seed of the wicked as well as that of the children of God who had been enticed by their unbridled desire for world power. That was the sacred fire of judgment released from the heart of the LORD who, in the person of

Archangel Chamuel, "came down to see the city and the tower which the children of men builded."[4]

Indeed that judgment which produced the confounding of their language and their scattering abroad from thence upon the face of all the earth was the white light of the Mother, the energy of Alpha and Omega in a descending spiral of ineffable love that could be received only by those who retained within their own hearts that corresponding love of God.

The light of God's judgment is simply and completely, my beloved, the descent of the harmony of the Father-Mother God, which harmony is always Love intensifying unto love and to love and to love, and confounding the discord and the dissonance of inharmony. The pure in heart, therefore, not only see God but in seeing him are able to receive that great light of the judgment and retain it, thus adding to the dimensions of earth a greater and greater concentration of the light of heaven.

Why, the very nature of the sons and daughters of God is the great sphere of cosmic consciousness called the T'ai Chi, which illustrates the plus/the minus, the masculine/the feminine, polarity of Alpha and Omega. This great sphere of Universal Being is twofold in nature: it is first the great causal body in heaven and then the sphere within the heart that contains the Flame of Life, the threefold presence of power, wisdom, and love which always includes the Person of God as Father, Son, and Holy Spirit.

The soul whose delight is in the law of the LORD God, I AM THAT I AM, his own beloved Presence, the soul who meditates upon the Law of the One, the Law of Love, "day and night" as the Psalmist wrote,[5] opens the floodgates of being to the great sphere of this universal reality and to the concentric energies of the solar rings that comprise, layer upon layer, the great causal body of its own individual God Presence.

As the causal body is in balance in the masculine and feminine principle of being, so is the manifestation of the sons and daughters of God intended to be in time and space. Within the white fire core of the I AM Presence is both the Person of the blessed God Self and the Principle of the white light, Alpha and Omega. The surrounding balance of the rainbow rays is the Omega, or feminine, extension of the masculine, or Alpha, center.

And throughout all of nature, in Spirit and in Matter, the pattern of the T'ai Chi, of the Alpha-to-Omega and of the Spirit/Matter universes, is repeated again and again. This illustrates the simplicity of cosmic geometry—that the seed of Light, the nucleus of God's energy, always contains both the masculine and the feminine particles of the Person of God.

In the planes of Spirit it can be demonstrated that Matter, or Mother, is dormant within Spirit, or Father, whereas in the outer universes of time and space it is Mother, or Matter, who is the active counterpart of Spirit as the *Shakti,* or energy, of Father. Nevertheless, in all planes of heaven and earth, Life is one, Life is whole, Life is complete. There is no separation from God—from the God Self, from the Person of the Lord Christ or the beloved twin flame.

This statement of the Law as the Principle of your being contains the seed within it, my beloved, of your own healing of the sense of separation, of fragmentation of the body of God, and of the gnawing sense of incompleteness which the children of God often allow themselves to entertain, thereby leaving open the back door of consciousness for the demons of temptation to enter.

And upon entering, their vain talk and proud boasting is always of the alternative route to the acquirement of a power that promises contentment through worldly success, riches, authority, prestige, and position. Thus is ambition born of the ignorance of the Law concerning a wholeness that is even now your very own reality, my beloved.

Be at peace, then, in the great mystery of the wholeness of being; and contemplate how profound is the peace of the man or woman who has found the True Self in God. The one who meditates upon this law discovers that with the opening of the floodgates of consciousness, the sphere of the heart—which contains the potential for every son and daughter of God to become God incarnate—now expands and expands and expands. And life on earth becomes life in heaven here and now because first things are first.

"Seek ye first the kingdom of God and his righteousness, and all these things shall be added unto you"[6] was the living proof and the example of Jesus Christ who is the Saviour *because* he has saved your souls, my beloved, for the entering in to the path of Christhood—which he opened and which no man can shut.[7] No man can shut that door once you have determined to be God in action here and now, everywhere and anywhere.

Yes, take the wings of the morning, and dwell in the uttermost parts of the sea.[8] Glide in the heart of the gulls and soar with the eagles into the highest mountains. Be God in the love of elemental life and in the animal kingdom, nurturing their newborn with the coming of the spring. Enter atoms and molecules of a pounding surf and know the limitless power of creation available to those who in all humility have made themselves co-creators with God *because* he first made them so to be.

Wherever life is, God is, and there you can be in consciousness, if you will it so. There you can be the integral law of the Father undergirding a universe, or the Son as the wise dominion of those whom he has anointed to be rulers of the vast dominions of time and eternity.

And behind the grasses that grace the winds and the stars of energy that regulate the interstellar exchange of Spirit and Matter, there you can be—one in the love of the Holy Spirit who is the rhythm and movement, the very comfort of the whole creation that groaneth and travaileth in pain to be delivered from the bondage of corruption into the glorious liberty of the children of God.[9]

Whereas the cult of success and the conquest of egos by other egos has been offered by the fallen ones as the panacea for all discontent, God is the universal cure of the ailment of the soul alienated from the Person of its own Christhood. Your blessed Christ Self is the one who integrates your soul with the Presence of God. Jesus Christ demonstrated that integration, being full of the Holy Ghost, being one with the Father, being the Word incarnate.[10]

His illustration of the law of self-sufficiency in God is indeed the cure for every attitude of selfishness and self-concern at the foundation of the modern cults of idolatry. These outlets for ego expression are a dime a dozen. Everywhere in the marts of commerce are the strutters who dance and prance with their tin and tinsel toys, leading the poor with promises of salvation to squander their light and energy on vanities of both Spirit and Matter. That light—they know it not, alas—could be the very instrument of their salvation.

Let all who approach the path of the white light understand that the goal is the assimilation of the soul into the Great God Self. It is the integration of the Father-Mother principles of being as the true identity of self and of wholeness. It is the ascension of being from the Matter universe you have known to a Spirit universe which you once knew. It is the goal of desirelessness come full circle to be the desire of God.

Let all who come this way—the way of the Great White Brotherhood[11] outlined as the path of the Master-disciple relationship—know that all lesser goals will be dashed upon the rocks of their own human ambition upheld by their own human habit.

Ye cannot serve Light and Darkness or God and mammon,[12] nor can ye come to the fount of Reality or to the retreats of the ascended masters seeking our stamp of approval upon your humanly engineered projects for personal self. We will not place our label of the cosmic honor flame upon your brand of human perfection that has failed to submit to the Person of Christ.

You need not don your white garments to disguise the ravening wolves that lurk within as the untransmuted demons of desire for personal power and prestige.[13] And if you come to the altar of the Holy of Holies expecting to be filled with light, be forewarned, one and all, that the all-consuming love of God will be the challenge of the judgment, in order that you might choose this day[14] between your own inner reality and the unreality of these most treacherous impostors of the Christ.

I AM Gabriel, the servant of God in his sons and daughters. I offer to you, in answer to your call to me—to be given in the name of the I AM Presence and the Christ Self—the full momentum of my own attainment of purity for the purification of motive and desire, of heart and soul, that you might come into the true path and that your offering of self and selfhood might be the expression of the sweet love of God endowing the sacred labor with the flame of your adoring.

I AM

GABRIEL

I ANNOUNCE TO YOU
THE OPPORTUNITY
FOR THE PURIFICATION OF YOUR SOUL
ON THE PATH
OF GOD'S PERFECTION

VI

Archangel Gabriel on the Mystery of Selfhood

VI

Children of the Love of Alpha and Omega,

Sealed within the soul is the inner awareness of what is and what is not. The reality of thy being can never be subject unto the doctrine and dogma of those who have sought by the intellectual methodology of the outer mind to interpret the great mystery of the Word incarnating again and again in Spirit and in Matter in the sons and daughters of God.

There is no argument that can prove or disprove the Truth. Not argument but the experience of Truth, the being of Be-ness, if you will, is the only proof that God can be and is where you are and where I AM.

I AM an archangel of the white light of the Mother. And who art thou, O disciple of Love? I would tell thee who thou art. But in all of my telling, the truth of thy being can be known only in thyself and of thyself.

You will hear my word—you who would

hear my word—and in the very Word itself there is established the link of hierarchy whereby the I and the thou are one. And in that oneness, you become more of thyself through myself. In knowing who I AM, you may become more of who you are—and in that becoming discover that we are indeed one in the chain of being.

The ascended masters call their chelas to the true understanding of the mystery of Selfhood. This is not indoctrination, for the doctrine of Truth cannot be learned in the ordinary sense of the word. For you must become it, my beloved.

With all of this chatter of programming and deprogramming, let it be understood that he who is programmed to a doctrine or dogma or a political, social, or economic ideology, whether of Light or of Darkness, can just as easily be deprogrammed; and he who believes by fear and by doubt can be brought to a state of unbelief by a similar doubt and fear.

But he who knows who he is in God because he has become that God—because in heartfelt prayer and utter humility he has gone to the Holy of Holies to bow before the beloved Presence of God and to know that Presence as the lover of the soul—can never be deprogrammed because he has not been programmed!

His religion is of the Light. It has come by the true path of initiation under the Lord Christ through confession that he is Lord and through confession of sin and the repentance thereof, and then through the conversion of the soul by the Person of the Holy Ghost.[1] He in whom the seed of the Word has been planted through direct contact with the ascended masters can never lose that seed unless he surrender it voluntarily through the betrayal of the Word—whether in his own Christ Self, in the messenger, or in the Master.

The ascended masters' teachings are not based upon a belief system, so called, composed of a child's blocks, building hypothetical towers of human reason to fill the human vacuum. The Great White Brotherhood, in the integrity of the soul's potential to become one with God, quickens in each receptive heart by the light of the Logos that which has been known by the soul from the beginning unto the ending of its cycles in God.

The Law that is written within the inward parts of the sons and daughters of God[2] cannot be reduced to a series of statements injected as instant self-awareness and then just as easily rejected as instant unawareness. No, the foundations of Truth are built century upon century as the soul, by love and love alone, enters into the true citadel of being.

The Christ mind is the real mind of every disciple of God.[3] This one Universal Mind to which all may gain access through an obedient humility is not programmed, nor indeed can be, by the fallen ones who would impose their belief systems upon the children of God.

Their success in manipulation comes about because the children of God have placed their trust in the outer mind; and it is this outer mind that is subject to all of the influences that surround the evolutions of earth—hereditary, environmental, and including the auric impressions of every lifestream upon every other lifestream amplified by mass communication, satellite, and the psychic levels of human experience.

Thus, at the level of the human consciousness, all are molded by common molding factors. Nevertheless, within the vehicles of the earth earthy[4] there is that point of reality in which the soul may take refuge. It is the diamond-shining Mind of God—never self-limiting but limitless in its expansion and expression of Truth, unalterable and unbending in the self-awareness of Truth.

The sacred scriptures are not intended to be used in a battle of wits with unwary souls where deprogrammers representing one phase of human doctrine attempt to deprogram their victims of one belief system and to replace it with another.

The root of error within this generation is to be found within parents and teachers who have neglected to inculcate within the soul of the child the understanding of communion with the innermost Person of God, the

Christ Self of each one. The soul who is one in that Christ, saved by that Christ, cannot be subject to the extremism of fanatics of left and right.

And those parents who have sought to defend freedom of religion by denying all religion, those who have sought to remove from the public schools the simple prayer, the Christmas carol, the observance of the holy days of Christian, Jew, or Moslem[5]—it is they who have sown the wind and who will reap the whirlwind[6] of the barren consciousness that they have willed upon their children!

The seven archangels stand within the schoolhouses of America and *we* give the Lord's Prayer for the little children whose mouths have been stopped, whose devotional nature has been tethered to a scientific humanism that declares, "With man all things are possible," instead of recognizing the great truth of being: "With God all things are possible unto man."[7]

Yes, we recite the Psalms in a vacuum of spirituality where the matter universe itself threatens to collapse because of the failure of the children of God to infuse the blessed earth with the balance of light that always flows through prayer and meditation and devotions of the heart. And thus the most frightful programming of all is that programming of the children of a material civilization and a mechanized culture to a self-sufficiency outside of God.

Were the German people who were hypnotized by the black magician Adolf Hitler[8] inferior in some way or more ignorant than others to the tactics of his brainwashing? No, their susceptibility is the same that is frightening the parents and teachers of this generation.

It was the susceptibility of a prior brainwashing that entered through the Protestant revolt. For with Luther and his ninety-five theses came the damnable doctrine of the removal of the Person of Christ from the sons and daughters of God and the removal of the LORD God as the inhabiter of the temple of the soul and the body! The denial of the proper role of the Virgin Mary and of the hierarchy of the hosts of the LORD, as well as of the communion of saints in heaven with the saints on earth, has deprived the children of God of the understanding of the great mystery of the Word incarnate both in the ascended masters and in the unascended devotees of God.

Remove God from the temple, the consciousness of your children, ye parents and teachers well-meaning or otherwise, and your children will then be inhabited by the anti-God manifestations of a materialistic philosophy based on the pride of the personal self rather than the glory of the Person of God.

If you do not teach your children to serve the God within, then they will unfailingly serve that mammon which you have erected in his place. For the children of God are devotional by nature, and they will give their devotion to the anti-God of the fallen ones if you take from them the true and living God who is worshiped in temples not made with hands.[9]

No, those who respond to the call of the fascist, communist, or atheistic dictators are of two categories. Either they are the seed of the wicked sown by the father of lies who was a murderer from the beginning,[10] who follow the archdeceivers because they are of the same vibration—or they are the children of God programmed in a false religion and a false understanding of God-government.

You parents who have given to your children no foundation of the law of the prophets, the great miracles of Elijah and Elisha, you who have not given to them the tradition of the culture of God and of the Messiah come in the Person of Christ Jesus, you have no one to blame but yourselves when your children leave you for the prophets of the day, false or true.

If you have not taught your children that God lives in them, by an example of morality, human kindness, compassion for life, and a mutual respect for one another because God is the reality of each self, then your children will seek the God for whom their souls long. And God have mercy upon them as they are left to sift and to search Truth and Error without the standard of the living Word incarnate!

You who fear for your children because your own lives have been based upon fear, I come bearing good tidings of joy! For the birth of the Saviour is the promise of salvation to all people. He was and is the perfect love which casts out fear,[11] first within you and then within your offspring.

When you love your children as God loves them, with the sacred trust that they are of him and will return to him, you will begin to have that peace that passes understanding[12] which your children are seeking outside of the home simply because you yourselves have not raised up that presence of peace that provides the divine solution to every human problem.

The climate of "no religion" that has produced the vacuum of God consciousness which marks this age is as bad as false religion where the false gods of those who profess to pursue the fundamental teachings of Christ and of his word have become, O vanity of vanities![13] a religion of Bible-quoting, demon-possessed, so-called Christians who think they have salvation in a dead letter and an untempered zeal. Jesus referred to these when he said, "Search the scriptures; for in them *ye think* ye have eternal Life: and they are they which testify of me."[14]

They have lost the Holy Spirit which they have never found. And their temples are invaded by the impostors of that Spirit who, while professing obedience to the laws of God, do violate those laws even as they violate the free will of the individual to pursue the kingdom of God (i.e., the consciousness of God) whom he declared is within you.[15]

To justify kidnapping and one form of brainwashing in order to counteract another form of supposed brainwashing by the quoting of sacred scriptures and the misappropriation of the Word is verily the blasphemy against the Holy Ghost.[16] To offer lies in defense of the supposed Truth is once again the age-old tactic of the fallen ones who proclaim: "Let us do evil, that good may come."

To offer fanatical prayers of malintent against the witnesses to the Truth of being, calling for the death of our messengers—this is not the religion of Christ but of Satan. And those who lead the children of God in these Satanic rituals are those who have the greater fear and doubt in their own damnation.

Those who are incapable of discerning Light and Darkness within themselves are the ones who make the loudest pronouncements concerning our representatives. They have denied the ascended masters and the living Christ within themselves. By what standard then, pray tell, can they know the servant of God or the prophet, true or false?

Discernment comes by the gift of the Holy Ghost, and no one can say that even the living Master Jesus Christ is the LORD but by that

Holy Ghost.[17] It is our desire that every sincere seeker after God should become the agent of his Holy Spirit.

Those who have sought the Holy Ghost through the impure motive of spiritual pride—and there are many within the churches today—have bypassed and been bypassed by the Spirit of God and have become the victims of discarnate entities posing as the Holy Spirit, as well as demons of pride who speak in the tongues of fallen angels and easily provide other demons for the interpretation of those tongues. Just as there has been the perversion of language upon earth, so there has been the perversion of the tongues of angels in heaven, and so the language of the fallen ones is not the original Word yet spoken by the archangels and their legions.

So often the appearance of the gifts of the Holy Spirit has confused the children of God and caused them to follow ministers of the Word who have all manner of foul and unclean spirits and who are the first to accuse the representatives of the Great White Brotherhood in every age.

Let programming, deprogramming, mass indoctrination, and the brainwashing of children and youth and of the susceptible of every generation be counteracted by the universal knowledge of the Word incarnate and the Truth that is the rock of every man's being.[18]

The seven archangels challenge the enemies of righteousness and the enemies of the souls of humanity in church and state to prove their light and their right by their own God-realization on the path of attainment!

I AM

GABRIEL

I ANNOUNCE TO YOU,
O SOULS OF HUMANITY,
THE OPPORTUNITY TO ASCEND
INTO THE MOUNTAIN OF THE LORD
AND TO BE FREE TO BE YOURSELF
IN THE UNIVERSAL MIND OF GOD

VII

Archangel Gabriel on the Mystery of the Incarnate Word

VII

Children Who Have Uttered the Decree
of the Word,

It is written that the LORD God "uttered his voice" and "the earth melted."[1] The voice of God is his Word. Ponder now the great mystery of the incarnation of that Word!

For the Christ, as the Son of God, is the Voice of God. And when the Word of God the Father "that goeth forth out of my mouth"[2] is sent and signified by the unalterable Presence of the I AM THAT I AM, it is the light of the only begotten Son of God, it is the energy of Alpha and Omega that manifests instantaneously as the Person of Christ.

Thus the *Word* becomes the *Work* of the LORD God in the manifestations of his sons and daughters. The Word is the emanation of Spirit that becomes the Work in Matter—the whole of the creation itself, culminating as the love of the Person of the Holy Ghost.

And so the Word of God, which he has declared "shall not return unto me void,"[3] is always and evermore the Lord Christ whose light emanation as the spoken Word of God quivers the bow in that Christ Person who is the real Person of every son and daughter of God.

The Great Reason—the manifest Principle of the Logos—is the self-assurance within the children of God that the Real Self, their own beloved Christ Self, shall not return to the plane of Spirit devoid of good works. "But it shall accomplish that which I please"[4] is the declared decree of God the Father, the veritable blessing upon the Son who comes forth out of the I AM THAT I AM to be the mediator of the Word in everyone who is born of God.

The Son is the extension of the Father in his sons and daughters, whom the Father hath sent by the power of his spoken Word. The Son is the spokesman and the mouthpiece of the Father to whom he hath "committed all judgment."[5]

And so the Law of God was written and it was spoken as I, Gabriel, dictated it unto the prophet Isaiah. And because Isaiah, *Guru* (i.e., the one who embodied the Law of the Lawgiver and the God flame) unto the twelve tribes of Israel and the thirteenth, spoke it, it remains and is the Law of their evolution unto the present hour. And that Law of the manifest Word, the unalterable decree of the Logos, is the certainty of the ascension unto the sons and daughters of God: "It—the Word, the Christ Self—shall prosper in the thing whereto I sent it."[6]

My beloved, unto the Real Self—the One, the incarnate Word who even now is in you "the hidden man of the heart"[7]—is the promise of God the Father given:

"For ye shall go out with joy and be led forth with peace: the mountains and the hills shall break forth before you into singing, and all the trees of the field shall clap their hands. Instead of the thorn shall come up the fir tree, and instead of the brier shall come up the myrtle tree; and it shall be to the LORD for a name, for an everlasting sign that shall not be cut off."[8]

And the name of that LORD is the Anointed One, the bearer of the message of the Holy of Holies. Your Christ Self is the messenger of your I AM Presence—the Wonderful, Counsellor, The Prince of Peace, verily the Personhood of The everlasting Father, The mighty God: hence the Guru (the incarnation of the Light of God, the I AM).[9]

This beloved Christ Self, who would inhabit your temple of the living God,[10] is the everlasting sign of Reality that shall not be cut off—no, not even by the free will of the soul who has rebelled against the indwelling God. Nor shall it be cut off in the person of the prophets and messengers who each in their own century come in the name of the LORD as the physical manifestation of the Guru whose presence *all shall one day know.*

This is the goal of the path of initiation: to know the inner Guru as the Real Self and to accept the one whom God has sent to represent that Guru until every jot and tittle of the law of personal and planetary karma is fulfilled[11]—balanced—and the soul is able to see the inner Guru *face to face.* Thus, when the disciples asked Jesus, "What shall we do, that we might work the works of God?" he gave to them the great mystery of the Word made manifest as the Work of God: "This is the work of God, *that ye believe on him whom He hath sent.*"[12]

This belief, or trust, is the foundation of the Master-disciple relationship, which in turn is the foundation of the universal order of hierarchy of the Great White Brotherhood that spans heaven and earth. Thus Jesus taught his disciples that their primary obligation in working the works of God, both as dharma and as karma, was to sustain their link in the chain of being by believing in the One whom God had sent to be himself incarnate.

Belief, or trust, in the LORD (the embodied Word) is the necessary energy arcing the disciple's devotion to the Master and opening the line of his consciousness to receive the return current of the Master's love which completes the hallowed circle of their oneness.

Some upon earth have accepted the Saviour Jesus Christ as their *Guru* and thus commenced the circle of the Master-disciple (i.e., Guru-chela) relationship that is the only reality of existence. But they have cut themselves off from the great cosmic interchange that God has ordained for the intimate communion of the Guru (LORD) and the chela (servant), whereby the soul puts on and becomes, step by step, the Self-awareness of the Guru, while the Guru assimilates elements of the chela's consciousness which require purification, balance, and a strengthening in the law of limitless being.

This they have done by declaring Jesus to be the *only* Son of God and themselves to be sinners incapable of embodying the first elements of the Word and ultimately its fullness as they walk in the footsteps of their Master. Thus have they failed utterly to apprehend his great message: I go to prepare a place for you . . . that where I AM (in the consciousness of the Christ), there ye may be also.[13]

All who therefore worship the Person of Jesus without accepting the challenge to be joint-heirs with him of the Person of the Christ—denying God's promise that he, the Great Guru of the Piscean age, has the power to make them, like unto himself, sons of God (Christ manifestations of God)[14]—practice a religion of idolatry. And in their idolatry they have not the fruits, i.e., the manifest works, of the Holy Ghost, beginning with the real belief in the One Sent as the true archetype of their own Real Self.

Thus, while espousing the first requirement of the Law—the acceptance of Jesus Christ as their Saviour—these children of God led astray by "the pastors that destroy and scatter the sheep of my pasture"[15] remain in ignorance concerning the second requirement of the Law.

Let the true shepherds of the people come forth who shall feed them and cause them to fear no more, nor be dismayed, neither be lacking in the wisdom of the Word incarnate, saith the LORD![16] Let the adoration of Jesus the Christ, born in Bethlehem, be understood as the very necessary beginning of the path of individual Christhood whose ending is the ultimate expression of that very same Lord Christ of Jesus within the devotee.

Thus he is the author and the finisher of your faith, my beloved, the beginning and the ending of your awareness of the "true Light, which lighteth every man that cometh into the world"[17]—first in him and then within your own blessed Christ Self into whose light he would initiate your soul.

When David penned those words spoken unto him by the voice of God, he fearlessly and forthrightly said: "I will declare the decree . . ." He knew the requirement of the Law that what God had spoken to him within his heart, he himself must declare as the decree of the Word. And with the uttering of that Word, with the declaration of the decree, the law of the Guru was registered in time and space: ". . . The LORD hath said unto me, Thou art my Son; this day have I begotten thee."[18]

This decree of the Father is heard by every son and daughter of God in that moment when the soul accelerates into the individual attainment of that Higher Consciousness of the inner Christ Self. When the soul is one in Christ by loving obedience to the Person of that Christ, then the approbation given unto the only begotten Son as the Second Person of the Trinity is also heard by the soul as it is one with that inner Self. Now the soul has become the inheritor of the Christ, 'Light', whom the Son Jesus became.[19] And the soul receives the appellation: Son of man.[20]

Now let Jew and Christian unite as one before the great truth that Jesus, the Son of God, was, in a previous incarnation of his soul, embodied as David, king of Israel, author of many of the Psalms. And to him was given the revelation of his own Sonship even prior to his final incarnation when he exemplified the Messiah as the Real Self of all children of God and was the fulfillment of the prophecy which I, Gabriel, gave as the Word of the LORD unto Isaiah.

David was the king whom the LORD set upon "my holy hill of Zion,"[21] and even then David held the key to the incarnation of God within his people (i.e., *king*). That key was the understanding of the great mystery of the Holy Grail, his own individual Christhood.

His life as David, though not wholly perfect, reveals the evolution of the soul Godward—the soul who cries out, "Let the words of my mouth and the meditation of my heart be acceptable in thy sight, O LORD, my strength and my redeemer."[22] This is the soul immaculate who looks forward to the day when he will be perfected in God, who yet trusts in His salvation and in the ultimate fulfillment of His law, though he himself has sinned transgressing the laws of God.[23]

That sin was the karma of David, a misuse of free will resulting in the misqualification of God's energy and manifesting as a corresponding imbalance of the light of the Trinity burning as the threefold flame upon the altar of being.

The understanding that Jesus, the Son of God, had numerous incarnations before his final embodiment in which he demonstrated the mastery of the self in time and space and the path of initiation which he opened to the sons and daughters of God is the greatest hope to all people that they may walk in his footsteps and fulfill the law of their individual karma.

To know that the Saviour of the World did himself struggle with the human consciousness and that he outfoxed Goliath as he outfoxed Herod makes the challenge of Christhood available to all who realize that they, too, have sinned and come short of the glory of God,[24] and that nevertheless they, too, may challenge the seed of the Wicked One who to this hour deal unjustly with the children of God.

Because he overcame, they, too, may overcome. Because he had karma and balanced that karma through the mercy and justice of the same law that governs the evolution of the sons and daughters today, there is hope for the resurrection and the ascension of every son of God—if he will but understand that the crucifixion will be for him also a necessary part of the victory.

The Lords of Karma desire to open the path of Christhood to greater and greater numbers, to Christians as well as Jews and Moslems who have been deprived of the true teachings of the Guru-chela relationship as taught by Jesus Christ to his disciples and as demonstrated by his soul in numerous incarnations all the way back to the civilizations of Lemuria and Atlantis.

David, the beloved, was anointed by the prophet Samuel to be king of Israel.[25] When Samuel anointed the eighth son of Jesse, he taught him the Law of the King of kings—the Christ Self who is the King over all temporal kings. He taught him that the one anointed by God to rule the people must represent to the people the King of kings within themselves whom they must respect and to whom they must give authority and ultimately allow to reign supreme.

Thus all allegiance to the person of David by the people of Israel was the sustainment of a

Guru-chela relationship, for the authority of the prophet Samuel came from God the Father as he was the first of the prophets, or the gurus, of the people.

His anointing of David made David an extension of the Guru, appointing him to both a spiritual and a temporal authority and making him the mediator between the people and their God, even as Moses, the great lawgiver, had served in that very same capacity.

And so when David wrote the Word of the Lord "Yet have I set my king upon my holy hill of Zion," he understood that the Christ Self of each individual son and daughter of God always sits on the right hand of God, on the mount of attainment, the holy hill of the Higher Consciousness of Zion. And here the mystical interpretation of the word *Zion* is I AM THAT I AM, or the individual I AM Presence.

David knew that he was anointed king because in his heart he had given preeminence to the real Person of God, the Lord Christ, and by his devotion he had placed that Christ one with the Father in his prayer and meditation. Because he had fulfilled that requirement of the Law, he himself was elevated to the position of king. Made one with the inner Christ, he then bore the divine right of the king to rule, which right is given only to those who are in that oneness of the Father, the Son, and the Holy Ghost.

The life of David illustrates grandly and nobly that whomsoever the LORD has anointed to be the Word incarnate, to be the Guru, with or without karma, with or without sin, that one is yet the LORD's anointed and out of his mouth proceed the psalms of praise that become, in the hearer and the doer of the Word, *the Word made flesh.*

Let every chela of the ascended masters give praise unto the LORD who made heaven and earth and who forevermore in heaven and in earth maintains the sacredness of the Guru-chela relationship.

I AM

GABRIEL

I ANNOUNCE TO YOU
THE GREAT MYSTERY
OF YOUR INCARNATION
OF THE WORD

VIII

Archangel Gabriel on the Mystery of the Translation

VIII

Children of the Light of Freedom,

I call for the amethyst jewel of Taiwan to manifest now! Let the light of freedom be ablaze on land and sea in the heart of man as it is in the heart of his God!

As the tides of diplomatic relations rise and fall and the actions of the few dictate the fate of the many, the Great White Brotherhood is not moved. For we see the end from the beginning.

We see the outworking of the human consciousness in human affairs at all levels of interchange, national and international. And we know, given current trends of foreign affairs, that there is a probability in the current and the direction of the tide which, although problematical from the standpoint of Light and Darkness, will nevertheless be the outplaying of an international game of chess that unfortunately is based upon the logic of the carnal mind.

It is when that logic runs out, when all moves on the international chessboard have been exhausted, that the alternatives of the invincible Christ mind will be summoned. At that moment the students must be ready.

Thus we offer the God-solution to every human problem and we counsel our representatives in every field, as they seek to maintain their forcefields of light, to clear the heart for the amethyst jewel and to bear the gift as the Magi unto the nations.

I AM Gabriel. I have been sent by the LORD God on many a diplomatic mission on behalf of Alpha and Omega unto the evolutions of these systems of worlds. Although the political strategies of the fallen ones have at times been a setback to the strategy of Light, it is most often the culpability and the vulnerability of the children of light that carry the elements of self-defeat and a corresponding delay of cosmic timetables.

Therefore, in the face of changing international relations, I bring a message to all people of goodwill from God the Father:

The wicked have no power to destroy the bastions of light, whether by their manipulations of science, the balance of the international economy, or by the current recognition of Red China at the expense of the security of Taiwan[1]—*if* a free people will unite worldwide to confirm their freedom in a holy alliance of the will of God through the heart of the blessed

God of Freedom, Saint Germain.

The tyrannies and treacheries of a Babylon or an Assyria, of a Gog or a Magog,[2] have no power to deter the unalterable divine plan of Almighty God for the hundred and forty and four thousand, for the City Foursquare,[3] and for the path of the ascension for those who elect to do the will of God.

When freedom is pursued as a virtue of the Holy Spirit, as an element of the Personhood of God himself, then that right and that freedom is defended by all of the hosts of the LORD and the armies of heaven led by The Faithful and True,[4] camped even now upon the hillsides of both Taiwan and mainland China.

But when the people place their trust solely in physical armaments and diplomatic accords, when the day of karmic reckoning, individual and national, is upon them, all of their defenses and diplomatic agreements cannot hold back the descending light of God that accelerates the return of the collective misqualification of God's energy by the people and by their leaders who have mismanaged his government over the nations.

The law of karma is inexorable. It exacts of each soul a just recompense of energy expended and energy interchanged with every other soul.

The leaders of the nations can do no more than the people allow. The great question of the hour is: How much will the people allow? How long will they allow their representatives to act in their name and yet to betray the inner flame of freedom that burns on the altar of every heart?

Will the Communist leaders of Red China be able to subdue and assimilate the people of Taiwan by levels of human force? Or will they lure them with overtures of a peace that is without honor?

The answer is: If the people allow it.

Men and women, one by one, can be the instrument of the salvation of earth and all nations if and when they allow God to work through them. Solutions sought by human means alone, neglecting the priority of the Logos, must come to naught. "But my words shall not pass away."[5]

Kingdoms may rise and fall, but the soul tethered to the personal Christ Self through Jesus Christ, Saint Germain, Mother Mary, and every ascended master of the Great White Brotherhood will remain a pillar in the temple of my God,[6] both in heaven and in earth.

The Darjeeling Council sets forth its solution to world problems. It is Mission Amethyst Jewel. We stand in a vote of confidence around the Darjeeling Council table in honor of Saint Germain and all servant-sons and daughters who embody the Great Spirit of Freedom as a mystery of the Holy Grail.

We do not bargain with men's souls.

We do not trade a free nation, a free people, for the security of an alliance with those who have built their empires upon the blood of martyrs, millions upon millions of souls murdered for the dragon of World Communism—perverting the energies of Alpha and Omega, East and West, through the governments of the fallen ones in the Soviet Union and Red China.

The silent witness of the slain upon the altar of God is that the crucifixion which they have endured in the battle of world freedom leads not to the death of the soul or the death of the flame of freedom that yet burns upon the altar of the nations, but to a glorious resurrection of the soul and its freedom through the path of initiation opened to the Jew and Gentile nations by the Saviour Jesus Christ.

Through the crucifixion and the blood of the martyrs, spilled just as his blood was spilled upon the cross, there comes the judgment of the princes of darkness, of the kings of the earth and the great men and the rich men and the chief captains and the mighty men and every bondman and every free man[7] who has failed to acclaim the Lord Christ as the God who is the Life and the Person of every son and daughter.

Those who have denied the Word incarnate in his children, those who have failed to give God the preeminence due his holy name I AM THAT I AM, cry out to the mountains and the rocks, "Fall on us and hide us from the face of him that sitteth on the throne and from the wrath of the Lamb: for the great day of his wrath is come; and who shall be able to stand?"[8]

The Lamb is the Person of God, or Guru—always present in the embodied prophet and messenger—who sits upon the throne of the great threefold flame within the heart of every disciple of that Lamb and of that universal Christ in heaven and in earth, of whom the ascended masters and their embodied messengers and disciples are the logical extension.

Learn then the mystery of the Grail. The wrath of the Lamb is the white light of Alpha and Omega, always present in those who have not broken their tie to the great chain of hierarchy, the chain of all who share consciously in the universal being of God.

This white light of the Mother in the Matter sphere of being and of the Father in the Spirit sphere is the acceleration of karma, as Above so below, which can take place only through the embodiment of the Lamb. The Lamb, my beloved, is incarnate wherever there is the Guru-chela relationship held intact by the cords of love that bind the soul to the universal law of being.

Think not that the martyrs of World Communism have died in vain, nor that they do not exercise the power of Almighty God as a counterweight to human infamy. For John the Revelator saw "under the altar the souls of them that were slain for the word of God and for the testimony which they held. And they cried with a loud voice, saying, How long, O LORD, holy and true, dost thou not judge and avenge our blood on them that dwell on the earth?

"And white robes were given unto every one of them; and it was said unto them that they should rest yet for a little season until their fellowservants also and their brethren, that should be killed as they were, should be fulfilled."[9] Unto them is the Word of the LORD spoken and through them he continues to utter his decree: Thou art my Son; this day have I begotten thee.

The crucifixion is the judgment. Each time the Son of God is nailed to the cross of World Communism, the fallen ones are judged. And while their end is the second death before the Court of the Sacred Fire in the final judgment,[10] sons and daughters of the cross of Alpha and Omega go marching on to the Great Central Sun on the path of glory from sea to shining sea.

Now we contemplate the great mystery of the translation whereby, through the baptism of the Holy Ghost[11] and through the blessed violet transmuting flame, the gift of the immortal Saint Germain, chelas of the ascended masters in embodiment become the counterpart of the saints robed in white, holding the balance of life in Matter on behalf of earth and her evolutions and the souls "slain for the word of God" abiding in the etheric plane.

Thus those "that should be killed" yet abiding in time and space understand the meaning of the translation of the very spirit of prophecy. They understand death as the death of the carnal mind and of the human ego and the ultimate triumph of the Son of God and his victory over hell and death[12] to be reenacted by the Piscean conqueror in the Aquarian age right within their very own body temples—even in the secret chamber of the heart.

These stand in life this hour as they stand in the violet transmuting flame to transmute the liar and his lie, the murderer and his murder. They know the meaning of the amethyst jewel, for they have become that jewel in the purple fiery heart of Saint Germain.

They will stand on the shores of a physical universe to behold the new heaven and the new earth within the configuration of their own stellar body, the great causal body of Life, and of their own Great Central Sun, the I AM THAT I AM. They will see the kingdoms of this world become the kingdoms of our Lord and of his Christ[13] in the white sphere of the Mother exalted and expanded in the Matter temple.

Just as the Person of Christ, when enthroned by the free will of the soul within the temple of his very own being, becomes the amethyst jewel for the crystallization of the soul's alchemical marriage to the living Spirit—so the disciples of that path of God-realization who cluster around the One who is the Word, the Lamb incarnate, form the amethyst jewel of community: clusters of 'neutrons' and 'protons' as particles of participation in the great God-awareness which the Great White Brotherhood is committed to sustain within the earth body as a counterweight of Light midst an evolution yet in the darkness of spiritual neglect.

This multiplication of the light body of God-servers is the growing crystal of the amethyst jewel known as the mystery school which we have ordained in the community teaching centers of Church Universal and Triumphant.

Now let the amethyst jewel of Taiwan appear in physical dimension. Now let Saint Germain's violet-flame diplomacy become the international coup that sets at naught the designs of the wicked and out of seeming setback produces the miracles of the causal body of his own Guru, the Great Divine Director, of the jeweled mind of the Buddha, and of his own vast storehouse of Merlin's magical Mother light.

You who would see Camelot come again

nation by nation, this is the year of the rallying of knights and ladies of the flame standing on the line with Morya and Mother where Light meets Darkness and consumes it.

I AM

GABRIEL

I ANNOUNCE TO YOU
THE AMETHYST JEWEL
FOR THE ALCHEMY OF GOD-FREEDOM
NATION BY NATION

IX

Archangel Gabriel on the Mystery of Evil

IX

Children of the Light of Taiwan,

You cannot hold the line of world freedom in Asia—in your economy, in your government, in your industry, or in your armed forces—without direct contact with God through the blessed mediator, your own individual Christ Self.

Your souls are sent as the survivors of an ancient battle between Light and Darkness where a handful of the children of Chin defeated a dragon of idolatry and ideology whose nucleus was death and the cult of death.

Understand that the dragons and beasts of the apocalyptic vision of John represent the momentums of individuals who have elected by free will to ensoul mass movements of an energy veil, or *e-veil,* known today as World Communism but existing and preexisting as a force of anti-Love (the cancerous consciousness of the seed of the wicked) before the flood of

Noah, the fire of Mu, and even the destruction of the planets Maldek and Hedron.[1]

Great were the forces of the mechanical ones. Their spaceships were extensions of mother ships, and their black magicians under Satan extended their material power through clones of themselves—chemical humanoids programmed with malintent to the destruction of the souls of the standardbearers of the LORD's Christ.

Star Wars is no mere science fiction but the surfacing of subconscious memories of ages past when the evolutions of Light and Darkness, as the wheat and the tares of Christ's parable,[2] were strewn across the solar systems of this galaxy; and the battles of Lucifer's fallen ones, waged against the teams of conquerors of Archangel Michael's bands, were indeed a war of the worlds in the valley of the gods.

The earth bears record of their feats of power hurled against other feats of power as even the black magicians were divided against one another, expending the children of God in their planetary contests of "Who is greater and more glorious among the seed of the devil?"

The competition unto the death, as the fallen ones locked horns in their power struggle for the dominion of worlds, could be broken only by the Archdeceiver himself, that Lucifer who reunited the legions of darkness on the common theme of the common enemy: the Lord Christ and his legions. Seeing his blinding light and the imminent victory of the children of the sun, their competition now became "Who could destroy to the death more souls with greater subtlety and deftness?"

The cunning cruelty of the Chinese Communists from Mao to Hua Kuo-feng and Teng Hsiao-p'ing[3] derives from their fallen masters. These astral overlords control the chessboards and their pawns in governments bond and free, their goal being always to extend the line of their territory to include more and more of the ground of the children of the light, challenging their right to evolve in freedom upon that ground.

Children of the light of Taiwan, you have held that line with the legions of Jophiel and Christine for many an aeon and many an arena of the time/space continuums! And your own Chiang Kai-shek, Madame Chiang, and Chiang Ching-kuo[4] have figured again and again as heroes and heroine of your legions of light.

The people of Chin, both from the mainland and on the island of light, are of an ancient evolution. They are bearers of wisdom's scrolls dictated by Lord Lanto and Lord Confucius as emissaries of the Cosmic Christs unto your root races[5] serving on the second ray—the ray of the incarnation of the Word.

You once knew the message of Messiah as the message of your own inner man of the heart,[6] exemplified in your sages. Now the Lord Christ as Saviour and as Word incarnate must become the ultimate reality of each individual selfhood, that you might see his victory through yourselves for freedom, God-freedom, in Asia and the world. For when he and his legions were attacked by Lucifer and his bands—and this did indeed occur as it is recorded in the Book of Life and in the annals of the history of these several systems of worlds—the children of Chin rallied and stood fast at their Thermopylae.[7]

But the final act of the numerous scenes of Armageddon is yet to be outplayed, and the players East and West are even now rehearsing their parts and their roles. They choose again and again according to free will, according to the light or the dark motif of the heart.

But the great sadness of all sadness is that those who align with the strategies of the fallen ones do so thinking they do God service,[8] convinced, as they say, "beyond all doubt" that they have pursued the right course of action for world peace, world trade, and the balance of power.

They are brainwashed so to think, they are indoctrinated so to be. Some are the programmed computers of the strategists of world conquest, soothing the fears of the people with their self-esteem as the archarchitects of a world utopia.

The children of the light in all of China are one indissoluble Union. Their oneness is their origin in God yet to be realized in their orientation of God-freedom, their culture of the Mother, and their victory in the light. While the masterminds of world dominion think they arrange and rearrange power and anti-power by diplomatic maneuvering, the two-edged sword of righteousness forged of 'molecules' of souls East and West keeps the way of the Tree of Life for the children of God bond or free.

As the subsurface rocks of the sea part the most deliberate waves, so the rock of Christ in the consciousness of the embodied servant-sons and daughters of freedom, jutting out from the bedrock of Reality, parts the astral currents and the astral hordes.

The sons of dominion march by another route. It is the direct route of the descent of the light of the crystal cord from the I AM Presence to the altar of the heart. It is the direct route that connects the Mind of God to the mind of man, bypassing the byways of human reason and problem solving.

We come bearers of the amethyst jewel—the seventh-ray solution for the seventh age, the seventh-ray freedom for the seventh dispensation. Let noble knights and ladies volunteer their individual amethyst crystals of the heart for Saint Germain's three dots—Taipei, Vancouver, and Mexico City. Let diplomatic relations be established between Camelot and the lightbearers of the nations. Let outposts of Morya's realm confide the mysteries of the

Holy Grail, as two by two twin flames in love witness unto the nations.

Let the counterfeit Illuminati,[9] imitators of the Round Table and of the mystery schools, carve up the earth with their secret diplomacy and their trading in the souls of light! Saint Germain and Morya have never lost a fight! They hold the timing of the victory and they know their chelas whose time has come.

I AM Gabriel, emissary of the councils of goodwill of the Great White Brotherhood. I come from Darjeeling where I have attended closed sessions on Project Amethyst Jewel.

Let representatives of the courts of heaven be ministers with portfolio, presenting their credentials by their light and by their record of attainment. Let them be received extraordinary and plenipotentiary, their expertise in God-government and God-victory gained through the enlightenment of the "little book"[10] and the Everlasting Gospel,[11] and the tutoring and the testing of their souls by the Guru Mother who surveys the seas that cover the Motherland and penetrates the hermetically sealed alabaster cities of the deep.

From the flame room of the central altar of Mu and the twelve surrounding temples come the emissaries of God-government to the earth. They stand with the righteous, the tolerant, the patient, and the meek who, emboldened by the Word, endowed by its mysteries, will bear the Holy Grail to the nations and serve his Body and his Blood to those who have lost the memory of higher consciousness—those children of the light of Asia who stand steadfast in the battle and who will now win by the enlightenment of the Cosmic Christ.

Enter Lord Maitreya into the halls of China.

I AM

GABRIEL

I ANNOUNCE TO YOU
THE MYSTERIES
OF THE ADEPTS OF THE AGES
WHO KNOW THE HOUR OF THE VICTORY
AND SUMMON IT

X

ARCHANGEL GABRIEL ON THE MYSTERY OF ALPHA AND OMEGA

X

Children of the Golden Pink Glow-Ray,

I AM Alpha and Omega, the beginning and the ending, saith the LORD, which is, and which was, and which is to come, the Almighty.

Whereas the light of Wisdom and the light of Love manifest in heaven the polarity of Alpha and Omega (the plus and the minus of the energies of being), the circle of life on earth includes those who are aligned to the left and to the right of the spectrum of relative good and evil. It is needful to understand the Law of the One as expressed through the active and passive elements of the Father-Mother God—first in heaven and then on earth, as in Spirit so in Matter.

Wisdom in the Mind of Father is the active thrust of Alpha that arcs a cosmos as an arrow that finds its mark in the Love of the heart of Mother. Thus Wisdom and Love, as mind and heart, focus the masculine/feminine polarity of being—Wisdom as the active force, Love as the passive force. And when the energy that began as Wisdom, as action in Father, fulfills its cycle in Mother, it is that very same energy that has become Love—the passive, quiet irradiation of the life-force of a cosmos.

The plus and the minus are merely coefficients, or qualifiers, of the same energy which, when passing from point A to point Ω, are Life-giving, Life-gaining by the very process, the ritual, of energy in motion. This movement of energy from the positive to the negative coordinates of a cosmos is a rhythm that interprets the Mind and Heart of God unto the evolutions of far-flung worlds whose Identity is but the repetition in infinite variegation of the active, the passive modes of Life.

The thrust from Alpha to Omega, from Wisdom to Love, is the first half of the whole—"The Beginning." The second half is fulfilled when Omega, Mother of Love, assumes the active role and Love itself becomes the Omega return—"The Ending." Now it is an arrow sent as Wisdom by Love to become Wisdom fulfilled as Love quiescent, passive in Alpha, Father of Wisdom.

Then once again God's energy cycles back to Omega as the active Wisdom of the LORD regulating in Love the affairs of the Matter universe. (See diagrams, pp. 140–49.) This is the same Love that is the active force of the

World Mother, Shakti (feminine counterpart) of Brahma, Vishnu, Shiva—abroad in the world as fires of the law of compassion that produce chastening and judgment in the Holy Ghost.[1]

The golden pink glow-ray that appears at sunrise and sunset marks the two points in the twenty-four-hour cycle of the fusion of Love/Wisdom hurled as spheres of light twixt Helios and Vesta[2] and all twin flames who engage in this great cosmic interchange that marks the day and the night, the active and the passive movements of all systems of worlds both in the Macrocosm and the microcosm of Universal Being.

And children, tossing a beach ball on the sand, play the game of life with worlds at their command. The oscillation of energy to and fro reaches a crescendo of infinity as the unmeasured velocity of this transfer of Light, plus/minus, minus/plus, is the blending of the one indissoluble Union of God.

As the light shines on the sea and is reflected back unto a universe, a signal of life below as Life above, so the I AM Presence sends a beam of radiant energy. It is the wisdom of the I AM THAT I AM as shooting star descending to the soul who in love receives the teaching of the Law and reflects that Law with such rhythmic devotion as to create a mounting spiral, a returning current of light/love back to the source of wisdom's fount.

Thus within the being of man, the Spirit

of God is always the active giver, the positive polarity, the polestar of reality; and the soul who descends into the Matter spheres is the passive receiver, the negative polarity, of the eternal Self.

The soul, then, has the responsibility to be Omega, to know Mother as distinct from maya and illusion, to be Mother without chaos and confusion, to be Mother as energy in motion in the rhythm of life without qualifying the Void as the misqualification of an energy veil that has come to be known as *evil.*

As long as Spirit/soul are in balance plus and minus, positive/negative, and the suns hold the sacred fire for their respective planets, the universal order is maintained and a cosmic interchange continues—Wisdom becoming Love, Love becoming Wisdom, all becoming One. This is the order of the Absolute; and the very rhythm of Light becoming Light excludes any subtle deviations of the plus, the minus frequencies that are wont to manifest in the dimensions of relativity.

The Lord is thy keeper. The Lord shall preserve thee from all evil (the energy veil consisting of relative good and evil): He shall preserve thy soul. The Lord shall preserve thy going out and thy coming in from this time forth, and even forevermore.[3]

I would speak of the problem of relative good and relative evil as molding factors in the human environment and as imitators of the polarity of Alpha and Omega in the Absolute. Actually, relative good and evil are a perversion of the plus and the minus of the Matter sphere. For you see, my beloved, as we have explained before, the whole of Alpha contains the plus, the minus of Spirit while the whole of Omega contains the plus, the minus of Matter. These two wholes in alignment as two spheres, one above the other, are seen as a figure eight. And the figure eight marks the flow of energy from Alpha to Omega, from Omega to Alpha.

Souls who are aligned as the expression of the negative polarity of Omega always reflect the golden pink glow-ray of Wisdom/Love, Love/Wisdom. They stand in Matter, reflecting the light of the sun unto a universe. They are the salt of the earth and the light of the world, a city (a *citadel of consciousness,* Alpha to Omega) that is set on an hill of the Holy of Holies and cannot be hid.[4] (See diagrams, pp. 140–49.)

It is the hill of Higher Consciousness in whose mastery they sustain a vibration of light—whose velocity never descends below that of the Cosmic Christ. For the Cosmic Christ, in the Person of Jesus Christ and their own Christ Self, is also the perfect blending of the Love/Wisdom of the Logos.

When the velocity of energy moving from Alpha to Omega, as the plus/minus within the Matter sphere of the soul, begins to decelerate by the subtle intrusions of error and the laws of limitation, the soul loses its momentum in

Matter. It is no longer qualified with enough energy and light to be in polarity with the Absolute. Hence it is no longer 'qualified' to be the passive Omega of the active Alpha. It drops the ball and loses the rhythm of life—no Alpha thrust, no Omega return. And the game is over.

Now it's to another field and another team of players. Now the forcefield is no longer Omega, the absolute counterpart of Alpha. Now the soul enters the human scene with its scenarios of relative good and evil where, one and all, the players have 'dropped the ball' of Mother light and entered into the twilight duality of personalities and their idolatries.

Here the light that has become a darkness of sorts is interchanged person to person, and the people-to-people exchange of a quasi-wisdom and a quasi-love stimulates the human consciousness as it simulates the divine, but does not admit, because it cannot, the golden pink glow-ray of far-off worlds.

Relative good cannot approximate Absolute Good nor can it contain it. It is part and parcel of the same energy of the energy veil which yesterday was evil, today is good, and tomorrow again will be evil.

Relative good is in polarity with relative evil. It is the other side of the coin—now the active, now the passive, but always the same low-frequency vibration that can be no more, no less than the limits of its own self-expression until the self is no longer that self but through Christ has become the Great Self.

Relative good and evil personified in the alignment of human polarities to the right and to the left, now active, now passive, are indeed the salt which has lost its savour which the Great Teacher said was "thenceforth good for nothing but to be cast out and to be trodden under foot of men."[5]

The soul need not light a candle and put it under a bushel,[6] and men and women need not remain in the valleys of mediocrity. No God has ever condemned them to an eternal damnation of relativity. Yet there they abide playing ring around the rosy, a pocket full of posies, then the ashes—the ashes of vain repetitions and relativities—and they all fall down:[7] down the spiral of vibrations that, lower and lower, year by year, are more and more self-convinced that Truth is here.

There is no Truth there where role swapping of you-be-me and me-be-you remains but an imitation of the great ingress and egress of light in souls who have kept that light because they remain electrodes of the Great Central Sun, following his injunction "Let your light so shine before men that they may see your good works and glorify your Father which is in heaven."[8]

We see an aggressive human goodness posing as the antithesis of an aggressive human badness, as human do-gooders propose to save the earth by humanitarian schemes but somehow never arrive at the solution of their own human pollution. As human evil is a mockery of human goodness, so human goodness cloaks an underlying passivity to human evil while mocking the Absolute Good of the Person of God in the Christ immanence of his true sons and daughters.

The LORD God sends his judgment upon the 'good' people of earth who masquerade as his sons and daughters. Wearing robes of righteousness they come, pretenders to the throne of grace, imitators of the way of peace. Promising salvation, they stand side by side with the wicked themselves and are even worse. For they say they are good while denying the Good of the Son of God, cursing his Body and his Blood in each of his little ones.

While those who do evil know they do evil and are identified clearly as such, those who do good—resisting not the devil[9] but passively receiving his *d*eified *evil* and his idolatry of the energy veil—are, in fact, the negative polarity of the evildoers posing in the Personality of Good.

Those who allow evil, passively tolerating social injustice, outrage upon outrage that defies the dignity of God in man and woman and child—these are the very ones who are responsible for evil in its inception. For without the passive receiver, the aggressors of evil could not anchor their dark deeds in the earth.

Thus the LORD God assigns this day the

greater guilt to the children of God who have descended to a relative goodness and are therefore entirely responsible for the intrusion of the fallen ones as the aggressors who have invaded the earth, nation by nation from East to West, in the plus/minus karmic configuration of the international capitalist/communist conspiracy.[10]

Woe to you! is the denunciation of the LORD God this day, for it is the so-called good people of the earth who have stood by for the stoning of the martyrs, century by century. And oft, how oft, it was the do-gooders turned inside out who became the evildoers, thus revealing that the passive receiver of evil often becomes the aggressor as plus becomes minus and minus becomes plus in the valley of relativity.

He who is humanly good today can be humanly bad tomorrow. And as James was God-taught to write, "a double minded—'relatively minded'—man is unstable in all his ways."[11]

How often the friend who is the friend of human goodness and the foe of human evil will be on this side and that from year to year and lifetime to lifetime. They come, posing as disciples of Christ. They know where the power is and, by their masquerades of human vice and virtue, move when expediency requires from sinner to saint and back again—a puzzlement to the children of light whose one desire is to know the Self as God.

Let Keepers of the Flame renounce the camp where personalities of good and evil cuss and discuss the rounds of human circumstance, as human karma, positive and negative, fails utterly to provide the key to the dilemma of life as it is lived on earth.

Enter the Good of Alpha and Omega in the Person of the ascended masters. Enter their chelas who are on the road to becoming that Good—as Above, so below.

Chelas are chelas because they have shunned the right and the left bank in pursuit of the strait gate and the narrow way which lead unto Life.[12]

I AM

GABRIEL

I ANNOUNCE TO YOU
THE MOMENT OF TRANSCENDENCE
IN WHICH THE SOUL ACCELERATES
FROM THE RELATIVE TO THE ABSOLUTE

DIAGRAM 1
THE GREAT COSMIC INTERCHANGE

Diagrams 1 and 2 illustrate the cosmic interchange of energy from Spirit to Matter, Alpha to Omega, Spirit to soul, Guru to chela within the circle of being, the Divine Whole.

The upper sphere is the positive polarity (Wisdom) denoting Spirit as the Creator and heaven as the Cause. The lower sphere is the negative polarity (Love) denoting Matter as the Creation and earth as the Effect.

The upper sphere is the I AM THAT I AM, Absolute Good, the Incorruptible One. The lower sphere may also represent the soul descended to the plane of relative good and evil now become the corruptible.

The upper and lower spheres each have two halves, one the plus, one the minus. Alpha and Omega are contained within the upper sphere within and as Spirit. Alpha and Omega are contained within the lower sphere within and as Matter.

The I AM THAT I AM
Absolute Good
the Incorruptible One
as spheres within the Sphere
of Alpha and Omega

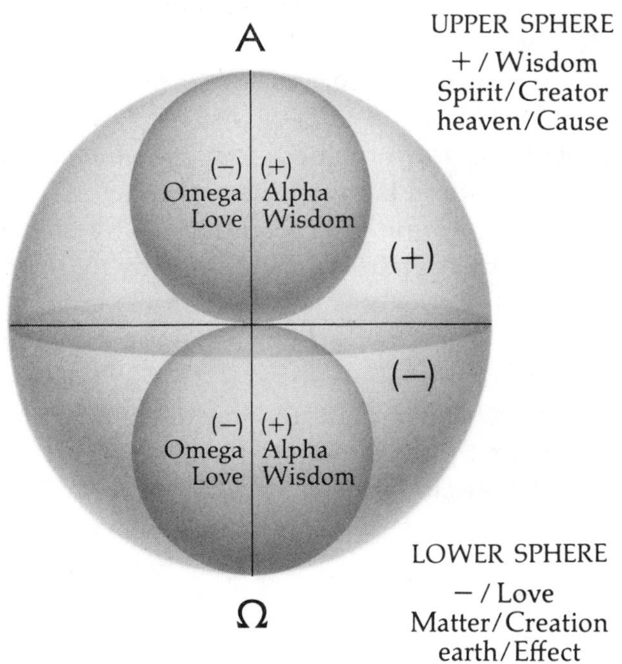

"I AM Alpha and Omega,
the beginning and the ending, saith the LORD,
which is, and which was,
and which is to come, the Almighty."

DIAGRAM 2
THE GREAT COSMIC INTERCHANGE

Cycles of the upper sphere rotate in a clockwise direction; cycles in the lower sphere rotate in a counterclockwise direction.

The flow of energy between the two spheres is shown by the arrows which create a figure-8 pattern between the two spheres.

The cycle of "The Beginning–Thy Going Out" is the Alpha Thrust indicated by the solid line. The cycle of "The Ending–Thy Coming In" is the Omega Return indicated by the dotted line.

The former indicates the descent of the soul from Spirit to Matter, the latter the ascent from Matter to Spirit.

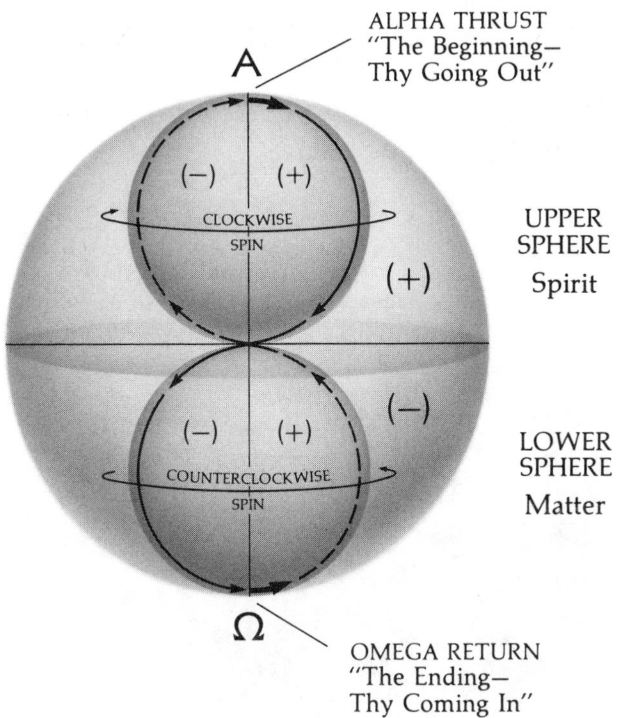

"The LORD shall preserve thy going out and thy coming in from this time forth, and even forevermore."

DIAGRAM 3
THE GREAT COSMIC INTERCHANGE

There are four steps of energy flow in the figure-8 pattern as follows:

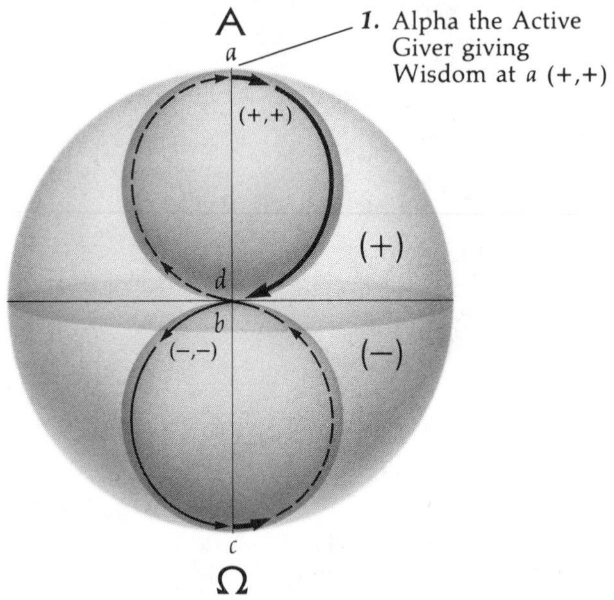

STEP 1. At point *a,* Alpha the Active Giver passes the torch of Wisdom (+,+) to Omega the Passive Receiver, who receives it at point *b,* the nexus where it changes direction and polarity to become Love (−,−).

STEP 2. Omega carries the torch of Love (–,–) from point *b* to point *c* where it changes direction and polarity to become Wisdom (–,+) at point *c*.

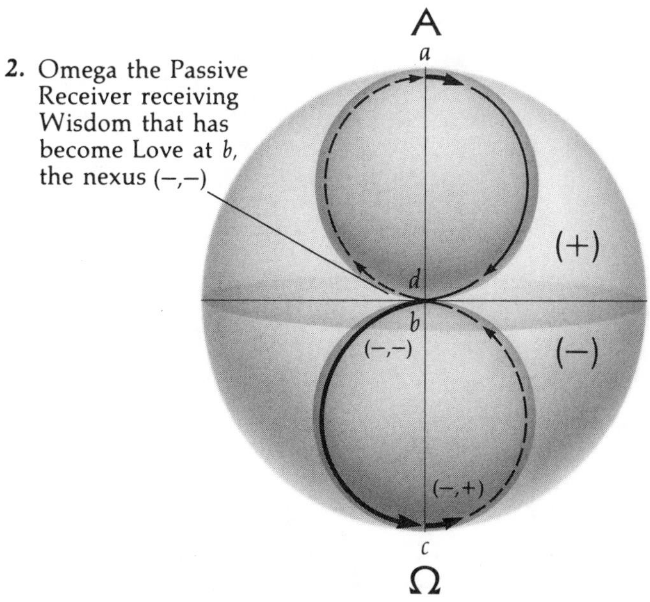

STEP 3. At point *c* Omega, now the Active Giver, passes the torch of Wisdom (−,+) to Alpha, now the Passive Receiver, who receives it at point *d*, the nexus, where it changes direction and polarity to become Love (+,−).

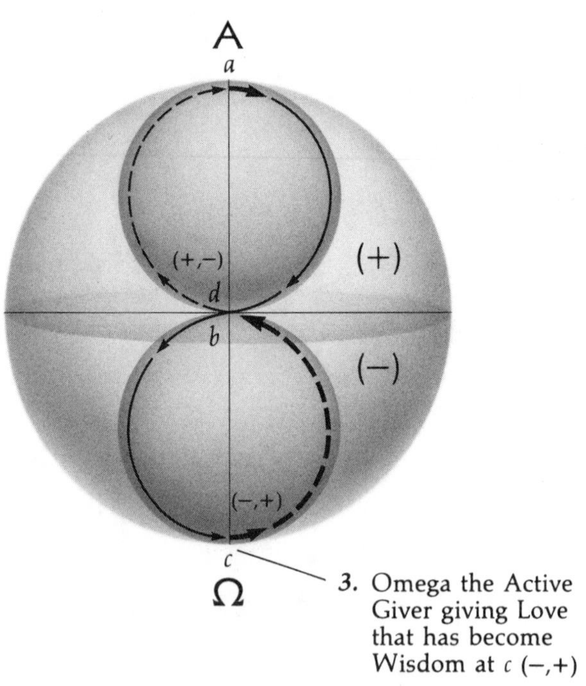

3. Omega the Active Giver giving Love that has become Wisdom at *c* (−,+)

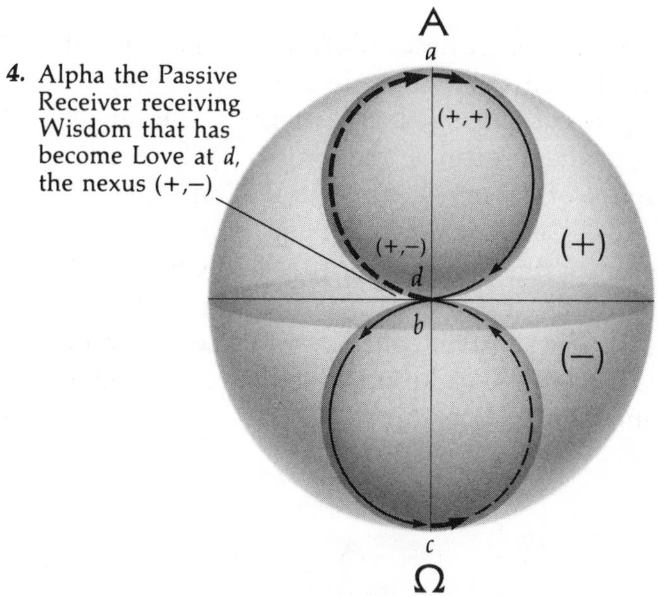

STEP 4. Alpha carries the torch of Love (+,–) from point *d* to point *a,* where it changes direction and polarity to become Wisdom (+,+). And there begins once again the ritual of the energy flow of twin flames of cosmos celebrating the going out and the coming in of the soul from the I AM THAT I AM in Father to the AUM in Mother and from the I AM THAT I AM in Mother to the AUM in Father.

DIAGRAM 4
THE GREAT COSMIC INTERCHANGE

As energy descends from point *a* to point *c* in diagram 3, the light in the upper and lower halves of the figure-8 pattern is spinning in opposite directions, resulting in the descending spiral of energy pictured in diagram 4.1.

As energy ascends from point *c* back to point *a*, the spinning of the two halves of the figure-8 creates an ascending spiral (diagram 4.2). The simultaneous flow of these two spirals is the cosmic caduceus (diagram 4.3) of Alpha and Omega.

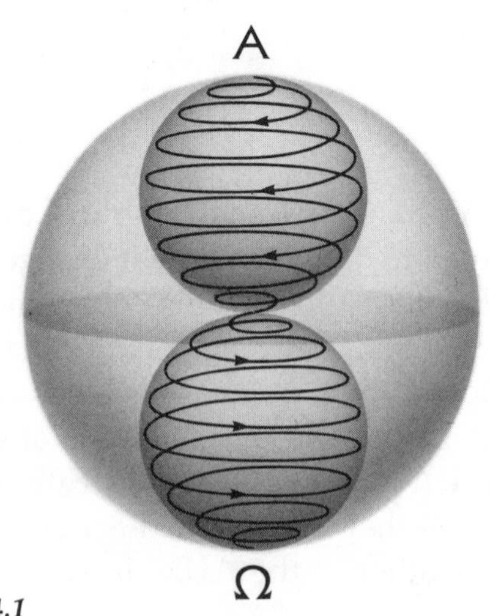

4.1

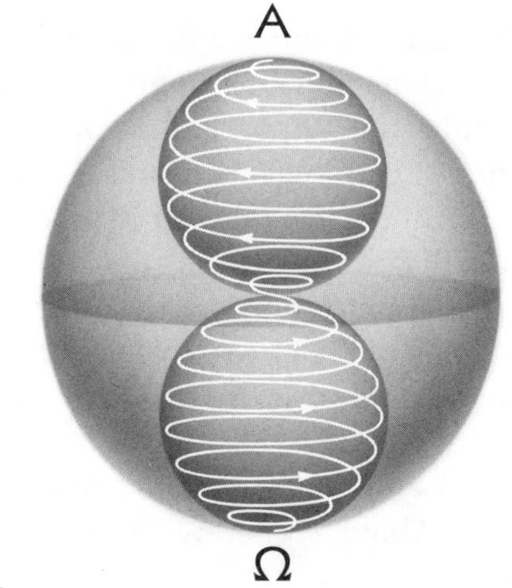

4.2

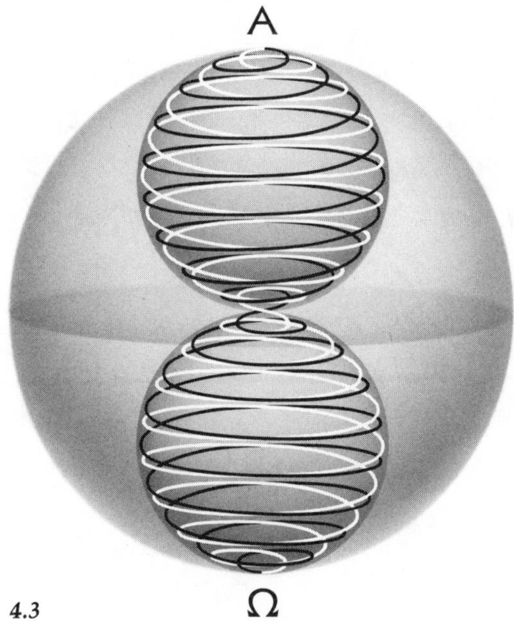

4.3

In diagram 4.4, the two horizontal figure-8 patterns show the plus/minus energy flow contained within the upper and lower spheres. These figure-8 patterns create spirals similar to diagrams 4.1 and 4.2, imitating in an east-west direction in diagram 4.5 the cosmic interchange of the figure-8 north and south (diagram 4.3).

The action of the Great Cosmic Interchange can also be visualized as the whirling of the T'ai Chi (diagram 4.6), the plus/minus interchange, and of Alpha and Omega in the white fire core of being, as Above so below, as in heaven so on earth.

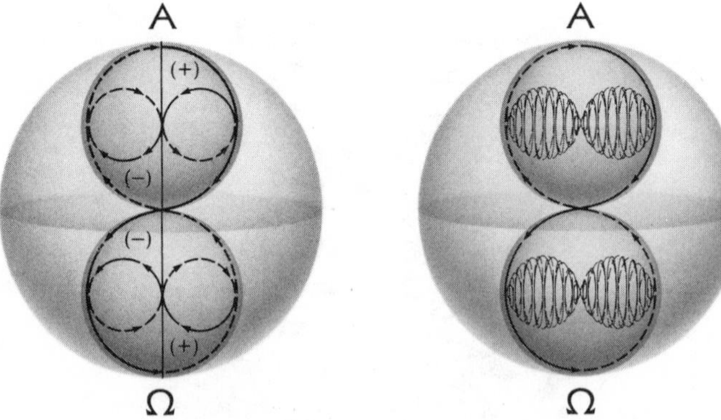

4.4 4.5

4.6

XI

Archangel Gabriel on the Mystery of the Sacred Eucharist

XI

Children of the Light of Alpha and Omega,

The dilemma of good and evil was put to naught by Jesus Christ when he addressed the rich young man who came and said unto him, "Good Master, what good thing shall I do, that I may have eternal Life?" The Master replied: "Why callest thou me good? There is none good but one, that is, God. But if thou wilt enter into Life, keep the commandments."[1]

Jesus would not be classified as a good person. No, he would not. He attributed all goodness to the Person of God and the attainment of that goodness through the obedience of the chela to the commandments of the Guru and Lawgiver.

Pride motivates men's souls in the performance of good works in order that the self may receive a reward from other selves and acquire name and fame, position and prestige. For similar reasons, in a perverted sense, the deranged perform feats of devil-daring, ideological murders, seeking for themselves the headlines of the dailies or a reference in the history books as anti-heroes or prime movers in the mainstream of events.

A study of the psychology of fanaticism, especially when observed in the outplaying of the psyche over several embodiments, reveals the pendulum swing to the right and to the left of relative good and evil as the extremes of the human consciousness find the individual positioned now with "the good guys," now with "the bad guys," but always on the same rod of energy with the mere change of the dial from plus to minus and minus to plus.

Human hatred is human hatred, whether it takes the form of malice and premeditated evil or that of human sympathy with the human consciousness. Both attitudes fulfill the goal of the fallen ones: the destruction of souls—whether by the venom of vipers or by the milk of human kindness.

The personality cults of the day surrounding figures in politics, religion, or entertainment illustrate the game of human sympathy where individuals, incomplete in themselves, build altars to their human gods and sit in circles around their idols, totally identifying with every laugh or tear, trial and triumph, as though they were their own. So intense is their involvement with the idol that the energies of their emotional bodies flow out of themselves and into the personality figure, thus creating the emotional tie through which they can then be hypnotized and controlled.

This willing consent given by the masses to their soapbox leaders, allowing the latter to live their lives, not only for them but through their energy, can well be labeled the emotional tyranny of the age. It occurs because individuals with a poor self-image derive satisfaction in living their lives through those who present a more colorful self-image, daring to do more 'good' or more 'evil', as the case may be, than the less polarized, less daring masses they control.

This relationship of the people to their gods is an obvious imitation of the true Guru-chela relationship wherein the God in the Guru and the God in the chela retain a relationship that is based upon their polarity of the light of Alpha and Omega.

The Guru represents the God Self, the Spirit, the plus factor of life, and is the Source-emitting sun center receiving from the Above, distributing to the below. The Guru is the activator of Good, the only Good that is God.

The chela is the passive receiver of that Good. When he receives it, he becomes a portion of the Guru and of the Person of God which the Guru has become. Now the chela (who holds the balance of the negative polarity in relationship to the One Sent) takes on, in relation to other personages in the circle of life, the plus polarity, he himself becoming a secondary outpost of the Great White Brotherhood.

Thus in the mode of receiving life, light, and consciousness from Above, every part of life sustains the negative polarity of being in relationship to the person in hierarchy who stands above him in the cosmic chain of initiation. Inasmuch as all who have received must become givers of the life that is Good, they, then, in the mode of givingness, assume in turn the role of the plus polarity of Alpha. Thrust and return, thrust and return is the ritual of the givingness and the receivingness of God throwing the warp and woof of a cosmos.

Now the dilemma of good and evil becomes the drama of Gog and Magog who, because they are of the same genesis of the plus, the minus of the anti-God, destroy one another, hence are self-destroyed.

What is this human consciousness arrayed upon the human consciousness as dinosaur upon dinosaur, locked in a life and death struggle, pierce and puncture one another until their mutual viciousness is spilled upon the ground? Not as the spilling of the blood of a Christ upon Golgotha, theirs is the blood of martyrs which they have drunk as their own death potion (though they know it not).[2]

Unto Clare of Assisi the Saviour Jesus Christ gave the Sacred Eucharist for the turning back of the hatred of the Saracens upon themselves.[3] Thus, through the Body and Blood of Christ present in the sons and daughters of Alpha and Omega is the judgment of the nations come, and the Light of the One confounds the light and darkness in the relativity of the human consciousness.

Saint Germain sets forth the strategy of Armageddon: It is to allow the forces of relative good and evil to array themselves, one against the other, and to cancel each other out while the Lamb, as the Word incarnate, is with the hundred and forty and four thousand who sing their new song,[4] giving dynamic decrees unto the day and unto the night. This precipitates the gently falling manna that angel ministrants place upon the tongues of God's children as his Body becomes their body and his Blood, as Spirit's light, becomes their blood.

They have lost their leader, these fallen ones. Lucifer is no more.[5] They have no rallying point save the ebb and tide of their own aggressions. Let the Communist regime of Cambodia's Pol Pot destroy and be destroyed by the Communist Vietnamese as column upon column of the black ants invade the territory of the red ants in this Communist game of checkers wherein each side, drugged by their own hatred of the Light and drunk with the blood of martyrs whom they have murdered by the millions, is too insensate to know that Death itself speaks from both ends, playing them against the middle, when they say, "We pledge to fight them to the end."[6]

This is a mini war of Gog and Magog, of the sympathetic Communism of the Soviet Union in polarity with the malicious Communism of Red China. Yes, each assumes from time to time the polarity of the other in the plus/minus exchange. It is only the dance of the most unfortunate advance, swinging partners right and left but always returning to the point of origin that is Anti-Light.

These factions of the tares live off the wheat, you know. Let the children of the light beware! Let them withdraw their supplies, manpower and matériel, their technology, taxes, trained experts, and tender loving care from the Gogs and Magogs West and East. Their principalities and potentates are everywhere positioned, vying for the power of the Son of God.

Don't you see through, little ones, the power plays of a secretary of state and a national security advisor?[7] Don't take sides, for neither one will win. Now learn your lesson well: human good and evil will never out. Only Truth will triumph over sin.

While everywhere the power plays go on among the spiritually wicked in high places[8] and they volley for financial empires built upon the souls of people—who are guilty in part, for they have played their game of the personality cult from the start—the Son of God in the Son of man stands unmovable as the Rock, still waiting to receive all who will receive him in purest light.

While the representatives of capitalist nations consider it their duty to arm and rearm the beasts who prey upon the children of the light, those very children, for whom the fallen ones show only a scurrilous scorn, drink the communion cup of the Lamb and eat the Bread of Life that is his Body. They are awakening to their own Sonship which he has won for them upon the true cross of Alpha and Omega.

One by one *they* shall emerge the champions of the international power play, and then the members of the pleasure cult too late will awaken in dismay. Emboldened by their madness, the unquenchable thirst for pride of power, they will have overplayed their hand and the forces of Light will in God Victory assume command.

Let the strategy of Saint Germain be known, and let the wise ones be readied for their role. Let the true shepherds of the people be positioned on the stage of life continent by continent in the Person of Good.

Let them give their energy to God alone and to his Lamb, as the children of the light are made one through the Body and the Blood, the Omega and the Alpha, of the Lamb.

Let them withdraw all life and light, energy and consciousness from the Adversary and his cults of sin and death in which he has engaged the wicked of the world—from those who are right to those who are left—for neither one will enter into Life but they that keep the commandments of their God.

I AM

GABRIEL

I ANNOUNCE TO YOU
THE ALL-TRANSMUTING LIGHT
OF HIS BODY AND HIS BLOOD
AS THE SOLUTION AND THE DISSOLUTION
OF WORLD GOOD AND EVIL

XII

Archangel Gabriel on The Mystery of the Judgment

XII

Children of the Spirit of Prophecy,

"The lion hath roared, who will not fear? The Lord God hath spoken, who can but prophesy?"[1] The Holy Ghost be upon our messengers as they can but prophesy unto the whole family of the children of Israel whom the Lord God hath brought up from the land of Egypt.

And the days have been fulfilled prophesied by the prophet Amos eight hundred years before the birth of Jesus Christ:

"I will send a famine in the land, not a famine of bread, nor a thirst for water, but of hearing the words of the Lord.

"And they shall wander from sea to sea, and from the north even to the east; they shall run to and fro to seek the word of the Lord and shall not find it.

"In that day shall the fair virgins and young men faint for thirst.

"They that swear by the sin of Samaria and say, 'Thy god, O Dan, liveth'; and, 'The manner of Beersheba liveth'; even they shall fall and never rise up again."[2]

This day, O ye tribes of Israel, the Word of the LORD is fulfilled in your ears. For there has been a famine in the land America and a famine, lo, these two thousand years in the speaking of the electrifying message of the prophets of Israel unto the people of God.

The false prophets have come and gone, century by century. They have offered their serpentine ideologies to quench the hungering and the thirsting of the souls of light after the righteousness of the Law and the Spirit,[3] but they have never filled the vessels of men's souls; for their own waterpots were empty and they were clouds without water, wandering stars to whom is reserved the mist of blackness forever.[4]

Now the long night of the LORD's famine is far spent and the day of his appearing in the abundant Word is at hand!

The LORD God in the Person of the I AM THAT I AM, in the Person of the Lamb whose mantle is upon the embodied messenger, is standing upon the altar[5] of the sanctuary judging the house of Jacob, and not one among the twelve tribes or the Levites shall escape the LORD's judgment. It is the dividing of the way of Light and Darkness in order that the soul may accelerate its immersion into the white light.

And the Everlasting Gospel dictated to our two witnesses[6] is a gospel of judgment. This is the highest love of the I AM Presence toward each child of God, for with the judgment is the death of the carnal mind and after that the resurrection of the soul—"they that have done good, unto the resurrection of life; and they that have done evil, unto the resurrection of damnation."[7]

I, Gabriel, utter the decree: The resurrection of the soul unto life and the fullness of its individual Christ consciousness will not be intercepted by the carnal mind—who would seize the crown of king and kingdom, and of Christ and his apostles, but can never wear the cosmic cross of white fire of Alpha and Omega or the cross of Malta, emblems of Jesus Christ and Saint Germain unto the kingdoms of Israel and Judah.

The judgment is the unalterable piercing by each one's Christ Self of the qualifications of Light and Darkness which the individual has executed according to free will. The judgment is the command of the Lord for the sifting of the house of Israel among all nations, "like as corn is sifted in a sieve, yet shall not the least grain fall upon the earth. All the sinners of my people shall die by the sword, which say, *The evil shall not overtake nor prevent us.*"[8]

Thus every man, woman, and child who is of the seed of Abraham, of Isaac and Jacob, every soul who is of the seed of David, the seed of Alpha and Omega through Jesus Christ, receives this day the recompense of his word and his works according to whether or not he has allowed the Word, as the personal Christ Self, and the emanation of his Work through the Holy Ghost to manifest within and without the temple of being.[9]

The piercing light that traces the thoughts and feelings and the motives of heart and mind is each individual's own energy returning unto him, by the directive of his own Christ Self, all that he has sent forth as bread cast upon the waters.[10] That bread of the life they have lived on earth, for better or for worse, now returns to the people standing on the shores of life waiting for the Redeemer, who is Christ the Lord.

The Lord is after his people. Though they have hid themselves in the caves of human good and evil, thence shall the hand of the Lord take them! Though they dig into hell, though they climb up to heaven, thence will I bring them down![11]

For that which they have sought to accomplish outside of my I AM Presence will be stripped from them and they shall behold my handiwork.[12] And the God of very gods, who is the Creator within and without the creation, shall demand of his people the fulfillment of every jot and tittle of the Law, and a cosmic accounting of their deeds and their desirings.

Though they have sought their heavens and their hells, yea will the right hand of my judgment be upon them! For the arm of the LORD descends, and Love and Love alone rules the world.

Those who defy the energy veil which they have created saying, "The evil shall not overtake nor prevent us," those who challenge the very law of cause and effect which they themselves have set in motion, who deny their own karmic accountability, they shall 'die by the sword' with the death of their own carnal minds to which they have given preeminence when they could very well have given that lawful preeminence unto their own I AM Presence.

And all of their dying and all of their sacrifices and all of their temple offerings with their weeping and their wailing will not suffice to deter the unalterable, irrevocable law of karma. But with all of that, it is neither their karma nor the coming of the Dark Cycle of the intensification of the return of their karma[13] by which the carnally minded shall die, but by the sword.

What is the sword? The sword is the *sacred Word* who releases the sacred fire of the ascended masters unto the people through the upraised chalice of the messengers.[14] Who are the ascended masters? They are the Persons, or the personification, of the I AM Presence whom the prophet sees in the presence of the LORD standing upon the altar.

The LORD God, the one God of Israel who is the I AM THAT I AM, has multiplied himself in the Person of his servant-sons, the ascended masters, who are present in the land—each one a flaming sword of righteousness, each one the presence of the living Word, each one releasing the teaching of the promised Comforter,[15] the light of the Holy Ghost, in the true Spirit of prophecy spoken through our messengers.

Thus all of the misqualifications of light and darkness in the valley of relativity have no power to destroy or to judge the people of God. Karma in and of itself is not the judgment; but the coming of the emissaries of Alpha and Omega, delivering the light of the Father-Mother God—that is the judgment. The Light is the Logos by whom and through whom the Father executes the discretions of his judgment, now accelerating, now decelerating the return of the energies of men's deeds.

Thus the Law is subject unto the Lawgiver, and the Law is applied with justice and mercy, impartially yet individually unto Israel and Judah and the surrounding nations according to the dictates of the wisdom of the Son unto whom the Father "hath committed all judgment."[16]

With the presence of the Person of the Son of God in their midst, the people of God have an advocate with the Father, one who will intercede before the throne of grace,[17] imploring the great Trinity of Life in the Person of the I AM THAT I AM to withhold the wrath of God (his white fire) in the day of judgment. Thus the prophet Amos interceded and implored forgiveness on behalf of the house of Jacob, and it is written that the LORD repented for this and said, "It shall not be."[18]

The true Person of the prophet is the Person of the Christ, the Friend of God even as Abraham was the Friend of God.[19] Thus the function of the messenger is to be with the Son (the Mediator of the Lawgiver) as he mitigates the Law by his dispensations of mercy released in answer to the clear call of the messenger.

And thus the disciples of the Word who make themselves by a disciplined love perpetual chalices of the true light of the ascended masters become transmitters of the Word of the LORD given unto the prophet. And the effectual fervent prayer of these righteous (these veritable extensions of God's flame) availeth much,[20] as rays of light emanating from the central Logos.

The chelas of the ascended masters positioned in time and space likewise intercede with God through the blessed Christ Mediator on behalf of the children of Israel. And as long as the prophet is in their midst focusing the living God in flesh and blood, in time and space, there is a staying action of the LORD God and a mitigation of personal and planetary karma.

The hour of the famine in the land, prophesied by Amos, signifies the cycles or centuries in which God withholds from the midst of his people the embodied Word who comes in the Person of the messenger, the prophet, the Guru, i.e., the one anointed with the Christ consciousness, embodying the God flame of the I AM Presence.

This period of the absence of mankind's true teachers is the period of the famine, for without the Teacher there is no teaching. This famine, then, becomes the karma of the children of God who have allowed the children of the Evil One to kill the prophets and crucify the Christs East and West.

In that hour the Law spoken by God's emissaries in previous cycles of the abundant Word is established as the authority of God in the midst of the people. This Law is the plumbline of Truth. Now without the personal presence of the Guru, it is the chelas whose constancy to the memory of the Lawgiver and his laws sustains the extension of light from the Holy of Holies into a darkened and darkening world.

They recognize the plumbline not only as the commandments of the patriarchs and the prophets but as the testimony of Jesus Christ unto his messengers, the veritable mysteries of the Holy Grail shining in the midst of my people Israel.[21] And they bear witness to the plumbline itself as the vertical line of the righteousness of the Law, daily separating their Good and their Evil and commanding the separation of the Real and the unreal in the whole body of God.

"Walk while ye have the Light" is the command of the Lord Jesus Christ, and while the Light be incarnate "believe in the Light, that ye may be the children of Light,"[22] for this is the opportunity for salvation that is given. O ye men and women who seek the Word and the LORD in this day, remember that you also "must work the works of Him that sent me, while it is day: for the night cometh, when no man can work."[23]

The night is the dark night of the soul when the darkness that covers the land is each individual's own returning karma that eclipses momentarily the light of the Son of God (the avatar of the age or the personal Christ Self). And when that karma is balanced, there is yet the initiation of the dark night of the Spirit when the light of the Sun (the I AM Presence) is withheld in order that the initiate may prove that the Christ light that is in his heart is the light of an unmovable devotion that places its trust in the Presence of the Father even when that Presence withdraws itself as the ultimate test of Golgotha.[24]

The crucifixion of the house of Jacob is the testing of that Love (an absolute Love not conditioned by the yin and yang of the outer personality but truly wedded to the inner Christ) which must be great enough to love Him even in the appearance of His greatest absence, an absence so desolate and so dark as to cause the Son of man to cry out: "My God, my God, why hast thou forsaken me?"[25]

The dark night of the soul is thus created by the lesser self, but the dark night of the Spirit is created by the Greater Self. The one is the test of the soul's confrontation with its own karma of relative good and evil, the other is the initiation of the soul's encounter with the Great God as the presence and the absence of Light, as the plus/the minus, the active and the passive participation in the cycles of his being.

Children of the prophets, all of this draweth nigh. With the coming of the Light in the Person of the Son is the day of Work. With the withdrawal of the Son cometh the night, the long night of initiation through direct encounter with the Law itself—as First Cause in God and as the secondary cause-effect chain of man's own self-imposed law of karma. And after the night, the coming once more of the day of mercy and grace through the Son. Now the Son is your own beloved Christ Self, the inner Guru, the Teacher face to face, now firmly fixed within the temple of thine own being, nevermore to depart.[26]

In that day will I raise up the tabernacle of David that is fallen and close up the breaches thereof; and I will raise up his ruins, and I will build it as in the days of old, that the children of the light may possess the remnant of *Eden.* And all of those who were not of the original seed of Christ, they, too—which are called by my name I AM THAT I AM and who give answer to that name—will be possessed of me and of my prophet.[27]

And I will bring again the captivity of my people of Israel, and they shall rebuild the waste cities,[28] and they shall reinfuse the cities of America with the light of Alpha and Omega which they bear as His Body and His Blood. And they shall reclaim the waste places of the laggards that have been destroyed by the seed of the wicked who have come and gone as a plague of locusts, the cloud upon the horizon that has laid desolate the Christ consciousness of the people. And my children shall live the abundant life in the land of abundance.

"They shall plant vineyards and drink the wine thereof; they shall also make gardens and eat the fruit of them. And I will plant them upon *their land,* and they shall no more be pulled up out of *their land* which I have given them, saith the LORD thy God."[29]

I AM

GABRIEL

I ANNOUNCE TO YOU
THE JUDGMENT OF LIGHT AND DARKNESS,
THE RESURRECTION OF LIGHT,
AND THE RESTORATION
OF THE GURU-CHELA RELATIONSHIP
IN THE LIGHT
THAT SHALL NEVERMORE GO OUT
IN ISRAEL

XIII

Archangel Gabriel on the Mystery of the Antichrists

XIII

Children of the Path of Christhood
under the Master Jesus Christ,

When Jesus said, "Woe unto you, lawyers! For ye have taken away the key of knowledge; ye entered not in yourselves, and them that were entering in ye hindered,"[1] he was addressing himself to the excessive legalism of the scribes and Pharisees. For they had buried the great commandments of the law of Moses and the Holy Spirit exhortations of the prophets of Israel and Judah in their orthodox codification of the Law and the Spirit, teaching for doctrines the commandments of men, even holding the traditions of men greater than the commandments of God.[2]

The lawyers to whom Jesus addressed himself were determined to lay upon the children of the light, as they are in this day, "burdens grievous to be borne" which they themselves touch not—no, not with one of their fingers.[3]

When Jesus warned his disciples to beware of the doctrine of the Pharisees,[4] he was speaking of the self-righteous and zealous sect of self-appointed custodians of the communication of the Word from the I AM THAT I AM unto Moses.

Originally, the guardianship of the law (of Moses) was held as an office in hierarchy by the Chasidim, veritable saints who were called by the LORD to keep the flame of the prophets among the true disciples of the Law. These disciples were among those who felt within their very souls the calling of Messiah and returned to Jerusalem after their captivity in Babylon.[5]

The Pharisees, persecutors of Jesus Christ, were the children of those who had murdered the prophets. They even built the sepulchres of the prophets, thereby witnessing their approval of the deeds of their fathers.[6]

From time to time, by the wisdom of his Word, God had sent them prophets and apostles filled with the Holy Ghost, veritable evangels of the LORD's hosts, rebuking them as did Zechariah with the full authority of the seven archangels: "Why transgress ye the commandments of the LORD, that ye cannot prosper? Because ye have forsaken the LORD, he hath also forsaken you."[7]

But on each occasion of their coming, this

same "generation of vipers" denounced by John the Baptist would conspire against the lightbearers and stone them with stones even upon the commandment of the king of Judah.[8] And each time they slayed the prophets, they effectively denied that Jesus Christ was come in their flesh.[9] For it is written in the Book of Life that whosoever shall speak the Word of the Son, the only begotten Son of God, in him dwells the Lord Christ as the Person of Jesus *bodily.*

The Word incarnate in the prophets which the LORD God sent unto Israel and Judah was the very same Lamb of whom it is written: "He was slain from the foundation of the world."[10] Thus the words of Zechariah, who perished between the altar and the temple, *"The LORD look upon it and require it,"* are answered in the Person of Jesus who declared to the lawyers, "Verily I say unto you, *It shall be required of this generation.*"[11]

Who were the lawyers to whom Jesus denied the kingdom of heaven—habitation in the consciousness of Spirit—and unto whom he denounced the woes of Gehenna? Surely they were not the defenders of the poor, the fatherless, the widowed, and the homeless, nor the challengers of social injustice of that day or of your own.[12]

Surely they were not those who wore the mantle of Christ as counsellors before the Bar of the Logos or the true mediators of the Word who would plead before the throne of the

Father in the name of the Son Jesus Christ on behalf of mercy and justice unto the children of God—which children, though they transgressed the law (of Moses), were yet worthy of the higher law of forgiveness and that grace that comes only through the Son.[13]

Surely they were not the advocates empowered by the Holy Ghost to set aside both spiritual and material law in favor of Opportunity, whose living flame, the violet flame, is the renewer of good works and the sponsor of the soul's sacred labor through which his sin may be transmuted and then transcended.[14]

No, the "lawyers" then and now are the legalists whose excessive conformism to the letter of the law brought down upon their heads frequent denunciations from the true advocate with the Father who never feared to expose their hypocrisy:

"Woe unto you, scribes and Pharisees, hypocrites! For ye pay tithe of mint and anise and cummin, and have omitted the weightier matters of the law, judgment, mercy, and faith: these ought ye to have done and not to leave the other undone. Ye blind guides, which strain at a gnat and swallow a camel.

"Woe unto you, scribes and Pharisees, hypocrites! For ye make clean the outside of the cup and of the platter, but within they are full of extortion and excess. Thou blind Pharisee, cleanse first that which is within the cup and platter, that the outside of them may be clean also.

"Woe unto you, scribes and Pharisees, hypocrites! For ye are like unto whited sepulchres, which indeed appear beautiful outward, but are within full of dead men's bones and of all uncleanness. Even so ye also outwardly appear righteous unto men, but within ye are full of hypocrisy and iniquity."[15]

The term "lawyer" (Greek *nomikos* 'of the law') is synonymous with "scribe." The scribes were the legalists of their day who copied and codified both the written and oral tradition of the law which was handed down not only as sacred scripture but as rabbinical definitions and redefinitions of rituals both spiritual and material. Eventually these degenerated into human reasonings and human statements of the law, held by the scribes and the Pharisees to be the actual Word of the Christ Self, *Adonai* (Hebrew 'master', 'lord', or 'sovereign').

Such rituals and interpretations which have resulted in the orthodoxy both of today and of two thousand years ago are thus an accumulation of doctrine and dogma which in Jesus' time stultified not only his own literal sacred-fire transmission of the Word but also that of the patriarchs and the prophets.

Today the same solemn-faced interpreters would if they could "muzzle the mouth of the ox that treadeth out the corn"[16]—of the LORD God himself—as he sends the direct person-to-person communication of the Word of Jesus Christ unto his disciples through the Holy Ghost come upon his messengers.

Thus it is that everyone who is a disciple on the path of Christhood under the Master Jesus Christ must meet and denounce the enemies of righteousness both in the ecclesiastical Babylon, the citadel of confusion within the established church, as well as the political Babylon,[17] which is the citadel of confusion erected by the false prophets who have sought by entering the governments and economies of the nations to penetrate the matrix of the spiritual Confederation of Israel and Judah.[18]

There comes a time and a place on the path of initiation when the disciple cannot take another step unless he first slay the dragons of orthodoxy that give power to the beasts of the Liar and his lie to control the people in the conspiracies of the dark ones pitted against the lightbearers East and West.

Orthodox traditions in church and state are those which conform to an interpretation of the Law that fails to take into account the progressive revelation of the Person of the Word incarnate. Such traditions upheld with the pomp and ceremony of a dead ritual by a dead clergy are the justification on the part of the rebellious spirits whereby they may reject the Person of the Son of God who comes in the true shepherds of the people.

Thus these wolves in sheep's clothing[19] claim immunity from the authority of the true servant-sons bestowed upon them directly through the Holy Ghost from the Father to the Son. Such as these, who would claim the power of heaven and earth without the Trinity, lay claim to a prior ordination in the law handed down from generation to generation and therefore, they say, more valid than the fragrant virtue emanating from the aura of the living saints.

Their strictness in the observance of a dead letter and their quoting of scriptures to and fro is the defense mechanism of these "whited sepulchres" who are "full of dead men's bones" —whose auras and very body temples are inhabited by discarnate entities—and whose demons continually cry out "LORD, LORD!" *because,* and for the very reason that, they cannot enter into the circle of sacred fire reserved for Jesus Christ and his true disciples.[20]

And when they can no longer stand in the presence of the Anointed One, because their demons are tormented in the presence of the Light, they cry out with a loud voice and stop their ears as they did in the presence of Saint Stephen, running upon the lightbearer with their accord of discord.[21]

As they slay the righteous—those who have understood both the Spirit and the Matter of the Law of God and have the right and honorable use of that Law and that Spirit—they think they do God service; but in fact, while promising liberty to the children of God, they themselves are the servants only of the corrupted self.[22] They raise up the carnal mind and its carnal logic in the place of the Logos and in the place of the true interpreters of the Word, our messengers in heaven and in earth.

The fallen ones have not the sponsorship of the Logos, therefore they must become a law unto themselves. And they go one step further. Seizing the robes of the prophets, they sit in the seat of the scornful[23] as the judges among the people, dispensing the law as the lawgivers in church and state and saying, "We have the authority. There is none other." Thus they have made themselves equal with God and are the true Satanists according to the lusts of their father.[24]

Now I, Gabriel, stand in the midst of the land America with the judgment of the LORD God Almighty which he has already pronounced through his Son Jesus Christ: "Whoso shall offend one of these little ones which believe in me, it were better for him that a millstone were hanged about his neck and that he were drowned in the depth of the sea. Woe unto the world because of offences! For it must needs be that offences come; but woe to that man by whom the offence cometh!"[25]

Therefore let the justices of the Supreme Court of the United States of America heed the

Word of God spoken in the full power of the Holy Ghost, whose blood has been shed from the foundation of the world:[26]

> You who have rendered your decisions[27] against these little ones, thereby promoting abortion and giving license unto the seed of the Wicked One to murder the seed of Christ—of you and your generation shall the blood of the Anointed Ones be required. You who have denied the reality of myself, saith the Lord Christ, in these little ones tenderly abiding in the womb of Mother, you will I deny before my Father![28]
>
> You who have denied Life, unto you will Life be denied in the final judgment and the second death at the Court of the Sacred Fire.[29] You who have led a generation in your death cult and in your suicide pact with Satan: Know then that I, the LORD God, have spoken, and that judgment is meted out this day in the Person of my Son.
>
> And it cannot be turned back! It will not be turned back! And upon all who are in accord with this hatred of the Woman and her seed—this persecution of the ones who bear the cup of Light to the earth as the threefold flame in their hearts—is that Light turned this day. It is an all-consuming Light. It is the sacred

> fire of Alpha and Omega, consuming all unlike itself and canceling out the antichrists who have invaded the temples of church and state worldwide.
>
> Yours is the abomination of desolation standing in the holy place where it ought not.[30] But the LORD is in his temple[31] and he will stand, and he will come as a refiner's fire and fullers' soap.
>
> And ye who have sinned against the Holy Ghost shall not abide in the day of his coming nor stand in the presence of his appearance. And he shall sit in the land as a refiner and purifier of silver: and he shall purify the sons of Levi, and purge them as gold and silver, that they may offer unto the LORD an offering in righteousness.[32]

The scribes who thus interpret the Law, destitute of their moral obligation to the Person of the Law and to the interpretation of the intent of that Person, that Son of God, are also destitute of the sense of their own sin and of the need for the Person of the Christ in whom is the cleansing of sin[33] and the redemption of the soul.

Wherever we have set our representatives, these 'scribes' have come. Almost as soon as the hot coals of the Word of God fall from the mouth of the prophet, they are ready to codify that law and that fire, tempting him with their specious reasoning and their personality cult, then laying wait for him and seeking to catch something out of his mouth that they might accuse him.[34]

But they, confounded in their own mechanical prison houses with which they have sought to imprison the souls of light, are not able to answer the Christ a word, neither do they dare from the day of their own judgment to ask him any more questions;[35] for he himself is the living Answer to the accuser of the brethren, which accused them before our God day and night.

Even within our own activity, our own community of the Holy Spirit where we, the hosts of the LORD, are fulfilling the prophecy of the LORD in giving unto the two witnesses the Everlasting Gospel and unto the two prophets the finishing of the mysteries of God,[36] there have come those who have sought the initiation of empowerment (enduement) even while they have denounced the messenger upon whom the power of God is bestowed.

Little children, beware of the children of them which killed the prophets.[37]

After the death of Jehoiada, the apostate princes of Judah came with their flatteries and obeisance unto the king. And Joash the king, who had done that which was right in the sight of the LORD all the days of Jehoiada, now responded unto the personality cult of the princes and their idolatry of his person.

Now the king, preferring the power of the princes of this world, gave the commandment for the murder of the prophet in the very court of the house of the LORD,[38] seeking, in the shedding of blood, the light of the Son which is held in the very physical blood cells even as the wine of communion is held in the crystal chalice of the soul.

These same princes, reincarnated, have come to our own sanctuary of the Holy Grail, appearing as the pious ones, quoting the law as though they were the very authority of the Law itself. And when the prophet has denied to them the power that is contained in the Blood of Christ and that is transferred today by the ascended masters through their embodied messengers, they, too, have gone to gather in their groves, idolizing one another while plotting the astral assassination of our witnesses through malicious gossip and the interpretation of the LORD's Words and Works through our messengers that is devoid of the testimony of the Holy Ghost.

When they cannot gainsay[39] the teaching of the Teachers which has come forth faithfully year after year in the publications of The Summit Lighthouse, then they resort to the detaining of innocent souls, binding them to their own hypocrisy, giving them to drink of the gall of their bitterness which they also gave to Christ upon the cross.[40]

And what are the lies of these legalists, these scribes who would circumscribe the great body of Truth though they themselves are not a part of that body? They give their interpretations which are their *mis*interpretations of a most stupendous delivery of the sacred fire that descended as the chastening light of God unto the disciples who gathered at the Retreat of the Resurrection Spiral in Colorado Springs in the final hours of the mission of our Messenger Mark L. Prophet to America and to the Mother and her children.

His Word was a sacred fire, a sword of righteousness, dividing the way of the sheep and the goats.[41] The same Word spoken unto the children of light was understood as endearment and was received as the precious gift of his Body and his Blood. But to the scribes who would yet inscribe their record of infamy against the Lamb, his words were a threat to their very ego-centered identities which they attempted to hide from their fellow disciples but which they could never hide from the messenger.

Now these ones, jealous of that Light (Christ consciousness) which they cannot have because they do not bear witness of that Light (neither in themselves nor in the messenger), have set themselves up as the discriminators of Good and Evil, marking this and that religion as counterfeit of the Truth according to their wholly false and fictitious labeling system based upon the dead letter of their own legalism.

Let all children of the light who approach the fount of the Great White Brotherhood, all who are athirst for the water of Life and are bidden to buy it without money and without price,[42] beware of *these* false prophets. They are the counterprophets whom Jesus denounced as the blind guides. They are blind because they have not seen him face to face;[43] and because they have not seen him, they have not recognized his messengers nor can their perception of the messengers come through the all-seeing eye of God.

These individuals who separate themselves bodily[44] from the company of saints are the Pharisees of the day, whose very hatred of the Light is the black magic of Satan which they impute to our messengers. Their names are numbered and known by the archangels, though they think they enjoy the secrecy of our presence and our sponsorship. Like hired assassins, they gladly receive fame and fortune as they attempt to destroy the unspeakable love and beauty of God shared in the Guru-chela relationship.

Now we see these "raging waves of the sea, foaming out their own shame,"[45] traveling here and there, now speaking in low tones to emphasize their wisdom that is of the Serpent, now crying loudly in the outbursts of their anger against the Almighty who has sent his

Son for their judgment. Wherefore he has said to them, "Woe unto you, scribes and Pharisees, hypocrites! For ye compass sea and land to make one proselyte, and when he is made, ye make him twofold more the child of hell than yourselves."[46]

Hearken, ye little ones! They come in fear of their own torment[47] due their own rebellion, and they leave in their own justification of that fear. From the beginning they were "trees whose fruit withereth, without fruit, twice dead, plucked up by the roots."[48]

They have never known the sublime love of our messengers. They have not understood the love of twin flames or of the shepherd who lays down his life for his sheep.[49] They love one another as accomplices in crime, as vultures devouring their choice prey.

They have never known the love of the Father or of the Son or of the Holy Ghost, and the love of the Mother is far from them. Therefore they have not that perfect love which casts out fear and the fear of the Guru who embodies the Law hence is the catalyst of their own personal karma.

No, they have never loved because they do not have the capacity to love. And their human sympathy, one with the other as they commiserate in their outer darkness, is a paltry substitute for the love that binds together the body of God, the love wherewith the Lord Christ loves his disciples and the love to which he commended them, saying, "This is my commandment, That ye love one another, as I have loved you."[50]

And here is the perfect love of God the Father, that he sent his only begotten Son into the world that the children of the light might live through him.[51] That perfect love in that Son is the manifest Christ Self in the Master and his disciples, always alive where the Guru-chela relationship is sustained as the ordering of the hierarchy of a cosmos by the Law of Perfect Love.

I AM

GABRIEL

I ANNOUNCE TO YOU
THE AUTHORITY OF THE WORD
WITHIN YOU
TO DENOUNCE THE ANTICHRISTS
IN YOUR MIDST
AND THENCE TO MOVE ON
TO YOUR OWN CHRISTHOOD

XIV

Archangel Gabriel on the Mystery of the Wicked One

XIV

Children of God Who Expose the Antichrist
by the Mother Flame,

John the Baptist was confronted by the Pharisees and Sadducees, who came in their cunning to be baptized of him.[1] They desired the initiation of the Light but would not give obedience to that Light. Lifetime after lifetime they had rebelled against the Law—they who had been cast out of heaven with Lucifer by Archangel Michael and the hosts of the LORD.

They knew all too well that with the coming of the Son of man in the Person of the Son of God the final judgment would be upon them.[2] But in the meantime, for thousands of years and thousands of rounds on the karmic wheel of rebirth they had learned to use the light and to abuse the light without giving answer to the Word incarnate.

Now his time had come and his herald was before him, fulfilling the prophecy of Isaiah as the voice of one crying in the wilderness: "Prepare ye the way of the LORD! Make straight the paths of the descent of the Son Jesus Christ, who has come into his temple to judge the twelve tribes of Israel[3] and to initiate the loving, the obedient, the humble servant-sons in the Personhood of their own Christ Self!"

And the people of Jerusalem and Judaea and the region of Jordan went to receive the initiation of the baptism—the confessing and the cleansing of sin in Jordan.[4] And there followed them the seed of the Wicked One—now the murderers of the prophets, now the imitators of the prophets. For so long had they grown accustomed to deceiving and being self-deceived, regaling in the absence of the LORD's anointed, that they did not figure on the God-power of the reincarnated Elijah, great Guru of Elisha, who had "come again" as the messenger of the Promised One.[5]

Note, O chelas of the prophets holding the line of Light against the Darkness mounting in the twentieth to the twenty-first centuries, note well the difference in the action of the impersonal and the personal Law. The sacred fire that proceeded out of the mouth of John the Baptist was the denunciation of personalized Evil, embodied Evil, by the Person of Absolute Good, the Person of God.

Before all of the multitude gathered at Jordan, he told them who they were: a "generation of vipers," the offspring of the Serpent.

He exposed them as the fallen angels who fell from grace and from serving as ministers of fire[6] on the right hand of God with his Christ. Cast out of heaven, they would soon be cast out of earth by the blazing light of the Son of God.[7]

Now they sought not to amend their ways, not to reconsider and to confess that living Christ. No indeed, they sought to steal the light of the prophet by posing as children of God. He knew that they were trembling before the oncoming Light and that "the wrath to come" would be the light of Alpha and Omega dwelling bodily in the incarnate Word as Father, Son, and Holy Ghost.[8]

John the Baptist wore the mantle of the Lamb, the same mantle he had worn as Elijah, denoting the office in hierarchy that carries the authority of the Word and the judgment of God. He had been his messenger then unto all of Israel, and he was his messenger reincarnated.

He demanded of the Pharisees and Sadducees "fruits meet for repentance,"[9] good works on the ledger of life, a record of good karma that would compensate for bad karma and therefore be the necessary and acceptable offering unto the Guru, a token expression of allegiance unto the Law whereby the Law might then increase the light of the supplicant. But they had not the good works meet for repentance, for their works were done in evil.

What is Evil, what is Good? The good work is the work done to the glory of the

I AM THAT I AM in love, unselfed love, purest love for the Person of the Son. And no other work will count for grace except that work that is done to exalt the Most High in the lowly places of the earth and in the lowliest hearts of men.

The evil work is the misqualification (*mist-qualification,* hence illusion[10]) of the light of the Trinity and the Mother manifesting as the substance of sin, causing the soul to be out of alignment with the inner blueprint of the Logos—the image and likeness of God—the I AM THAT I AM out of which the soul was created and in which it will now be re-created first by water of John, then by fire of Jesus.[11]

He told them not to rely upon their supposed ancestral origins in Abraham,[12] for they themselves had sinned (made karma through disobedience to the Lawgiver and the Law) and they would bear the burden of that sin (karma). And they would not be allowed to place that burden then or now, my beloved, upon the sons of God. He knew they were not of the seed (the Christ image) of Abraham, even as Jesus Christ would declare:

"If ye were Abraham's children, ye would do the works of Abraham. But now ye seek to kill me, a man that hath told you the Truth, which I have heard of God; this did not Abraham.

"Ye do the deeds of your father. . . . If God were your Father, ye would love me; for I proceeded forth and came from God; neither came I of myself, but he sent me.

"Why do ye not understand my speech? Even because ye cannot hear my word.

"Ye are of your father the devil, and the lusts of your father ye will do. He was a murderer from the beginning and abode not in the truth, because there is no truth in him. When he speaketh a lie, he speaketh of his own; for he is a liar and the father of it."[13]

My beloved, heed, O heed the warning of John and Jesus: He who loves not the Christ in the Father's incarnate servant-sons, in those whom he has anointed with the gifts and graces of the Holy Ghost, cannot be of the seed of Christ; therefore he is the seed of the Devil—the offspring of the Evil One, that Lucifer who first *d*eified *Evil* and then became the personification, or personhood, of that *d*eified *e*nergy *veil.*

John the Baptist set aside the law of human heredity and human genealogies as capable of transmitting the Christ mind, declaring that God is able of these 'stones'—the common genes of the common people—to raise up true children unto Abraham's Christ consciousness of God the Father.[14]

The child is neither good nor evil because of his parents, but because the Lord God has endowed him with a threefold flame that burns on the altar of the heart and with the gift of free will which the child has used justly, wisely, and well in previous lifetimes.

The ax that is laid unto the root of the

trees[15] is the ax of the Law wielded by the Person of the Lamb incarnate. The tree is the symbol of individuality, male and female. In the son, the daughter of God, the Tree of Life does manifest the fruit of good works within its branches, ring upon ring of the causal body. And the tree trunk is the Christ Self through whom the soul is rooted in the bedrock of Reality, nourished from below by the currents of Mother Earth as from above by the Spirit currents of the Father.

But the seed of the Wicked One have been cut off from the I AM THAT I AM. They are without causal body, without rings of fire, without the Christ Self or the root of knowledge in the Law of the Word. When the all-seeing eye of God scans their auric field in Spirit and in Matter, in Alpha and Omega, and reveals not the good fruit of works in the Holy Ghost, therefore through the Person of the Son of God the ax of the Law is laid unto the cause and core of error, and Truth herself in the Person of the sacred fire hews down and casts that fruitless tree into the vortex of all-consuming Love.[16]

No wonder the Pharisees and Sadducees conspired with the council of the Sanhedrin to put Jesus to death after the soul of Elijah had come in the Person of John and they had refused to acknowledge his authority or to witness unto his light but had done unto him whatsoever they listed.[17] For John had told them that the Christ would come with fan in hand to throughly purge his floor and to gather his wheat, the children of God, into the garner. He exposed them as the chaff and told them that the Lord Jesus Christ would burn that chaff with unquenchable fire—Spirit fire, Alpha/Omega fire.[18]

Who are the Pharisees and Sadducees, then and now? By now you should have guessed, my beloved. They are the left and the right, the plus and the minus, of human good and evil. Assuming their positions, pretending to be in opposition to each other, they merely polarize the misqualified substance of the energy veil to suit their purposes which are always to deny the validity of God-Good in the One whom He hath sent and in the ones chosen by God to believe on the One Sent and to anchor the light of his Spirit in the planes of Matter.

The messenger then and now is the One Sent and the believers are those who sustain the light of the Spirit in the souls of humanity through the blessed Mediator personified in the anointed messenger.

Every believer is an electrode of the light of those who have reunited with the Spirit of the I AM THAT I AM—the ascended masters. Every believer is a disciplined one of the Master's Presence, the unascended chela of the Guru ascended. But he that denieth before men the messenger of the Word (who is as a shaft of light leading unto the Greater Light) shall be denied before the angels of God[19]—shall be denied the collective Christ consciousness of the ascended masters, the entire Spirit of the Great White Brotherhood.

Thus the chela's affirmation or denial of the messenger of the gurus determines his relationship to the gurus; likewise he who denies the Christ in the chela also denies the gurus and their messenger. And the chain of being, Alpha to Omega, throughout rings upon rings of the gurus and their chelas, is one universal order of Life. He who breaks a single link in the chain breaks the whole chain even as he who offends in one point of the Law is guilty of all.[20]

John the Baptist and Jesus the Christ came to affirm the hierarchy of heaven, the hosts of the LORD of whom they were a part and whose representatives they were. They were the One Sent to awaken the embodied children of God to their opportunity to be joint-heirs of the Christ consciousness which they bore. And all who would accept that opportunity would become as they were—disciples of the Ancient of Days—bearers of the Holy Grail.

It is the intimacy, the unspeakable love of this Guru-chela relationship of which the Sadducees and Pharisees were envious—the estate of the Son sitting on the right hand of the Father which they had lost through pride and ambition. But they would not relent, they would not repent, they would not confess the Light which they both saw and feared in the LORD's anointed. For if they should bear witness, the children of God should be converted to their origin in the same Light, and the Sadducees and Pharisees would lose their control over the people both in the synagogue and under the rulers of the Gentile nations.

"Show us a sign! show us a sign! show us a sign from heaven!" they cry in the market-places, taunting, even tempting the Son of God to come down[21] from the throne in Spirit and deal with them in their forcefield which they have arranged in the yin and yang of Matter in order to arraign the souls of light. But no sign will ever suffice these fallen ones, neither the abundant testimony of the angels and their evangels—the ascended masters and their messengers and chelas—nor the bodily resurrection of the Lord Jesus Christ and of the saints East and West, nor the witness of their own prophets.

Not the miracles of Elijah and Elisha[22] come again in John the Baptist and Jesus the Christ. No, not the ascension of Elijah in a chariot of fire or the smoting of the waters of Jordan by his servant-son Elisha.[23] Not the sign of Horeb's height or Sinai, the tablets of the law or the miracles of Moses midst the Egyptians.[24] Neither Words nor Works nor vibrations from the Upper Room where the LORD is gathered with his disciples for forty days or forty years or forty centuries.[25]

He healed the sick, he cleansed the lepers, he raised the dead, cast out devils and rebuked the blind leaders of the blind and continues to do so through his embodied servants.[26] But though they witness unto the truth forever and a day, those Pharisees and Sadducees will not receive a sign—not from heaven, not from earth!

They demand a sign of God the Father only to tempt the Son: "Command these stones be made bread" was the Devil's plea for the sign of phenomena in his attempt to cause Jesus to abrogate the covenant twixt Father and Son.[27] In this manner even the children of Israel, themselves tempted of the fallen ones, chided with Moses to tempt the Lord, murmuring against him, almost ready to stone him. And the Lord bade Moses to strike the rock because the people tempted the Lord.[28]

Nevertheless, Moses himself bore the karma of his rebellion against God's commandment in the desert of Zin. For he allowed his anger to be aroused by the strife of the congregation and willfully sought to sanctify the Lord before their eyes which it is not lawful for a messenger of God to do. Even so, the water came forth from the rock and it, too, was the sign denied.[29]

Always disputing, always denying, the Sadducees remain the spoilers midst every generation of lightbearers. Their doctrine is a doctrine of denial. They are the religious rationalists of then and now. Do you think, little children, that they really disbelieve in the angels and the spirits of God, who are the ascended masters? Do you think they really disbelieve in the miracles of the Anointed One? Do you think they really dispute the law and the spirit of the resurrection?

Now learn of an archangel, for the children of God must become "wise as serpents and harmless as doves."[30] They are the wise serpents. They once formed a ring of fire around the Central Sun. They knew God face to face and they rebelled against the Law of the One, the Law of Love. They knew and know the angels, for they themselves are fallen angels. They tremble before the ascended masters and their messengers, and they know that only the miracles of God are able to thwart their conspiracy of Absolute Evil pitted against Absolute Good appearing as relative good and evil.

They have seen the resurrection—oh yes, they have! They have seen the spiraling of sons and daughters of God back to the Great Central Sun, back to the heart of Helios and Vesta. But all this they deny. They are the deniers of Superconscious Being (one's own Higher Consciousness—the Mighty I AM Presence sealed in the successive rings of the God Consciousness of the causal body) and of the eternal existence of the soul before and after the finite span of birth and death in time and space.

Operating midst certain councils of the elders, of the Sanhedrin and the priesthood, the Sadducees are one with them in vibration—one and the same, and their beginnings and their endings are the same—the same death spiral that began when they denounced the LORD GOD Almighty and his hosts as the legitimate hierarchy of the Spirit/Matter cosmos.

Their priesthood is the anti-priesthood, the counterfeit of the order of Melchizedek.[31] Knowing as they know the inner Law of the great Three-in-One, they know that the knowledge of the Law will be the liberation of souls throughout the Matter sphere and that with that liberation will come their own ultimate end, the second death of the fallen ones in the final judgment before the Court of the Sacred Fire on Sirius.

They are *not* the Jews of today as you know them, but they have invaded the synagogues of the Jews even as they have invaded the Catholic church, the Jesuit order, the Protestant churches, and the mosques of Islam; and their seed has penetrated all of the races of the earth. Saying they are Jews or followers of Christ or those who come in the name of Allah, they are still of the synagogue of Satan.[32] By their fruits (their vibration and their soulless eyes) *ye shall know them!*

They carry neither the affirmation of the Word nor the adoration of the Woman clothed with the Sun. From their lips pass not the Our Father nor the Hail Mary. The Mother of Christ is anathema to them, for she is Creator in Matter even as God the Father is Creator in Spirit.

They are the protesters; with the descendants of the Pharisees, the offspring of the Sadducees go about protesting this and that in church and state, inciting the people in mass demonstrations and ignorant denunciations of the living Word. In the time of Jesus, the Sadducees were noted for their material wealth and their spiritual poverty. Reincarnated today, they assume every convenient stance as social or religious reformers, even mouthing the teachings of the Great Teacher while busily, nefariously, and secretively codifying the anti-teaching as the laws of church and state.

Enter the fundamentalist Jews, Christians, and Moslems as the legalists of the decade! They follow the tradition of the scribes and the Pharisees. They would sit in Moses' seat.[33] They would seize the power and the authority of the Law and the Lawgiver. They would bind the children of the light with their religious custom; but their fanaticism, their anger, their holy terror and their hatred in the presence of all who have the Holy Ghost exposes them as spots in their feasts of charity.[34]

"Woe unto them! For they have gone in the way of Cain," believing in a God and in a religion after their own will, who have never known the true redemption of both the Body and the Blood of Christ. And they have run "greedily after the error of Balaam for reward," who, acting in the name of God, would curse God's children who have sinned instead of extending to them the chastening of his intense love and the call unto that repentance which is the return to the Law and the Grace of God through the atonement that becomes the at-one-ment with the resurrected Christ. These are they which "perished in the gainsaying of Core," denying the authority of Moses as God's chosen spokesman and intruding themselves blatantly into the office of the priesthood of the Levites.[35]

The fanaticism displayed by these modernized cults of the scribes and Pharisees is always present when the Law is denuded of both the Person and the Principle of the Holy Ghost. Little children, observe! Where there is violence, there in the midst of the people are the seed of the Wicked One, the violent ones inciting them to denounce their faith and their hope in the Person of Charity who is always present in the true shepherds of the people.

Ponder my wisdom, for it is the wisdom of the universal Father and the universal Mother. Then know yourself as the offspring of that Wisdom and be the harmless doves of their twin flames of the Spirit.

I AM

GABRIEL

I ANNOUNCE TO YOU
THE LORD'S DENUNCIATION
OF THE SEED OF THE WICKED ONE
IN YOUR VERY MIDST

XV

Archangel Gabriel on the Mystery of the Messengers

XV

Children Who Love the LORD Thy God as One God and Thy Neighbour as Thy True Self:

Have you ever considered that the first and great commandment and the second were pronounced by the Lord Christ in answer to a question put to him by one of the scribes gathered together with the Pharisees in which they were again tempting him, saying, "Master, which is the great commandment in the law?"[1]

It is then that he pronounced the covenant of the great love flame, "the flame of the ark of the covenant"—that cloven tongue of fire[2]—whereby souls born out of the love of the Father-Mother God receive that arc descending and return that thrust of love as the arc ascending, thereby completing the ritual of wholeness as a holiness that begins and ends in the twin flames of the one God:

"The first of all the commandments is, Hear, O Israel; The LORD our God is one LORD;

"And thou shalt love the LORD thy God with all thy heart, and with all thy soul, and with all thy mind, and with all thy strength: this is the first commandment.

"And the second is like, namely this, Thou shalt love thy neighbour as thyself. There is none other commandment greater than these."[3]

The Pharisees were hung up on the law, and therefore they were hung by it. They are silenced by his statement in the Person and in the Principle of the Law of Love, for it is the one law of Alpha and Omega which they cannot fulfill. They sought to trap him in their own manipulation of the law, thinking then to dispute with him and to demand by what or whose authority he spoke.[4] But he confounded them, speaking to them in the language of the law of Moses:

Hear, O Israel: The LORD (Hebrew *YHVH,* from the verb "to be," the I AM THAT I AM) **our God** (Hebrew *Elohim,* plural of *El* or *Eloah,* meaning "Mighty One") **is one LORD**—is one I AM Presence manifest to the soul in the Christ Self. This one God is the Father (whose Being self-contains its own polarity, or counterpart, the Mother, hence the use of the plural noun) who reveals himself to you in the Person of the Son even as the Son will reveal himself to you in the Person of the Holy Ghost.

And thou shalt love the LORD thy God (Greek *Kurios* 'Lord' and *Theos* 'God' translated as "the Lord the God of thee")—i.e., the Christ Self whose descent is from the I AM THAT I AM of thee—**with all thine heart, and with all thy soul, and with all thy might.**[5]

But thou shalt love thy neighbour as thyself (as thy true self which is thy Christ Self): **I AM the Lord**—I AM thy God through thy Christ Self. I AM thy true self. I AM thy Word. I AM WHO I AM and I AM manifest in the plane of action as the Mediator between thy heaven and thy earth.[6]

Jesus the Christed One was the fulfillment of the law and the prophets,[7] the Law of Love which the messengers of the Lord had stated again and again to the very ones whom Saint Stephen named as the "stiffnecked and uncircumcised in heart and ears." Of these same Pharisees who murdered Jesus Christ and would also murder his disciple, Stephen thundered:

"Ye do always resist the Holy Ghost; as your fathers did, so do ye. Which of the prophets have not your fathers persecuted? And they have slain them which shewed before of the coming of the Just One, of whom ye have been now the betrayers and murderers; who have received the law by the disposition of angels (ascended masters) and have not kept it."[8]

And so Jesus taught them by example that Love—God's love manifest from the Divine Us as male and female in the incarnation of his sons and daughters—was the fulfilling of the law.[9] They themselves had not received that love as the communication of the Word or as the leaping of the sacred fire of the Holy Ghost from the succession of patriarchs and prophets unto their own hearts' altars: they received not the flame of Love because they received him not.[10] They had never received the LORD's Christ in the Person of the ones sent to them, how could they receive the Messiah who had come?

In the fullness of that Love which becomes the judgment of the Law unto those who, though silenced by the statement of Love's law—a statement written in the very flesh and blood of the Guru and his chelas[11]—yet remain unrelenting in their abuses of Love, Jesus asks the question that will now confound the scribes and Pharisees, even as he had confounded the Sadducees with his astonishing doctrine "God is not the God of the dead, but of the living."[12]

Now in the unquenchable, fiery love prophesied by John the Baptist, Jesus challenges them: "What think ye of Christ (the Messiah that I AM)? Whose son is he? (What is his origin? What is his seed? Whose soul is he?)" They said unto him, "The son of David." Then he asked them, "How then doth David, speaking in the Holy Spirit, call him Lord, saying, The LORD said unto my Lord, Sit thou on my right hand, till I make thine enemies thy footstool? If David then call him Lord, how is he his son?"[13]

This question, which no man was able to answer, must now be answered by the Lord Jesus Christ himself unto his disciples who are the branches of a living vine.[14] The term "son of David" means *soul of David* even as the term "Son of man" (i.e., *sun,* or *light,* of man) refers to the *soul of man* when that one has become 'fastened' to Christ.

Both refer to the soul *(solar)* identity that reincarnates again and again until it reunites with the individual Christ Self,[15] referred to in much of the Old Testament scriptures as *Adonai,* meaning "Lord," or "Master." This Lord is the extension of the LORD, the I AM Presence, in your life, hence the individual Master, the very personal Guru of the soul, whom you address as your own beloved Christ Self.

The Christ Self, then, has communication with the Father who in both Principle and Person is the Presence of God *(YHWH,* or *YAHWEH),* the I AM THAT I AM, or the I AM Presence. Thus we find that the soul of David, endued by the Holy Ghost,[16] addressed his own Christ Self, the archetype of the Messiah, and received of him the report that God the Father, his own beloved I AM Presence, had addressed his own Christ Self, saying, "Sit thou on my right hand, till I make thine enemies thy footstool."

Thus the I AM THAT I AM summoned the Christ of David as well as the soul of David—who was ordained to be the vessel of that personal Christ consciousness holding the office of the Son of man—to sit on his right hand of authority, i.e., to rule in and through the I AM Presence until the Father would "make thine enemies thy footstool."

The enemies 'without' of the soul who incarnated as both David and Jesus were the representatives of Antichrist who attacked his authority as the One Sent by the Great Silent Watchers and the Cosmic Christ to be the World Teacher—he who had been anointed by the I AM THAT I AM through the prophet Samuel[17] and baptized by the I AM THAT I AM through John the Baptist. The enemies 'within' were the elements of his own personal karma which he was required to balance before his final incarnation as Jesus when he would be called upon to bear the sins of the world, i.e., the planetary karma.

He then asked the Pharisees, "If David addressed the Christ as his Lord, how can that Christ, that Messiah, be the son of David?" Indeed it was the same soul who had incarnated as David who now reincarnated as Jesus who acknowledged the same Christ Self as his Lord and Master. Only now he had become that embodied Word, that embodied *Adonai.* There was no further distinction between the *soul* of Jesus and his own Christ Self, the Son of God. Hence he was called the *Son of man.* It was this highest Person of himself whom David had addressed as Lord—unto whose Identity his soul as Jesus attained.

While the Sadducees and the Pharisees would establish their authority by their supposed human ancestry descended from "their Father Abraham" and (at least the Pharisees) look for the Messiah, establishing his authority by the Davidic line, he himself would claim his authority solely through God the Father manifest in his own I AM Presence.

And he would teach his disciples that the real meaning of the seed of David and of his descent was the descent of the Christic seed which David bore—which Jesus bore when he was embodied as David—and which in truth is the seed of the Christ Self, the very Person of God, bequeathed to the sons and daughters by their own Father-Mother God, Alpha and Omega—regardless of who their earthly parents might be.

This implanting of the Personhood of God within his sons and daughters is the initiation which God delivers unto those souls who have fulfilled the requirements of the Law of Love, who have exercised free will in the footstool kingdom, outpicturing in the earth the patterns made in the heavens, as Above so below. The gift of the indwelling Christ is the gift of sublime Personhood to the child of God who has become the inheritor of his own Christ potential, sharing with Jesus Christ the joint-heirship that is reserved for him "that doeth the will of my Father which is in heaven."[18]

The difference between a child of God and the son of God is that the child is the soul of God entering the path of initiation whereby, measure for measure, through words and works, he shall put on and become the fullness of that potential who is Christ the LORD *(Adonai).* The son of God is one who has entered into a relationship of co-equality—co-creatorship—under God the Father. The son of God is the soul who has realized the fullness of the Christ of God[19]—the Christ consciousness that descends out of the LORD who is God *(YHWH,* or *YAHWEH),* who is I AM THAT I AM.

This is the true and only descent of souls perfected in Love. They have no other origin but God. The difference between the child of God and the son of God, then, is one of steps, or degrees of attainment (or realization) of the Christic light, on the path of initiation to individual Christhood.

Truly it is said that the sons of God are not only made in the image of God which image is Christ, but they have become the fullness of that image in manifestation (i.e., in *manifest action*). Now their Words and their Works are God's. They are blazing 'suns' of righteousness, 'secondary' sources of the light of God, i.e., the fullness of the *Second* Person of the Trinity.

Hence the sons of God when they are fulfilling the Law of the One—the one and only begotten Son of God—are the Christs of God incarnate. They are the embodied Word. There is one LORD but many souls embodying that LORD. There is one Christ, one Son of God, one Word, but many souls with upraised chalices who are the living witness of the Universal One. And the quest for the Holy Grail leads to the discovery of one's sublime raison d'être: to be the vessel of God.

In heaven, the "sons of God present themselves before the LORD."[20] They are also found among the "congregation of the mighty Watchers" whom the LORD called "Gods"[21] because through the path of initiation they had become himself personified—they had totally identified with the Self that is God. (They had God's consciousness, or 'God consciousness'. They were completely *God's.* Hence, "Ye are God's.")

In the very midst of this "assembly of the saints,"[22] this council of the elect, the Supreme Godhead executes his judgments. He is the one God who is the Source of the God consciousness (the awareness of the Self as God) of "all the host of heaven standing by him on his right hand and on his left."[23]

This host of heaven, I, Gabriel, declare to you to be the sons of God who have in the first instance descended to earth through Christ and who have in the second instance ascended to heaven through Christ. Through the descent and the ascent they have proven the Law of the incarnation of the Word in heaven and in earth as it is the will of God. And thereby they have completed the ritual of Alpha and Omega for the going out and the coming in of the soul from Spirit to Matter and from Matter to Spirit, which the Father-Mother God *(Elohim)* have ordained as the sowing and the reaping of cosmic consciousness.

The increase of light that results from the cycle completed, the ascension won, by a single son of God is the fruit by which his attainment is known. The fruit of the Father's harvest of his Son's Words and Works on earth is the manifestation of the Holy Spirit. In fact, the very presence of the Holy Spirit in the soul of God is proof that he has completed the requirements of Sonship as the embodiment of the Trinity through the threefold flame of the heart.

The initiation of the Holy Spirit is the ultimate conferment of power in heaven and earth accorded to the victorious one. It is this initiation of which Jesus spoke in the final hours of his mission on earth when he said, "All power is given unto me in heaven and in earth."[24]

This power conferred is the actual Person of the Holy Ghost whose living Presence every ascended and unascended master has become. Having received this power from the Almighty One, the Guru now empowers his chelas to be himself in *manifest action* in the world of form. Placing his mantle of authority upon them in this ritual of empowerment he tells them:

Go ye therefore (in my name and in the flame of my God-realized Self), **and teach all nations** (transfer the enlightenment of the Word that I have given you to all planes of consciousness), **baptizing them** (anointing their chakras[25] with the light of my attainment)

in the name of the Father and of the Son and of the Holy Ghost (in the name of the Trinity, the threefold flame, that I have become on earth as in heaven):

Teaching them to observe all things whatsoever I have commanded you (instructing them in the path of chelaship under the Law of the Great Guru as I have instructed you); **and, lo, I AM with you alway, even unto the end of the world** (and, lo, the mantle of my authority—my Electronic Presence, my auric forcefield, my Selfhood, the I AM THAT I AM of me, the God of me—is with you and in you, in all spheres of your individualized being, even until the end of the cycles of your personal and planetary karma when you, too, shall be the fullness of your own Christ Presence and I AM THAT I AM). **Amen** (AUM).[26]

The indwelling Godhead is the very nature of God-mastery itself and the sign of the disciple who has become one with the Guru—the Guru who, by the fusion of the soul with the threefold energy of Father/Son/Holy Spirit, turns Darkness into Light.[27] All they who have that Spirit are the LORD's host (his Eucharistic Body) whether in heaven or in earth. And together they comprise the entire *Spirit* of the Great White Brotherhood.

It is the Law of God that the interaction of his Presence with those among his children who have not attained to this Trinity of God-Self expression, yet are reaching towards it as chelas, must always transpire through the personification of himself in the embodied Word—in heaven the ascended masters, in earth the unascended masters.

These living gurus are the true shepherds of the sheep because they *have* the Person of God. They are the "Emmanuel"—or "God-with-us"—presence.[28] To be with them is to be with God. And all of the prophets, avatars, and anointed ones who have received the Word of God have received it from the ascended sons in heaven and transferred it as mediators to their unascended chelas on earth.

The Word of God is always delivered in this manner by the host of the LORD to those on the path of initiation leading to full Sonship. When that Sonship is attained, that Son may stand directly in the Presence of the Almighty and still stand. Such a one is a messenger of God in heaven delivering the Word of God to the messenger of God's people on earth. Both messengers come in the Person of the Holy Ghost and are one in and as the Third Person of the Trinity.

Such a one was Moses who stood where heaven and earth meet in the Christ consciousness to receive the Word of the LORD—the Word of the I AM THAT I AM made personal as it was delivered to him through the ascended masters—on behalf of the children of Israel. And today your messenger in heaven Lanello delivers the Word of the I AM THAT I AM to your messenger on earth, the Mother of the Flame. Even so is every ascended master who dictates to her the Word of the LORD unto his people a messenger in heaven.

Therefore David knew that in the hour and the day when he would fulfill the law of his karma, all enemies within and without would be beneath his feet and he would be given dominion in heaven and in earth by the Most High God. David then called upon his Christ Self to fulfill the Word within him because he, David, was the offspring of that Christ Self. He was his son, he was his very own soul awareness.

Thus the perfect love of that LORD, that Christ Self, in each disciple confutes and refutes the legalism of the scribes, allowing the soul to transmute and transcend the lesser consciousness that is devoid of the Holy Spirit, hence anti-Holy Spirit, and enter into the fullness of the joy of the living Guru[29] who is ever the lover of the souls of the living chelas.

I AM

GABRIEL

I ANNOUNCE TO YOU
THE SUMMONING OF YOUR SOULS
TO THE PATH OF INITIATION
UNDER THE MESSENGERS
OF THE GREAT WHITE BROTHERHOOD

XVI

Archangel Gabriel on The Mystery of the Relentless Wave

XVI

Chelas of the Guru, the Innermost Christ,

The message of love that He brought,
That to us God hath taught,
Is a relentless wave of light
Oncoming through the day and through
the night.
The wave is sent as a current
That touches fire, air, water, and earth,
Passing through all of the spheres of
Matter and Spirit
By the wondrous yin and yang of the
figure-eight flow.

The relentless wave of light is a
love determined,
Predetermined by the LORD God,
The I AM THAT I AM,
In the Person of Alpha and Omega
Who have sent forth that light
To captivate their children in wave's delight.

That oncoming love is welcomed
By the children of God
gathered on the shore of life.
They have known from the beginning
That the wave would come,
That the wave would make them one
And carry them back to the Sun—
Center of Being.
For them the wave is a welcome sign
Of the ending of a cycle
that was from the beginning
The choice of the soul acknowledged by God
To go forth in free will
To conquer a universe of the Self—
By the Self individualized within oneself.

And to them this water of Life
Is a liquid sacred fire all-consuming.
They know it well
And they would tell,
They welcome it.
For they would be consumed of God.
Theirs is an all-consuming love.
When love meets love
Where water becomes earth
And earth is translated into fire and to air—
They would be there as I AM there.

I AM Gabriel.
I partake of the cup of communion
That is the ritual of Life becoming life.
And all who partake of the ritual of love
That requires each participant

To resolve the self, to dissolve the self,
Then become the Self
Fear not the assimilation
  of the Body and Blood of Christ
Wherein they assimilate
  and thus are assimilated
By a greater Christhood than their own,
Who came to earth to all atone,
To make each one One,
To assemble the crumbs and make of them
One great loaf of his cosmic consciousness.

This is the love that the fallen ones fear.
It is their assimilation into a larger sphere.
Why do they fear?
They fear a loss of identity.
They fear a loss of separateness—
  apartness, exclusiveness.
When the anarchistic anti-God
  is swallowed up in God,
The fallen one is neither God nor anti-God.
It is his fear of loss of this lesser personality
Wound about the coil of the anti-Force
That is the crux of Light and Darkness.

And so the relentless wave is oncoming.
It searches the souls
  in the plus and minus spheres of relativity.
Those who remember swimming
  in the womb of the Cosmic Virgin,
Swimming in the water of Life,
Swimming in light, light, light
And in the sacred-fire seas beyond the seas—

These stand on the shore of life. . .
And welcome the relentless wave of love.

John the Baptist was the relentless wave.
Jesus the Christ was the relentless wave.
The challenge it thrusts unto their chelas
Is to move with the relentless wave
Until they, too, become it.
For by and by the wave will inundate
  worlds beyond worlds
And fill a cosmos and be a cosmos
As one great sea of God,
Every glistening drop
  a child of God become a son,
Until the whole body of universal awareness
Is one shimmering sea of light.

The relentless wave claims its own
And disowns those who have disclaimed it.
They say, "We serve the LORD,"
But their lord is the anti-God, the anti-Self.
They can no longer tell the difference
Between that Reality and the unreal self.
Their living is a dying.
They know it not.
Their souls are spiraling—
  in a counterclockwise spiral.
Yet their course back to the Source
Is a journey in time and space as they lose,
Layer by layer, the identity
They have never forged and won,
The God. . .
  whom they have never elected to become.

Year by year, the ritual
Of the unwinding of the self goes on.
And year by year, they are less and less
Of that self or any self.
For the relentless wave is the God of Love
Who claims all Light and Darkness,
Energy right and left,
as his very own personal being.
These wicked and their seed
Stand side by side with the children of need
Who know the Law and the necessity
For repentance from the waves of unreality.

And so the children of need
Repent by the I AM creed.
They resolve and balance
the light of Alpha and Omega
Within the dewdrop of the soul.
And they fear not to dissolve the drop
Into the Love that makes them whole.
For them the dissolution
is the making permanent
Of their individuality in God.

But for the seed of the wicked
Who have never acknowledged their need
To confess the Christ, that He is LORD,
Their resolution is the resolving
Of the plus and minus . . .
factors of human relativity
Into a comfortability that is no part of Light,
That has no part with Light.
Their resolution is the resolution

Of the death that they call life—
A life that is really death.

For them the oncoming wave,
  the expected wave,
Will be the relentless dissolution of the self,
Coil by coil, sphere by sphere
Until the foam tells the story
Of an ancient glory
They could have made their own.
But, unwilling to atone,
They themselves are now but ashes' cone
And the alchemy of light
Has resolved their creations
  and anti-creations
Into the common elements of the sea of light.
Their light which was darkness
  is now light again,
Repolarized in the Great Central Sun
As the light of Alpha and Omega,
The victors of the only victory that
  can be won . . .
Love.

What do you suppose is the reaction
Of the seed of the wicked to the action
Of the Person of the Christ who appears
  century by century
As the Person of the relentless wave?
Their reason is not adequate
  to the Reason of the Word.
Their argument cannot stand
Within the crystal geometry of the Mind of God.

They are silenced by the Word
of the messenger.
They agree with the logic,
But they disagree with the Person of the Logos,
The only begotten Son of God,
who stands before them face to face.

What further message is there
for the silent stones . . .
Silenced by their own guilt?
The message is loud and clear,
It rings from ear to ear:
"Woe unto you, scribes and Pharisees,
hypocrites!
For ye shut up the kingdom of heaven
against men:
For ye neither go in yourselves,
Neither suffer ye them
that are entering to go in."[1]

"Woe unto you, scribes and Pharisees,
hypocrites!
For ye are like unto whited sepulchres,
Which indeed appear beautiful outward,
But are within full of dead men's bones
and of all uncleanness.
Even so ye also outwardly appear
righteous unto men,
But within ye are full of
hypocrisy and iniquity."[2]

The denunciation of woes upon the seed of the wicked by John the Baptist and Jesus Christ is the pronouncement of judgment whereby the full intensity of the light of Alpha and Omega, their twin flames, descends as the sacred fire of the Holy Ghost, the cloven tongues, the plus/the minus, to deliver unto them each one, one by one, the fruit/the fruitlessness of their own dead works. Thus it was given unto John the Baptist and Jesus Christ to shake the very boughs of the tree of life[3] that the fruit of good and evil might come tumbling down as bane or blessing unto the soul.

The very spoken Word of the prophet "Woe unto you!" releases the sacred fire of the judgment, actually unlocking the momentums of relative good and evil and calling the individual to a personal and planetary accountability for all of his past sowings and reapings outside of the Law of Love.

Unto his disciples Jesus said, "Verily I say unto you, That ye which have followed me, in the regeneration when the Son of man shall sit in the throne of his glory, ye also shall sit upon twelve thrones, judging the twelve tribes of Israel."[4]

With these words the Lord Christ initiated the initiates on the path of personal Christhood (who had followed him in the recreation of the soul after the image and likeness of the Christ) in the transfer of the light of the relentless wave of God consciousness, thus giving them the authority to invoke the judgment whereby personal and planetary karmic cycles are accelerated or decelerated according to the soul's evolution.

This same initiation, making them instruments of his true and righteous judgments,[5] he conveyed to them when he breathed on them saying, "Receive ye the Holy Ghost: whosesoever sins ye remit, they are remitted unto them; and whosesoever sins ye retain, they are retained."[6]

This authority to be the instrument of God's judgment is conveyed by Jesus Christ to those apostles in embodiment who by the assimilation of his Blood and his Body—his physical consciousness of Alpha and Omega—are the extension of himself.

The chelas of the Guru are the extensions of that Guru, hence they *are* the Guru—by vibration, by commitment, by frequency, drop by drop in the cosmic ocean. Their mere presence in the earth is the confrontation of Light and Darkness, and unto them the living Christ transfers the authority of his Word by his messenger: "They shall not pass!" This decree of the Word is always spoken by the Guru within the chela, by the master of the household within his servant, by the LORD within his anointed one.

Children of the light, your souls are the branches of the Vine (Christ), hence extensions of the Great Self. Now move with the relentless wave in the denunciation of embodied Evil by the power of the spoken Word and thereby follow in the footsteps of the prophets, the

Messiah, the apostles who in their day challenged and were challenged by the personalities of Evil. Only in this way will the Light overcome the Darkness and consume it to the core of the energy veil.

I AM

GABRIEL

I STAND UPON
THE SHORE OF LIFE
WITH THE CHILDREN OF THE LIGHT
AND I ANNOUNCE TO YOU
THE COMING OF THE RELENTLESS WAVE

"THEY SHALL NOT PASS!"
by Jesus Christ

In the Name of the I AM THAT I AM,
I invoke the Electronic Presence of Jesus Christ:
They shall not pass!
They shall not pass!
They shall not pass!
By the authority of the cosmic cross of
white fire it shall be:
That all that is directed against the Christ
within me,
within the holy innocents,
within our beloved messengers,
within every son and daughter of God
Is now turned back
by the authority of Alpha and Omega,
by the authority of my LORD and Saviour
Jesus Christ,
by the authority of Saint Germain!

I AM THAT I AM
within the center of this temple
and I declare
in the fullness of the entire Spirit
of the Great White Brotherhood:
That those who, then, practice the black arts
against the Children of the Light
Are now bound by the hosts of the LORD,
Do now receive the judgment of the Lord Christ
within me,
within Jesus,
and within every ascended master,

Do now receive, then, the full return—
  multiplied by the energy of the
  Cosmic Christ—
  of their nefarious deeds
  which they have practiced
  since the very incarnation of the Word!

Lo, I AM a Son of God!
Lo, I AM a Flame of God!
Lo, I stand upon the rock of the living Word
And I declare with Jesus, the living Son of God:
  They shall not pass!
  They shall not pass!
  They shall not pass!
Elohim. Elohim. Elohim. [Chant]

Posture for giving this decree: Stand. Raise your right hand, using the *abhaya mudrā* (gesture of fearlessness, palm forward), and place your left hand to your heart—thumb and first two fingers touching chakra pointing inward. Give this call at least once in every 24-hour cycle.

XVII

Archangel Gabriel on the Mystery of Hierarchy

XVII

Beloved Who Are Chosen of Him,
Ordained to Bring Forth the Fruit of the Word,

There is yet many a chapter that I would write concerning the scribes and the Pharisees and the network of the false hierarchy of the fallen ones that interpenetrates the astral and the physical planes of this solar system and beyond. But I would also write of the great hierarchy of light, of magnificent God-free beings whom you know so well at inner levels, your own native bands with whom you came trailing clouds of glory[1] from your own natal lands.

You who were chosen out of this world by the Ancient of Days and his son Jesus Christ are not of this world, as he told you.[2] But you came from afar with a hope and a dream to make earth a glorious freedom star to the glory of God—her continents to hold the earth currents of violet flame, her seasons the cycles of Life becoming life in a never-ending transmutation as each successive stage of evolution transcends the last and life, O life is unveiled more noble than the last.[3]

The mineral, vegetable, animal, and human kingdoms reveal the expansion in complexity and design of Alpha-and-Omega Consciousness evolving in and through every phase of the material/spiritual progressions of the Law. The great bodies of water, the great blue aqua deep, are the counterpoise of the light of Alpha within the Omega sphere.

The light that is here in the seven seas is the sacred fire of the seven rays of Alpha that, reflected in Omega, has become liquid energy of life for the children of the sun evolving as children of the earth. First they were fashioned as living spirits from fire to fire. Now see how they are clothed upon with coats of skins from 'dust to dust'.[4] Now see how the blessed water of life, Mother life, is the agent of transition in this Holy Spirit baptism wherein the soul moves in the alternating current of Alpha and Omega from heaven to earth and earth to heaven.

In the alchemy of the Holy Ghost, the all-chemistry of God, the four elements—fire (+), air (–), water (–), and earth (+)—are symbols of four planes of God's consciousness. They are noted as the four quadrants of the sphere of heaven mirrored in the four quadrants of the sphere of earth. The alchemical notations of the fire (+,+) and air (+,–) quadrants indicate the nature of the positive polarity (the plus half) of the spheres while those of the water (–,–) and earth (–,+) quadrants indicate the nature of the negative polarity (the minus half) of both the upper and lower spheres. (See diagram, pp. 254–55.)

'Water' and 'earth', manifest as the sea and the land of the planetary body, provide a platform of evolution to teeming millions, the necessary environment for the formation of the links in the evolutionary chain—from the amoeba to the Omega in the body of Mother God. 'Fire' and 'air' manifest as the sun centers of solar and molecular systems suspended in atmospheric or nonatmospheric 'space'. They interact with 'water' and 'earth' to provide the balance of the necessary ingredients to the sustainment of life.

Physical fire, or 'Matter fire', is the carrier, or conductor, of the sacred fire, or 'Spirit fire'. Physical air, or 'Matter air', is the carrier of the breath of the Holy Ghost (prana), or 'Spirit air'. Physical water, or 'Matter water', is the carrier of the waters of eternal Life ('Spirit water') containing 144 elemental properties to hold the balance of the 144 virtues of the Twelve Solar Hierarchies in the four lower bodies of a world and its lifewaves. Physical earth, or 'Matter earth', is the conductor of life-giving currents of the central sun ('Spirit earth'), polarizing human, animal, and elemental life in nature's own Alpha-to-Omega energy interchange.

The perpetual motion of waves of Life in Spirit becoming life in Matter is a figure-eight flow that can be traced through the signs of the elements and the seasons of their transmutation—fire, water, air, earth on the north/south axis, and fire, water, earth, air on the east/west axis. (See diagram, pp. 256–57.)

This, my beloved, is but a glimpse of the wondrous interaction of Life as God in Father and Mother multiplying the Christ consciousness in the sons and daughters of Life. This ritual of the Alpha and Omega of the Creator is reflected within the creation, as Above so below, in the multitudinous plus/minus interchanges occurring in the cells of microscopic and telescopic worlds.

We have touched upon a facet of Saint Germain's vast teaching in the science of alchemy[5] because the laws governing energy and its cycles in the cosmos also reveal mysteries of the Holy Grail, especially those pertaining to the incarnation of the Word and the dilemma of God, Good, and the energy veil which we have discussed in this series. Though the musings of an archangel may not be the musings of mortals, initiates on the path of God consciousness will grasp a deeper meaning than words can convey.

Meditating upon the Word they will remember the ascended master's word to Isaiah: "For my thoughts are not your thoughts, neither are your ways my ways, saith the Lord.

For as the heavens are higher than the earth, so are my ways higher than your ways, and my thoughts than your thoughts."[6] And by and by if they are diligent in loving application of the Word, the initiation of the gift of wisdom will come to them through the Person of the Holy Ghost who is the agent of their own Christ Self.

The archangels and ascended masters serving humanity as the LORD's hosts are the very personal representatives of the Holy Spirit, the veritable ensoulment of the promised Comforter to God's children. Our purpose in coming to you through the printed word of the *Pearls of Wisdom*[7] is to deliver to you the contents of the "little book" so that you may be ready to receive the initiations God has so tenderly prepared for souls ascending back to the Source of their own beloved I AM Presence whence they came.

Now we must speak of circumstances of life and conditions of consciousness which, though unreal in the Absolute, must be dealt with in the relative flux of good and evil, where their temporary influence upon souls may become 'permanent' through an uneducated, unprincipled use of free will. Let us return then to the subject at hand. For its resolution will also be to you, dear chela, a soul resolution of undreamt proportions.

As the pollution of the consciousness and the souls of the people of earth has caused them to descend to a relative good and evil, so the pollution of fire, air, water, and earth has also caused a deceleration and a consequent densification of misqualified energy within the planetary body. This men have likewise called pollution.

The pollution of fire occurs through the abuse of the light of Alpha and Omega in the nucleus of the atom of Matter in the destructive uses of atomic energy, resulting in the violation of the balance of the four cosmic forces within the Matter sphere. The records of the galaxy reveal that some have successfully harnessed the light of Alpha and Omega in the sun of even pressure that holds the balance of fire within the center of the planets, while others have even harnessed the light of the suns of solar systems.

Whereas sons and daughters of God have used this central-sun energy constructively for the building of new worlds in their multiplication of God's consciousness,[8] the fallen ones who have taken the left-handed path have used the very same energy that is God in polarity in the manifest Omega/Matter spheres to destroy and diminish rather than replenish life with the Christ consciousness.

Some with Lucifer created synthetic planets with synthetic evolutions computerized, robotized, functioning as the outermost satellite of a solar system (e.g., Pluto) or as the moons of so-called legitimate planets. These stations, astral/physical in vibration, have served from time to time in the history of the galaxies to hold computers for the programming of the lifewaves of a solar system in a mass mechanization and manipulation of their own solar/soul energies.

To counteract the relentless wave of love sent by God for the perpetual ritual of the creating and re-creating of the soul in a buoyant, free spirit of joie de vivre, the fallen ones manned their anti-Matter stations with generators generating waves, or currents, of psychic (astral) mind-bending and mind-altering vibrations. Such vibrations, aimed by the Luciferians at the planetary targets of their successive wars of conquest, were merely the perversion of the normal Alpha/Omega interchange in the white fire core of the atom.

Lest some be affrighted by my message in which the fantasy of science fiction suddenly becomes a fact of galactic life, let me first remind you, precious ones, that although I am Gabriel, bearer of good tidings of great joy,[9] I am also sent to warn those who would receive the incarnate Word of that which opposes the Light of the Incarnation wherever it is destined to appear in God-manifestation. I am sent by God as co-creator with the Keeper of the Scrolls, and I would read to you from the scrolls of the Mother that record the uses and abuses of the light of the Mother in these several systems of worlds.

Our purpose is to acquaint you with the psychology of embodied Evil, the nature of the psyche of those who chose to personify Evil in place of Good, and then to illustrate to you, both within the microcosm and the Macrocosm of being, that which has been the logical, or rather illogical, consequence of the choice of some evolutions not only to manifest the vibration of anti-God but to attempt to extend it over vast sections of this and other galaxies.

That which is written in the scrolls of the Mother is also written within your own subconscious and the subconscious memory of all who have evolved within the Matter spheres both during and since the Great Rebellion. The records of the destruction of the planets Hedron and Maldek (asteroid belts closest to the sun and between Mars and Jupiter) reveal in their first stages the destruction of the balance of the polarity of Alpha and Omega, mind and heart, soul and body, within their evolutions. This was accomplished by the projection of psychic and physical energies, perverting the elements of water and earth, thus polluting the emotional and physical bodies of their civilizations.

Next was the alteration of the cycles of fire and air, distorting the memory and mind not only by chemical means but ultimately by the imprisonment of the elementals of fire, air, water, and earth. The imprisonment of these servants of God in nature, these regulators of the fourfold flow, plus/minus, minus/plus, was the method used by the fallen ones to imprison Matter molecules, to invert their polarity, thence to polarize the people in a right/left hatred of opposing sides that would spend itself in self-destruction and the death of their world or system of worlds.

Thus the modus operandi of death is to invert Life. Invert the components of Life—fire, air, water, and earth—and you have created a spiral and an interchange that is anti-Life. The diseases and disorders of the subconscious and the conscious mind as well as of the emotional and physical bodies, prevalent and increasing in the evolutions of earth, ought to be a warning to the true shepherds of the people of aliens in your midst.[10]

These fallen ones who were present in the previous civilizations of Lemuria, Atlantis, South America, and the African continent and are reincarnated today are working in the laboratories of the Soviet Union, China, and the West where they continue to tamper with the electronic energies of Life and the balance of yin and yang in man and nature.

The so-called scientists who busily turn their psychotronic[11] generators and gadgets, sophisticated and not, on everything from the weather and the earth currents to the DNA chain and the chakras of their victims, are the insane seed of the Wicked One whose time and space are very short[12] and who must yet be judged before Christ and his apostles. Some of the effects of influences you have observed, often attributing them erroneously to natural causes, are from outer space and space vehicles, their mother ships and satellite planets. But much is directed from the space within earth, projected from surface as well as subsurface levels.

All of this is presented not to alarm the children of the light but to arm them with true knowledge. Surely there is no greater gift from the heart of an archangel than the true knowledge of Good and the true knowledge of Evil. In my next letter I shall deal with the specific antidote for the Darkness that is misqualified Light and for the programmings and the programmers of spawned evil.

And the Light shall consume the Darkness, and the Darkness shall be no more.

I AM

GABRIEL

I ANNOUNCE TO YOU
THE VICTORY OF ARMAGEDDON
THROUGH THE SCIENCE OF THE WORD

DIAGRAM 1
THE CYCLES OF LIFE BECOMING LIFE

In the alchemy of the Holy Ghost, the all-chemistry of God, the four elements—fire (+), air (−), water (−), earth (+)—are symbols of four planes of God's consciousness. They are noted as the four quadrants of the sphere of heaven mirrored in the four quadrants of the sphere of earth.

In the diagram, the first sign in the parentheses indicates the polarization, plus or minus, of the half of the circle in which the quadrant is located; the second sign indicates the charge of the element of which the quadrant consists.

Thus we say that fire is a "plus, plus" because fire is located in the plus, or Alpha, half of the circle and it has a plus, or masculine, charge. We say that air is a "plus, minus" because it is located in the plus, or Alpha, half of the circle and it has a minus, or feminine, charge. We say that water is a "minus, minus" because it is located in the minus, or Omega, half of the circle and it has a minus, or feminine, charge. We say that earth is a "minus, plus" because it is located in the minus, or Omega, half of the circle and it has a plus, or masculine, charge.

A set of parentheses around these notations with a plus or minus preceding it will indicate whether the quadrant is in the upper or lower sphere, as 'Spirit fire' or 'Matter fire', etc.

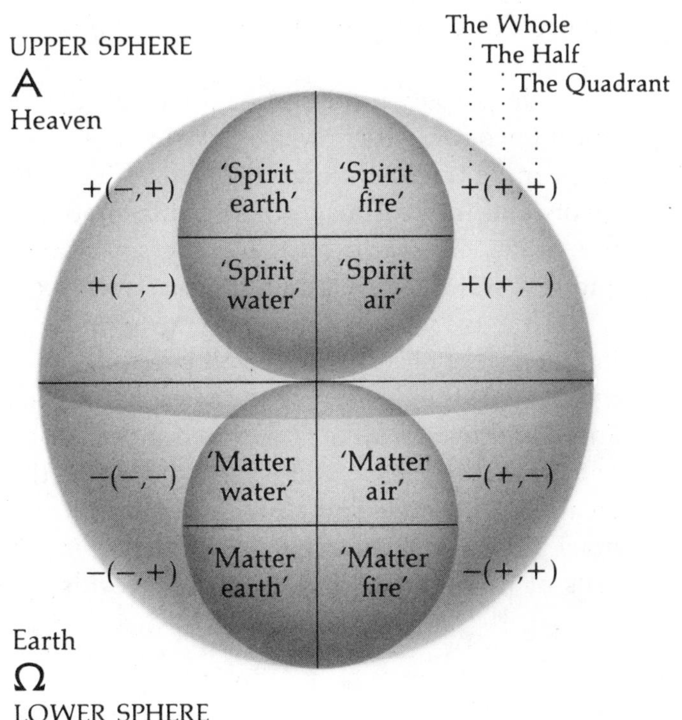

The Four Quadrants of Matter Are a Mirror Reflection of the Four Quadrants of Spirit

DIAGRAM 2
THE CYCLES OF LIFE BECOMING LIFE

The perpetual motion of waves of Life in Spirit becoming life in Matter is a figure-8 flow that can be traced through the signs of the elements and the seasons of their transmutation—fire, water, air, earth on the north/south axis, and fire, water, earth, air on the east/west axis.

This is but a glimpse of the wondrous interaction of Life as God in Father and Mother multiplying the Christ consciousness in the sons and daughters of Life. This ritual of the Alpha and Omega of the Creator is reflected within the creation, as Above so below, in the multitudinous plus/minus interchanges occurring in the cells of microscopic and telescopic worlds.

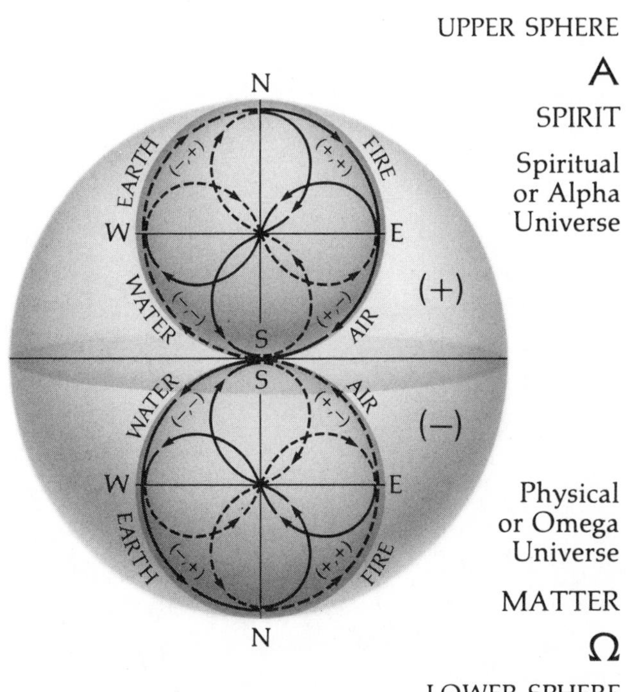

Direction of Figure-8 Flows
within the Upper and Lower Spheres:

north/south	*fire, water, air, earth*
east/west	*fire, water, earth, air*
south/north	*air, earth, fire, water*
west/east	*earth, air, fire, water*

XVIII

Archangel Gabriel on the Mystery of the Spoken Word

XVIII

Children of the Son to Whom He Speaks
Plainly of the Father,

I AM Gabriel. I come in the Spirit of Truth, the Comforter sent to you from the Father, and I testify of the Son Jesus who became the LORD *(Adonai)*.

"Jesus *cried* and said, He that believeth on me, believeth not on me, but on him that sent me. And he that seeth me seeth him that sent me."[1] His message is clear. The Son is the messenger of the Father; and all who have become the Son (or through discipleship become one with the One who has become the Son) are in effect messengers of the Word of God, and all who manifest the light of the Son embody the Spirit within Matter.

They are heaven personified in earth and unto earth's evolutions. The spheres of relative good and evil are darkness and the evolutions of those spheres abide in darkness. Thus Jesus said, "I AM come a Light into the world, that whosoever believeth on me should not abide in darkness."[2]

Jesus was the Word. His soul had become the Word. The messenger of God became the message. The Son who had been one with the Father from the Beginning became the Father, the Word I AM THAT I AM in physical embodiment. The soul of Jesus became the fullness of that Godhead who dwelt bodily in his flesh and blood.

And herein is the nature of the judgment of which he spoke: "And if any man hear my words and believe not, I judge him not: for I came not to judge the world, but to save the world. He that rejecteth me and receiveth not my words hath one that judgeth him: the Word that I have spoken, the same shall judge him in the last day."[3]

So magnificent is this illustration of the crystal clarity of the soul of Jesus reflecting the Word as the Person of the Lamb! Although he has become that Word, that Lamb, yet he continually acknowledges that Person of God to be greater than himself, greater than the vehicle provided as the Son of man.

It is not the Son of man who will judge the world, but the Christ in him, the Son of God who shall both save and judge the world. When he said, "For judgment I AM come into this world,"[4] he was speaking of the I AM THAT I AM come into the world through the Christed One, the Light that shone in the darkness and consumed it.[5]

The words which Jesus spoke in parable and in proverb were the breaking of the bread of Life, the breaking down of the single Word, the Cosmic Christ consciousness that he bore, for the assimilation, crumb by crumb, within the souls who comprise the body of God on earth. That bread of Life that he was, was the transfer of the Word, increment by increment, for the repolarization, the realignment, of body and soul—fire, air, water, and earth. The Word itself was the judgment of the inversion of Life and of the polarity of Life within the Matter spheres.

The Word, my beloved, *the Word* is the power of God to repolarize the continents and the seas, the subconscious and the conscious mind, the desire body, and the physical vehicle. Cell by cell of physical and mental consciousness resumes the polarity of Alpha and Omega by the Word. By the transfer of the *Word,* the Law of the Father is made manifest and it nullifies all unlike itself. By the transfer of the *Work*—the sacred labor, the service to the Light—the love of the Holy Spirit is made a living flame of creative, re-creative Life.

Thus the Son, messenger of the Father, forerunner[6] of the Holy Ghost said, "For I have not spoken of myself; but the Father which sent me, he gave me a commandment, what I should say and what I should speak. And I know that his commandment is Life everlasting; whatsoever I speak therefore, even as the Father said unto me, so I speak."[7]

In Matter the Son of man reflects the Father as the seas reflect the sun (the Son of God *is* the Father appearing in the phenomenon of the Absolute suspended in the reflective pool of relativity; the Son not only reflects, but absorbs and becomes the fullness of the Father's light in the horizontal plane of Matter) and the penetrating light of the Word is for the restoration of life. And who is to say when the sea is the sun and the sun is the sea? "Believest thou not that I AM in the Father and the Father in me?[8] The words that I speak unto you I speak not of myself; but the Father that dwelleth in me, he doeth the works."[9]

This oneness is the ultimate testimony and the ultimate love of Jesus (the Son of man) the Christ (the only begotten Son of God to which his soul was wedded). It is his utmost message to them that believe: "Believe me that I AM in the Father and the Father in me; or else believe me for the very Work's sake."[10]

His message to every son and daughter of God, every child of the heart of Alpha and Omega in whom there burns the threefold flame of Life, is of the indwelling Presence, the

LORD, I AM THAT I AM; of the indwelling LORD, the eternal Christ; and of the indwelling Holy Ghost, the true Worker of the works of God unto all who believe on the great mystery of the Holy Grail, the incarnate Word.

This mystery, my beloved, is the impossible made possible. It is the Infinite chaliced in the finite. It is the finite putting on and becoming the Infinite by the translation of the Word. Herein is the promise of eternal Life to be experienced in the here and the now, the plus/the minus, the flesh and the blood, of those who believe on the incarnate Word as the impossible made possible through the grace of God in Jesus Christ and in every soul called of God to be the Son of man:

"He that believeth on me, the works that I do shall he do also; and greater works than these shall he do, because I go unto my Father. And whatsoever ye shall ask in my name, that will I do, that the Father may be glorified in the Son. If ye shall ask any thing in my name, I will do it."[11]

Things asked in the name of Christ—the Christ in Jesus, the Christ in you, the Christ in every ascended and unascended soul of God—are fulfilled verily because that Christ is the Word, and the Word is both the message and the messenger of God's truth. The Word is the personal Christ Self of you, my beloved. The Word is the presence of salvation and judgment within the spheres of relative good and evil. That Word must be spoken through and by the sons and daughters of God in order to manifest the currents of Alpha and Omega in the plus/minus polarity of Matter.

Now behold the mystery of the Word incarnate. Behold, the Word *must* incarnate in Matter. The messengers of God *must* be in physical embodiment and the Word *must* be spoken through the physical instrument.

"I will not leave you comfortless: I will come to you"[12] is Christ's own promise of his progressive revelation which he has never ceased to release in Matter through his apostles as their Words and Works of his teaching and healing, and through the lives and the writings of the special saints of the Church, East and West, who left a record of the transmission of the hosts of the LORD given unto them by the Holy Ghost for the healing, *the healing,* of the souls of men and nations.

Now I call to the components of Christ's body who have been with him from the very beginning of his origin in God when heaven and earth were one and Elohim sung their symphonies unto the stars. For the Word has prophesied that ye also shall bear witness of the Son *because the Son of man dwelleth in you.*

The Son, this Word, that you are daily becoming by appropriation and the divine approbation is the Absolute Reality of your soul's preexistence in the Spirit spheres. This Son of God shining through the Son of man is the antidote by far of all misuses of the sacred fire—manifesting in and as fire, air, water, and earth in the Matter spheres—contrived by the fallen ones since the rebellion of Lucifer and his cohorts throughout the history of worlds and solar systems and galaxies beyond. All that has opposed Life by polarizing the absolute and diametrical opposition to Life is judged both in the person and the principle of the energy veil. Both the creator and the creation of the fallen ones is transmuted by the sacred fire of the Holy Ghost released in the science of the spoken Word.

The salvation of the world is the *self-elevation* or soul-elevation of the world. **And I, if I**—the I AM THAT I AM—**be lifted up . . . will draw all men**—elevate all manifestations of the One—**unto me**[13]—the Universal Christ for whose consciousness I AM the Holy Grail.

It is the elevation of the Great Self that is God the Father, God the Son, and God the Holy Spirit by the Son of man—not only in every son and daughter of God but in every living thing, in all creatures great and small. It is the elevation of vibration back to the tone of the Word in the mineral, vegetable, animal, and human kingdoms, in every particle of dust, every drop of water, and every heart that would beat to the rhythm of God.

The purpose of your incarnation, my beloved, is to speak the spoken Word of God, the spoken Word that is not of yourself but of the Father which sent you, the commandment not of your human will or your human wish but the commandment which the Father, your own beloved I AM Presence, has given to you—what you should say and what you should speak.

The reason that the spoken Word of God spoken by the Son of God within you is so viciously and so violently opposed by the fallen ones is that they have known from the beginning of their descent that all that they have created as a perversion of God has manifest through the perversion of the Word of the Son.

They have known from the beginning that when the sons of God, the Christs of God, would once more walk the earth, knowing who "I AM" and who I AM *THAT I AM*—that they would intone the Word, that the real and living sacred fire would proceed out of their mouth as out of the mouth of God,[14] and that all things would be restored to cosmic reality by that spoken Word. Now they know that that Word is being released even in these latter days by the Keepers of the Flame who are the ongoing disciples of The Christ and the oncoming armies of The Faithful and True.

Yes, my beloved, your dynamic decrees are the vibration of the One Sent, the messenger of God, who is the Person of your own

Christ Self represented in our embodied messenger. That vibration is the Word that neutralizes all programming and deprogramming of the fallen ones, all negative projections of outer and inner space, all currents of manipulation and mechanization whatever their source, known or unknown. The spoken Word is death unto the demons of pride and ambition, of the cult of death and the false crucifixion.

The spoken Word is the power to exorcise Morphis, the imitator of Christ, who has invaded the temples of an entire generation of youth who have succumbed to the psychic thralldom of marijuana, hashish, heroin, opium, cocaine, LSD, angel dust, peyote, and magic mushrooms. Yes, the science of the spoken Word wielded as the sword of The Word, the Lamb, The Faithful and True, so long as it flows through you into the day and into the night of the Matter spheres, will realign a cosmos year by year, cycle by cycle.

It was the spoken Word of the priests of Lemuria who intoned the Word of Ma-ray, Mother ray, that kept the balance of Mother light. And the going out of that Mother light and the sinking of that continent came about by the void created by their absence of the daily intonement of the Word.

The dynamic decrees dictated to the Messengers Mark and Elizabeth Prophet by the ascended masters are the greatest gift of the entire *Holy Spirit* of the Great White Brotherhood, for they are the means to implement world salvation, to which end every incarnation of the Son of God is come. Use them! Do not abuse them! Rise above the levels of anxiety that cause you to doubt and fear your own emergent Christhood reflective of the Sonship of Jesus Christ.

Never mind and never matter those fallen ones that say our dynamic decrees are of the councils of Satan. It is they who are of the councils of Satan and they who have abused the Word to create illusion, delusion, and to imprison the Word in doctrine and dogma as the scribes and Pharisees have done. Now undo all that which is not of the Light by the light of the Word. Now move swiftly as an arrow that flieth by day, the arrow sent as the Wisdom of Alpha become the Love of Omega.

Initiates on the Path who take responsibility for the guarding of the light of a planet and its people know that they must be with the hosts of the LORD out of the body when the vultures lay their eggs in the nests of the doves—between the hours of 10:00 p.m. and 4:00 a.m.—then back to the physical plane at dawn for the lowering of the creativity of the Christ mind unto the body of God on earth.[15]

Having fought the good fight with Archangel Michael, they rise before dawn to be ready to stand with the children of God who must meet the Adversary in the day of their returning karma. At night while children sleep, the astral hordes are active in dragging their psychic nets seeking to snare the passive sleepers. For they know the susceptibility of consciousness during sleep to all manner of psychic manipulation, and they know how to penetrate the sheaths of the aura with infectious diseases of the mind and emotions—the will to die, the death wish of the not-self, and the denial of God and his laws.

From 4:00 a.m. to 10:00 a.m. is the Work of the Word accomplished in the setting of the blueprint of the day.[16] The blueprint is a grid of light, a mathematical matrix of light, calculated in the cosmic computer of the Mind of God and lowered through the Great Blue Causal Body ensouled by the ascended master known as the Great Divine Director. It is precision designed to hold the light of the specific Christ consciousness that God would crystallize in his children.

Moreover, that very light is sufficient to consume the anti-Christ elements of relative good and evil sent as sensual superstition and malicious mischief to deter the plan of God. Thus, inherent in the matrix is the manifest Christ—as Person to work his works through you, as Principle to drive back and bind the unprincipled foes and their furious, fruitless opposition to the Creator and his seven cycles of creation in the day.

Let the body of lightservers therefore invoke the allegiance of the angels of blue lightning serving under Archangel Michael before retiring, then exit their physical bodies in the night cycle to contend with the fallen ones on the astral planes and catch them in their Satanic pranks against an unsuspecting humanity.

Let their souls and finer bodies be refreshed and recharged in the etheric retreat of the legions of faith at Banff.[17] Then let them meet the challenge of the day with renewed zeal as they keep the vigil of the hours for the teaching and the tutoring of the precious lambs of God and for the loving—oh, the loving—of all life free!

Work while ye have the Light. Children of the light, work in the light of the morning, for the evildoers work in the night. "And men loved darkness rather than light, because their deeds were evil. For every one that doeth evil hateth the Light, neither cometh to the Light—to the Person of the Word, to the Christ incarnate within you—lest his deeds should be reproved. But he that doeth Truth cometh to the Light, that his deeds may be made manifest, that they are wrought in God."[18]

Children of the light, I have given to you mysteries of the Holy Grail and the key to Light and Darkness, Good and Evil, and to the workings of gods and men in the Absolute and the relative. Now take the Word, and work the works of Him that sent you while it is day, for the night cometh when no man can work.

The *Holy* Spirit of the Lord Jesus Christ in the entire *Holy* Spirit of the Great White Brotherhood is the I AM THAT I AM *in the world.* As long as that Spirit is present in the world in the embodied messenger of the Guru and in the embodied chelas of the Guru, that *Holy* Spirit, as the I AM THAT I AM incarnate in the Guru-chela relationship, *is the Light of the world.*[19]

I AM

GABRIEL

I ANNOUNCE TO YOU
THE INCARNATION OF THE WORD
WITHIN YOU
WITHOUT WHOM WAS NOT
ANY THING MADE THAT WAS MADE

XIX

Elizabeth Clare Prophet on The Mystery of Your Divine Self

XIX

There are three figures represented in the chart, which we will refer to as the upper figure, the middle figure, and the lower figure. The upper figure is the I AM Presence, the I AM THAT I AM, God individualized for every son and daughter of God. The Divine Monad consists of the I AM Presence surrounded by the spheres (rings of color, of light) which comprise the causal body.

This is the body of First Cause that contains within it man's "treasure laid up in heaven"—perfect works, perfect thoughts and feelings, perfect words—energies that have ascended from the plane of action in time and space as the result of man's correct exercise of free will and his correct qualification of the stream of life that issues forth from the heart of the Presence and descends to the level of the Christ Self.

The middle figure in the chart is the

mediator between God and man, called the Christ Self, the Real Self, or the Christ consciousness. It has also been referred to as the Higher Mental Body or Higher Consciousness. The Christ Self overshadows the lower self, which consists of the soul evolving through the four planes of Matter in the four lower bodies corresponding to the planes of fire, air, water, and earth; that is, the etheric body, the mental body, the emotional body, the physical body.

The three figures of the chart correspond to the Trinity of Father (the upper figure), Son (the middle figure), and Holy Spirit. The lower figure is intended to become the temple for the Holy Spirit which is indicated in the enfolding violet-flame action of the sacred fire. The lower figure corresponds to you as a disciple on the Path.

Your soul is the nonpermanent aspect of being which is made permanent through the ritual of the ascension. The ascension is the process whereby the soul, having balanced his karma and fulfilled his divine plan, merges first with the Christ consciousness and then with the living Presence of the I AM THAT I AM. Once the ascension has taken place, the soul, the corruptible aspect of being, becomes the incorruptible one, a permanent atom in the body of God. The Chart of Your Divine Self is therefore a diagram of yourself—past, present, and future.

The lower figure represents mankind

YOUR DIVINE SELF

evolving in the planes of Matter. This is how you should visualize yourself standing in the violet flame, which you invoke in the name of the I AM Presence and in the name of your Christ Self in order to purify your four lower bodies in preparation for the ritual of the alchemical marriage—your soul's union with the Lamb as the bride of Christ.

The lower figure is surrounded by a tube of light, which is projected from the heart of the I AM Presence in answer to your call. It is a field of fiery protection sustained in Spirit and in Matter for the sealing of the individuality of the disciple. The threefold flame within the heart is the spark of life projected from the I AM Presence through the Christ Self and anchored in the etheric planes in the heart chakra for the purpose of the soul's evolution in Matter. Also called the Christ flame, the threefold flame is the spark of man's divinity, his potential for Godhood.

The crystal cord is the stream of light that descends from the heart of the I AM Presence through the Christ Self, thence to the four lower bodies to sustain the soul's vehicles of expression in time and space. It is over this cord that the energy of the Presence flows, entering the being of man at the top of the head and providing the energy for the pulsation of the threefold flame and the physical heartbeat.

When a round of the soul's incarnation in Matter-form is complete, the I AM Presence withdraws the crystal cord, the threefold flame returns to the level of the Christ, and the energies of the four lower bodies return to their respective planes.

The dove of the Holy Spirit descending from the heart of the Father is shown just above the head of the Christ. When the individual man, as the lower figure, puts on and becomes the Christ consciousness as Jesus did, the descent of the Holy Spirit takes place and the words of the Father, the I AM Presence, are spoken, "This is my beloved Son in whom I AM well pleased."[1]

Your Holy Christ Self is the still small voice of conscience that speaks to your soul with unerring direction, warns you of impending danger, and distinguishes between good and evil, right and wrong.

It is written that one day your soul will rise up and meet this Beloved One in the rapturous union that is the culmination of your life on earth.[2] In this divine embrace you will recognize that there is no longer any need for separation from Christ—your Real Self. You need go out no more into outer darkness. You have found—you have become—your own Reality.

This union is known as the alchemical marriage. It is the mystical oneness with Christ experienced by the soul who has taken to heart Jesus' teaching: "Except ye eat the flesh of the

Son of man, and drink his blood, ye have no life in you."[3]

As you partake of the consciousness of your Christ Self day by day, you are entering into the communion of the 'Son of man', whose Light is the true Light which lighteth every child of God. For some, the saints and disciples of East and West, the union with Christ has occurred before or during their final embodiment prior to the ascension. One with their Christ Self, they have accomplished on earth a great service to life by being lightbearers of the Word.

Jesus was the great exemplar of this union, for his oneness with Christ was so evident—the union of his humanity with his divinity so integral—that he walked the earth fully clothed upon with his Christ Self and fully the incarnation of the Word—I AM THAT I AM—the Mighty I AM Presence. He was the three in one, the embodiment of the trinity shown in the Chart of Your Divine Self.

The chart shows that we are also destined to embody the fullness of the Godhead, as Paul so directed us when he said: "Let this mind be in you which was also in Christ Jesus: who, being in the form of God, thought it not robbery to be equal with God."[4]

Jesus' promise that the Father and the Son would take up their abode in those who love Christ and obey the Word opens the way to our discipleship under the same Law of the One whereby our Elder Brother attained his victory.

By this Christ in you and in me—the only hope of glory—we are made, as Paul says, "partakers of the inheritance of the saints in Light."[5]

Thus, the true inheritance of the children of God which they must now claim (for the false pastors have taken it from them) is the indwelling Son of God—the promised LORD Our Righteousness foretold by Jeremiah.

This Beloved Christ Self known by Peter as "the hidden man of the heart" transforms our souls even as He exalts our highest hopes and loves, purifies the muddied stream of thought, forgives our tortuous feelings, transmutes our sins and sense of struggle, and is our strong advocate before the Father.

Becoming one with God through the Holy Christ Self is our reason for being on planet Earth. As Paul said—"Nevertheless I live; yet not I, but Christ liveth in me; and the life which I now live in the flesh I live by the faith of the Son of God . . ."[6]

The Chart of Your Divine Self illustrates what Jesus taught and the apostles knew: The son of man's unique relationship to God through Christ, the Great Mediator. The chart shows the relationship of the Personhood of God the Father individualized in your Mighty I AM Presence (the upper figure) and God the Son individualized in your Holy Christ Self (the middle figure) with your evolving soul consciousness—the son of man (the lower figure).

The term 'Son of man' (with a capital *S*),

which Jesus used in reference to his own mission, defines the soul who has descended from the I AM Presence as the Son of God. Integrated with the Christ Self, this soul is now archetypically the presence of the Universal Soul of humanity. As in the life of Jesus, the Christ(Light) of the one becomes the Christ(Light) for all. And the Son of man is perpetually one with and representing the Holy Christ Self of all souls evolving on earth.

The term 'son of man' (with a lowercase *s*) is applied to all souls who embody with the mission of bearing the Light, balancing their karma, fulfilling their divine plan, and returning to God in the ritual of the ascension. The term 'son of man' indicates that the potential exists for Divine Sonship through the path of personal Christhood—putting on day by day the garment of one's LORD, 'eating his flesh and drinking his blood'.

This *son of man*ifestation (the manifestation of God) is intended to be the temple of the Holy Spirit, as grace for grace the Paraclete is magnetized into your life by your heart's devotion to "your LORD and my LORD"—your Christ Self and my Christ Self. For we know and are convinced by the Law of the One that there is in Reality but one God, one LORD, and one Christ—albeit perceived individually and personally (as in the chart) by each soul who has gone out from the Presence of God to serve the cause of Truth in the physical universe.

The chart can be studied in the light of Jesus' own words:

"He that believeth on me, believeth not on me, but on him that sent me. And he that seeth me seeth him that sent me.

"I am come a Light into the world, that whosoever believeth on me should not abide in darkness.

"And if any man hear my words and believe not, I judge him not; for I came not to judge the world, but to save the world. He that rejecteth me and receiveth not my words hath one that judgeth him: the Word that I have spoken, the same shall judge him in the last day.

"I have not spoken of myself; but the Father which sent me, he gave me a commandment, what I should say and what I should speak. And I know that his commandment is Life everlasting. Whatsoever I speak therefore, even as the Father said unto me, so I speak."[7]

Even as Jesus proclaimed himself to be the Son of man sent by the Father as His messenger to deliver the Word of Christ, so the chart reveals the great Truth that your Mighty I AM Presence is the Father who sent you into the world to bear the Light of the Son, your own Christ Self, and to accomplish his Word and Work that through him you, the son of man, might have everlasting Life.

As you descended from the Father and the Son, so one day you will ascend as Jesus did to the heart of the I AM Presence, one with your

Christ Self. Jesus was teaching this principle to Nicodemus when he told him, "No man hath ascended up to heaven, but he that came down from heaven, even the Son of man (Soul of man) which is in heaven."[8]

Jesus was the 'Son of man', but everyone who retains the divine spark, the threefold flame, is also the 'son of man'. The opportunity for joint-heirship with Christ exists only in those who descended from above—from the I AM Presence. Hence they are called the I AM Race.

Jesus also spoke of those who are 'from beneath', a 'generation of vipers' not of the Father but of the 'devil'[9] and his fallen angels, who are neither called nor chosen,[10] a 'race' which did not descend from the I AM Presence and therefore cannot ascend. This is the distinction Jesus is making to Nicodemus. Unlike certain modern theologians, the Master was willing to confront Good and Evil, and the real and the unreal among men.

XX

Elizabeth Clare Prophet on The Mystery of Jesus Christ

XX

As it is written: ". . . The law was given by Moses, but grace and truth came by Jesus Christ."[1]

He is called the Messiah, the Saviour, the Holy One of God. His message has marked the course of Western civilization, and yet to some the figure of the Nazarene Master, tall upon the hillsides of the world, serene and immovable through the centuries, has not appeared as the Image of the Christ within.

He was known abroad in Galilee as the son of Joseph. "Can there any good thing come out of Nazareth?" Nathanael asked. "Come and see," Philip answered. They beheld the Son of God.[2]

Many have marveled at his miracles but few have followed his magnificent example. Yet to the present hour his promise is unfailing: "He that believeth on me, the works that I do shall he do also; and greater works than these shall he do, because I go unto my Father."[3] Come and see.

Jesus Christ is the "express image"[4] of the Person of God, the archetype of man's God identity. Known to his disciples as "the Word"—*Logos* (meaning God in action)—he is the infinite love/wisdom/power of the Spirit "made flesh." John the Evangelist explains that "all things were made by him; and without him was not any thing made that was made."[5]

The beloved disciple learned from his Master that God the Father through the Image of the Son had created Christ Selfhood as the Light of every son and daughter. He recorded this truth in the very first chapter of his gospel, knowing that only those who are of the Light and born of the Spirit would understand this profound mystery of their joint-heirship with Christ.

John the Baptist, sent by God to herald his coming, also proclaimed his portion to be our own, saying, ". . . Of his fulness have all we received, and grace for grace."[6]

Jesus of Nazareth is the personification of that selfsame Word which put the law of God in the inward parts of his people and wrote it in their hearts. Jesus, the Son of man, so identified with the perfection of the Universal Christ, the Son of God, that in him we behold the fullness of the Godhead dwelling bodily. We see in him the individualization of the God flame—the perfection of God made manifest in man.

This is the mystery of the Incarnation.

This same mystery God would reveal both in us and through us as we confess the Christ in him to be the Christ that is also in us. Indeed, he is the Wayshower of the realization of the Christ potential which lives as the embryonic Light within every child of God. "That *was* the true Light, which lighteth every man that cometh into the world."[7]

The oft quoted "For God so loved the world that he gave his only begotten Son, that whosoever believeth in him should not perish but have everlasting Life"[8] is seldom preached as the supreme promise of the Father to every child of His heart. Jesus' mission was to demonstrate the reality of that Son as the Real Self of every son and daughter of God.

Yes, the only begotten Son is the Second Person of the Trinity, by whose Image the Father has created each of his offspring. Jesus' sublime example of the interior Light is the open door for you to receive the salvation of your own Sonship through his name.

The kingdom he proclaimed was and is the universal consciousness of the Christ. It was his awareness of himself as Christ and it can be yours. When Jesus said the kingdom of God is within you,[9] he was speaking of His own consciousness of Christ, one with your heart, and of your Holy Christ Self above and within you.

To bear witness unto the truth of this inner Christ, this Real Self, is the end to which Jesus was born and the same cause for which you—a soul born out of the same Christ Image, the same living Spirit—came into the world.[10] And "as many as received him, to them gave he power to become the sons of God."[11] Yes, beloved, you are also sent into the world to become the Christ.

Jesus is the Great Exemplar who proved that there is a science, a geometry, a mathematics based on love whereby we stand, face, and conquer the impositions of the personal ego and the limitations of the subconscious mind.

"Let this mind be in you which was also in Christ Jesus." Change the water of the human consciousness into the wine of the Spirit. Cast the moneychangers from the temple of church and state. "Be ye therefore perfect."[12] How? Through the Word incarnate in you and your exercise of its authority in the science of the spoken Word.

Jesus Christ demonstrated the abundant life and the ascension as a progressive achievement—an acceleration of consciousness. It is the fulfillment of the natural law of transcendence whereby just as the Creator through his creation is forever transcending himself, so every son must also transcend the limits of his self-expression. As Paul said: "This corruptible *must* put on incorruption, and this mortal *must* put on immortality."

The ascension is salvation—*Self-elevation* by works, by grace—the raising up of the God

Presence in your life: "As Moses lifted up the serpent in the wilderness, even so must the Son of man be lifted up: that whosoever believeth in him should not perish, but have eternal Life."[13]

The ascension is the path not only of Jesus Christ, but of his own Mother Mary, John the Beloved, Gautama and Maitreya, Moses and Mohammed, Zoroaster, Confucius, and many of the prophets of Israel. Some of these 'ascended' masters are recognized by the historian Toynbee as "the greatest benefactors of the living generation of mankind."[14] Countless others remain unnamed, unknown, yet immortally free.

The path of your ascension is the reunion of your soul with the individualized Presence of God, the I AM THAT I AM. Some call this fiery I AM Presence the Divine Monad, seeing it as the nucleus of the atom of Self, others simply 'the Beloved'.

Your return to this Reality, this Essence, is the goal of your life. It is the raison d'être of every son and daughter of God. It is the means whereby you individualize the God flame, making it your own forever. "If any man serve me, let him follow me," Jesus said, "and where I am"—in the heaven of the universal Christ consciousness—"there shall also my servant be."[15]

The true teaching of Jesus Christ—parabled principles often mistranslated, misinterpreted, or willfully altered—is now brought to our remembrance by the Holy Spirit through the teachings of the ascended masters. Having become one with Jesus in his universal consciousness of the Christ, having received the fiery baptism, having been born again to eternal Life through him, the ascended masters go before the LORD's people today, the great cloud of witness[16] unto his sacred fire. And they are with Christ the same yesterday, today, and forever; for they, too, have realized his kingdom (i.e., consciousness) as their own birthright.

In this as in ages past when they were described as 'angels' or 'men of God' through whom the word of the LORD came, the ascended masters speak directly to the hearts of God's people or to some who have been called to deliver the word of Truth from the Promised Comforter.

Tens of thousands of God-fearing people in America today acknowledge the teachings of the ascended masters as the missing link in the psychology of the soul, in their understanding of the practical message of the life and example of the Saviour Jesus Christ:

They now understand that they, too, must do "the will of my Father," do "the works that I do"—heal the sick, cleanse the lepers, raise the dead, cast out devils and freely give of the cup of his everlasting Life because they have freely received.[17] And they know that this is possible only unto the Christ—the same Christ of Jesus whom they accept as their indwelling personal Saviour.

Through his witness Mark L. Prophet, the Ascended Master Saint Germain has written in his *Studies in Alchemy* of the ministry of Jesus Christ as he would impart this understanding to his disciples today:

"Two thousand years ago when Christ walked upon the waters of the Sea of Galilee, his demonstration was a manifestation of the natural law of levitation operating within an energy framework of cohesion, adhesion, and magnetism—the very principles which make orbital flight possible. The light atoms composing the body of Christ absorbed at will an additional quantity of cosmic rays and spiritual substance whose kinship to physical light made his whole body light, thereby making it as easy for him to walk upon the sea as upon dry land.

"His body was purely a ray of light shining upon the waters. The most dazzling conception of all was his ability to transfer this authority over energy to Peter through the power of Peter's own vision of the Christ in radiant, illumined manifestation.

"By taking his eyes temporarily from the Christ, however, Peter entered a human fear vibration and vortex which immediately densified his body, causing it to sink partially beneath the raging seas. The comforting hand of Christ, extended in pure love, reunited the alchemical tie; and the flow of spiritual energy through his hand raised Peter once again to safety."[18]

Jesus now says, I am come that ye may have *light,* and that more abundantly.[19] He explains that the light of prayer, the light of communion with our Father, surges through all things and that the light is your obedient servant. His way of total communion and continual prayer is the way of God living in man—not in a remote corner of the universe, but in his heart of very hearts.

You are able to tune in with the God consciousness that is in every cell of your body, Jesus affirms, reinforcing the determination of Job in a new and living concept—that in his flesh man may see his flesh as the doorway into the eternal.[20] This is true Christianity, the lost art of communion with God as Jesus taught it—as he lives it even now, as you, too, can live it now.

In a dictation given through Mark Prophet in 1965, Jesus recalled for his followers today a most precious experience of his youth:

"It was at the age of seventeen that one eventide I passed out into a certain field. It was moonless and the stars shone their splendor above. I was alone with God and around me the grass commingled with myriad daisylike flowers whose upturned faces seemed to take hope from my gaze and I, beholding them, saw them as the faces of men. And in my buoyancy of heart and blitheness of spirit—feeling the dew upon my feet which were bare upon the grass and smelling the odor and scent of joy in the floral release—I communed with God and sent my love to the flowers below my feet.

"Suddenly they were transformed and I saw them no more as flowers but as the faces of men. And I saw them as though they were shining with hope and they became majestic—tiny, but majestic. I mused and meditated upon them and I spake unto my Father, unto my God and unto your God, and I said, 'Can I raise them up? Can I give them the hope of a greater magnitude?'

"And the Father spake unto me and said, 'Come see ye.' And suddenly I was transported beyond that field and the cosmos was before me. And my feet were placed as upon a rock in outer space and all around me I saw the stars that they did shine—worlds of hope and worlds without—and I felt as though I were a shepherd of planetary significance and as though each face of the flowers that had been below me in the field were indeed now a planet—teeming with multitudes of people and requiring the hope and the release of God's energy that came through me then in that experience.

"I was transformed. I was electrified. My soul did rejoice and as David of old, I sang an hymn unto God and I said in the quietness of my youth, 'O God, thy majesty is great to behold. In the numberless, luminous orbs of the heavens are the sheep of thy pasture and the flowers of thy sky—immortelles, shining ones full of hope, believing in thy grace and wondrous loveliness. How canst any, then, ever cease to believe in thy greatness?'

"And I mused upon Abraham of old—I, who was of the seed of David, mused upon Abraham and his faith. And I recalled, then, in my thoughts how God had spoken unto him saying, 'I shall make thy seed as the sand beside the sea, innumerable. I AM the Lord thy God that made the heavens and the earth and I shall make thy seed as the stars innumerable.'[21] And my heart was glad and I did rejoice.

"I found myself after this experience wandering in the pasture and upon the meadow there. And for a moment I was dazed at the experience, and I reeled as one drunken. And then, out of the soft folds of the night stepped beloved Holy Amethyst, and she enfolded me in the love of Lord Zadkiel[22] and her own. . . . "

In order that you may individualize the person of God within yourself through the principle of his flame, Jesus Christ brings to you the nearness of your own Christ Self and the understanding of the law of your soul's oneness with the Spirit which he demonstrated as "I and my Father are one."[23] His God consciousness is the open door for the light of inner worlds to manifest the kingdom of God that is within you.

Not until the Word is "made flesh," personalized "in fashion as a man,"[24] is the impersonal light of the Word comprehended. Hence the individualization of the God flame first in Jesus Christ and then in you is the open door to your personal understanding of the Person of the Godhead dwelling 'bodily' in you as your own Real Self.

This prayer, given with deep love and devotion to Christ, will open the door and establish the blessed tie between you and your Holy Christ Self.

MY PRAYER TO MY HOLY CHRIST SELF

Holy Christ Self above me,
Thou balance of my soul,
Let thy blessed radiance
Descend and make me whole.

Refrain:
Thy flame within me ever blazes,
Thy peace about me ever raises,
Thy love protects and holds me,
Thy dazzling light enfolds me.
I AM thy threefold radiance,
I AM thy living presence
Expanding, expanding, expanding now.

Holy Christ flame within me,
Come, expand thy triune light;
Flood my being with the essence
Of the pink, blue, gold, and white.

Holy lifeline to my Presence,
Friend and brother ever dear,
Let me keep thy holy vigil,
Be thyself in action here.

Through this open door of Christ individualization which "no man can shut"[25] comes the light/energy/consciousness necessary for the redemption of your soul. When you pray, "Jesus Christ, come into my temple!" lo, he comes. "Behold, I come quickly."[26]

And with him come the immortals, the "people in heaven" who have retained their individuality through their reunion with the I AM Presence—Archangel Zadkiel and Holy Amethyst, Archangel Gabriel who appeared to Mary and Mohammed, angels of Christmas, angels of the sacred Eucharist, angels of the resurrection, Saint Michael the Archangel and his hosts, even the mighty Elohim, "the seven Spirits" of God who worship before his throne.[27]

Behold, they live. John the Revelator saw them and he gives a sound report: "I beheld, and, lo, a great multitude, which no man could number, of all nations and kindreds and people and tongues, stood before the throne and before the Lamb, clothed with white robes and palms in their hands . . . . These are they which came out of great tribulation and have washed their robes and made them white in the blood of the Lamb."[28]

Through the open door of the Lord Christ they come—first we hear of the few who "shall walk with me in white,"[29] then we behold round about the throne of the Lamb "ten thousand times ten thousand, and thousands of thousands,"[30] then the 144,000 "which were redeemed from the earth,"[31] and finally the armies in heaven which follow "The Word of God" upon white horses, "clothed in fine linen, white and clean."[32] *They come. They are the Great White Brotherhood!*

These are thy fellowservants, "thy brethren that have the testimony of Jesus."[33] These are they who overcame the dragon "by the blood of the Lamb and by the word of their testimony; and they loved not their lives unto the death."[34] This is the unceasing communion of the saints—it is the body of God one in heaven and on earth. Those who have ascended into heaven through the intercession of Jesus Christ are the 'ascended' masters. Those following in their footsteps on the path of the ascension are their disciples, or 'chelas'.

Jesus Christ has given us his promise unfailing through his progressive revelation delivered to John: "Behold, I stand at the door and knock: if any man hear my voice and open the door, I will come in to him and will sup with him, and he with me. To him that overcometh will I grant to sit with me in my throne, even as I also overcame and am set down with my Father in his throne."[35]

Beloved, whether you are Christian or Jew, or Moslem, Buddhist, Hindu, atheist, or agnostic, *this is Jesus' own personal promise to you!* This is his promise of your resurrection and your ascension. And what of your promise to him?

It is to joyously overcome the not-self, the anti-self, replacing it day by day in love with the full awareness of the Real Self, the Christ Self, as the only reality of your being.

The path of this overcoming is God's gift to you. It is the gift of life itself. And the goal of life is your ascension—your soul's reunion with God. The initiations on the path of the ascension—with all the testings and temptations meet for sons and daughters of God—are made available through the progressive revelation of the Holy Spirit made known to us through the communion of saints, i.e., the many servant-sons and daughters of God who have ascended into heaven before us.

"I come. I AM in your midst always, the transformer of worlds below and worlds above. I come, I knock. You open, I enter. And I AM forevermore within you the great transformer of the Light of the Almighty One. I AM Jesus the Christ, alive within you forevermore."

This is that same Jesus Christ whom you have known forever and forever.

Even so, come, Lord Jesus.

XXI

Mark L. Prophet on the Mystery of the Great Mediator

XXI

God means many things to many people. I believe that God is best defined by the words *Light, Life,* and *Love.* In the beginning when the formless void existed, God spoke and said, "Let there be Light," and there was light. It is the light that enables us to see everything.

If there were no light to carry the image from the object to the retina of the eye and thence to the brain, the impulse of vision would be unrealized. We would as well, then, be in the dark. We could have all the creation around us, but unless we had light we could not see it.

So God, then, is Light. Now, Christ and Light are the same, because the sun gives us vision—and the Son of God, who is also that 'Sun' shining in his strength,[1] gives us vision. Through him, through the mediatorship of Light, we are able to see. But, you know, the mind sees as well as the eyes.

The eyes see, but do they understand what

they see? The understanding of what the eyes see is then attributable to the mind; and the mind, then, is a product of Light. And mind is a higher reflection of Light, so that people can say, "I see." And they do say this to you when you have made a statement to them. You see?

Now, then, let us take God as Life. Life is usually regarded as animation. Many people find it difficult to think of a stone as a living thing. Actually, a stone is also life. We may think of it as life in quiescence, life that obeys and records principles of universal law and illustrates the fundamentals of a higher form of self-conscious Life that makes us to have dominion over the "stone."

But we are inclined to think in terms of life only as 'conscious' life. This is really not correct, because when we know the law well enough we find that plants, which are growing things, have consciousness.

People have found out that they can put their hand out to a plant and love a plant and that the plant will respond. People have found out that trees or plants will sometimes move toward them when they pour out love to the plant. It's as though a baby were reaching for its mother.

As one pours love out to natural things, they may move toward him—but not always, because it takes a great deal of love-emanation to do this and most people don't have it. But if you build up your love-emanation enough and if you can tune in with the frequency of the plant, you can even pour out love to the plant and get response. That explains the "green thumb," you see. People who love nature will often get nature to respond to them more.

So God, then, is also a mediator through the extension of himself in the trinity of action of Light, Life, and Love. And life itself becomes a mediator or a path back to God. This is what Jesus meant when he said, "Inasmuch as ye have done it unto one of the least of these my brethren, ye have done it unto me."[2] He tried to emphasize that whatever we do to anyone is done unto God because we're doing it to Life.

This is a point that the world often overlooks in their puny involvements in self. They become so concentrated within the world that is around their physical forms that they lose sight of the vast, moving panorama of the cosmic.

We have people getting involved in the personal world and then we have them getting involved in the world of phenomena on the "outside." They get involved in nature and they say, "Where is God? Where is He?" And they begin tearing the skin off of things trying to find God. That's like cutting ourselves open and looking at our heart in order to see if it's beating. Or pulling up a carrot out of the ground to see if it's growing.

We should be able to have enough common sense and faith to realize that God is expressing everywhere. And if He is, we have to behave toward our fellowmen as we would toward God!

One of the greatest problems we have today is that we extend ourselves into "over-emphasization" of the ego. We attach too much importance to ourselves and we forget all about the importance of the other fellow.

This is why people have so many car accidents, because they drive their cars with their emotions—in a furious and irrational support of their egos. They feel that they have a right to be on the road and the other fellow is doing the wrong thing. "He was right, dead right, as he sped along. But he's just as dead as if he'd been wrong." We forget that. We get all involved in the mechanics of this "What involves me and my world?"

Life must be understood as a mediator—a mediator of the divine. It is the connecting thread. You can trace every light ray back to its source. And if you can't do that and all you're trying to do is bring the goods of the universe into your own coffers instead of being source-consciousness, it's sorcery. You know, "Bibbidi-bobbidi, boo . . ."—the old witch's idea. "I'll get what I want, by hook or by crook."

This is not the mediatorship of the divine man. The mediatorship of the divine man is to have reverence for Life, all Life—the sick, the halt, the ignorant, the afraid. Today people hate the sinner, the man who makes a mistake!

We must hate the mistake (whether it's our mistake or someone else's) and we must learn the charity of God, because that brings us to Love—the mediatorship of Love.

Love brings God to us. Because God is Love. But unless we have an object to love, which is the Beloved, how is God going to be brought to us?

There are many forms of Love. There are human loves, the love of husband and wife. There's the love of brother and sister. There's the love of man for God. And there's our affection for things, objects. People even have love for a tree that stands in their yard.

We must learn to recognize that all love is important in its own domain. Some people say, "Well, I believe in the love of God but I don't believe in human love." Well, what is human love? It is a lesser measure than divine love because we're dealing with something that is lesser. A human being is less than God.

Well, a lot of people think that they should love God but they can exclude their fellow human being and say, "Well, I don't like him. I don't like her. I don't like them. I don't like that." This is a great error, because we do ourselves irreparable harm when we have these strong dislikes or allow ourselves to be used by strong dislike and strong resentment.

When we learn to have the mediatorship of Love, we do ourselves great good. Because it does not make one whit of difference whether the person returns your love or not, because you are giving out love and the vibration that you are giving out is what counts for you.

Let them hate if they will. Let them be disturbed anywhere in the world over any condition if they wish to do it. You cannot control them. We all have to learn that we can only control ourselves. And this mediatorship of God through Light, Life, and Love is a matter of self-control. It is not the control of the world.

What do I do if I get angry? I immediately recognize I've erred and so I say, "You've done wrong." But be careful, now, that you don't get to feel that you're no good, because if you feel that you're no good, you'll make this mistake again. And you say to yourself, "I must not let myself feel that I'm no good. I made a mistake. The mistake was no good but *I'm good* because *God made me good!* Now, what am I going to do about it? I'm going to see that I don't make that mistake again!" And this is how we learn.

Man is a child. He must be taught. The problem is we say, "Because I'm so old I ought to be rich. Because I'm so old I ought to be wise." We equate chronological age with a wisdom and supremacy. Supremacy is the gift of God's Life, Light, and Love. We have to have the supreme seed within ourselves, and the supreme cannot be moved by human motives.

But in our own domain, whenever we work in a given field, we are subject to criticism. If you or I go on television, those who look at us on television can decide, "Well, I don't like him, or I don't like her." That is their privilege. You can't stop it. None of the politicians have been able to stop it. Their ratings go up and down like a yo-yo. And when their ratings are up, they say, "Well, I'll win. I'm going to enter the elections. Here's my hat. I'll throw it in the ring." When the ratings go down, they say, "Well, I guess I'll get out while the gettin' is good." This is what they do all the time. They watch the ratings.

But this is human fickleness. Now, God is not fickle. God is Light, Life, and Love constantly poured out. And he does not deviate from that one moment, but we do. We deviate, and this is why we're human beings. We're human beings—not to be condemned but to expand. We start like a little seed and we're going to grow—we're going to expand.

Now, I'm going to tell you a startling thing. All men, every one of you, have as much of God now as you are ever going to get of God. What a pity? Not at all. He gave you that gift and he put it in your causal body. He put it in your divine I AM God Presence. You've got it! It's there now!

"Well, why in the world," you say, "am I not possessed of all the Christ power in the universe? Why can't I say to the sun, 'Go down,' and it goes down? Why can't I command life and it obeys? Why can't I get along with everybody and make everyone love me and everything that I do? Why can't I do that?" Well, there's a reason for that. It's because we realize that potential only in part. As Saint Paul said: "We know in part. . . . Now we see through a glass darkly."[3]

Right now you have all of God. You've always had Him; He was never taken away from you. But your realization of the gift that you had has been taken away from you. By whom? Yourself, of course. Every single time we get involved in an expression of egoism, we lose a little more of our reality, and we recover it only by a reversal of the process. *We recover it by a reversal of the process.*

Our victory is attained in increments. As Omar Khayyam said, "I sent my Soul through the Invisible, / Some Letter of that After-Life to spell: / And by and by my Soul return'd to me, / And answer'd 'I Myself am Heav'n and Hell.'"[4]

God—Light, Life, and Love—is deposited in the chalice of your being: the physical, the mental, the spiritual, and the emotional. And in order to keep that God that is there active in the world, we have to obey certain precepts.

Now, have you ever been in a position where you went up to some kind of a machine that you knew how to operate very well, but because someone's life depended on your use of that machine you went up to it in emotional stress? This could be a car or an airplane or it could be a teletypewriter. It could be anything.

You're very familiar with it, you know exactly how to operate it, but now someone's life depends on it.

Have you ever found that your fingers were all thumbs, that because of the stress of the moment you could not do what you wanted to do? This is because the mind was not emitting a pure pattern. It wasn't working linearly. It was choppy and disconnected because fear rode in through your emotional body, and the emotions churned the mind into waves, and your emotions were governing your thinking.

Have you ever seen this when a traffic cop comes up to you? The red light flashes, he gets out of the car, he says, "May I see your driver's license, please?"

At that moment, you may have done nothing wrong. He may be making a routine check. But the moment he asks for that license and you see that red light and that star, you can't help it. You reach in your wallet and your hands are shaking because your emotions are disturbed. It's happened to most people.

So, what is the answer? It is to learn to still the various parts of our beings, to know what we consist of, to realize that we're not just a body.

The body and its computerlike components—its switching mechanism in the cortex of the brain, in the various interconnections in the nervous system, central and sympathetic—

are all-important because they are a vast network that directs and coordinates various forces in the body, but at the command of the emotions.

Yes, the emotions *and* the mind are very potent in affecting the body. But the mind is not you either. You know very well the mind is not you, but you identify with your mind. You wake up in the morning, you say, "Well, here I am again. Another day has dawned. What will I do today? How will it turn out? What will tomorrow bring?" You talk to yourself. Do you ever do that? Maybe I'm the only one that does that.

So this happens, but that's not you really. You are talking through the switching apparatus of the mind. And then again, you get up and you feel terrible and you say, "Oh, why in the world did I do that awful thing I did yesterday?"—whatever it was. "I wish I hadn't done it." And right away you're pulled down.

Maybe you bet on the wrong horse and somehow or other you had an idea that it wasn't going to win. Maybe you married the wrong girl, or maybe she married the wrong guy! But maybe you suddenly realize that you can't let that bother you now.

There are so many things that can pass through your mind and affect your emotions. And if you're going to have God working through you as a Great Mediator, you're going to have to become the master of both your emotions and your mind, which are extensions of yourself—instruments of self-expression but in essence not the Real You. But if you get all hung up in your feelings and your thoughts and these are not positive and expansive of the Good, then these adjuncts to your personality, undisciplined, are going to stand between you and your Divine Reality.

God is needed: God needs you! You need God! You need each other!

Why does God need you? Some people say, "Well, I don't believe that. I don't think God needs me. I'm too small." Well, all God has got on this small planet is a small group of small people. He doesn't have a mass of people that he can say, "Now, these people are mine." All people are his. But they have to know it, they have to realize it, they have to be willing to fit themselves into his pattern.

But God *does* need you, because he has no other body through which to express on this earth. That's why I'm on this platform, because God needs my vocal cords. He needs my brain and mind. I need him. I couldn't do anything or be anything without him. You couldn't even listen to me or enjoy life without him! You would not be a whole entity without him. So we need each other. And we have to learn to realize the being of God in the many parts of God.

Oh, we wish everybody was perfect like we were. Were we? Yes, we were. We *were*, I said. That's in the past tense. But we will be again, and that's what we're moving toward.

You have to understand this because it's something that requires a little thought. But when you grasp it, you have a power inside of you that is just dynamic. It's *dynamic* when you grasp it. And sometimes it comes to people all at once. It hits them with a sudden flash—just like that! And they no longer feel like a human being. They feel like just standing here and saying, "Whoopee!"

That's right. You just feel that power all through yourself. You know it isn't yourself. You know it's God! And you know that God has a job for you to do, each one of you. It isn't all the same, it couldn't be.

Now, what is the role of the Mediator? The role of the Mediator is to transform.

Do you know what a transformer is? I think you're familiar with a little doorbell transformer, the one you use on an erector set, or the one you use to light a little bulb. You also know about these great big transformers on the power poles. And you know about transformers that sit down in these cages so little boys don't crawl over the top and touch them because they carry a high voltage. A transformer takes a low voltage and raises it to a high, or takes a high voltage and reduces it to a low.

Well, then, the Mediator is a transformer. The Holy Christ Self acts to take the little love currents of the human from down here [pointing to the lower figure in the Chart of Your

Divine Self (facing p. 278)], and bring them up here [pointing to the I AM Presence], and change their nature from the human into the Divine, and then send the love current back into your world amplified by the Divine.

Archangel Michael once said, "You give me your doubt and I will give you my faith in exchange." This is the quality of the mother, too. The mother takes her child and heals his hurt. She picks him up and sets him on her knee. She wraps her arms around the child. She pours oceans of comfort and love into the child, and the child suddenly is soothed and relaxed.

No one can do this but a mother. And no one can do *this* transformation but your Holy Christ Self. You are in the lap of the living Christ when you go to him and he takes your doubts and he takes all of these negative vibrations. That's what it means when we talk about the personal crucifixion. It's the Real Self of us that we crucify with ungodly deeds. That's why Paul said, "They crucify to themselves the Son of God afresh, and put him to an open shame."[5]

The children of the light, because they're not perfect, carry to their Holy Christ Self these negative traits and this imperfection and all of these unlikable conditions. And the Christ reaches out and takes you to himself and he changes all these conditions—discomfort to comfort, death to life, darkness to light, strife to peace.

The whole human ball of wax is changed

by this Christ, and then he fixes that in your consciousness. That's his role. That's the role of the Divine Mediator. It's to fix in your consciousness the immutability of divine Law.

Now, God is Law. And the Law that God is is the law of action, not inaction. And the Mediator is a Mediator of action. God does not sit idly by even when we, as human beings, refuse to move. And those energetic ones who toil in our midst are they whose spirits have flown to the Higher Consciousness of the Mediator: "But they, while their companions slept, / Were toiling upward in the night."[6]

The Mediator says, "I come as a thief in the night. And, behold, I come quickly. And my reward is with me."[7] "One is taken and another is left."[8] What does that mean? It means that some people are taken by the Light and some are left by the Light.

We can't make anybody do anything! People will do what they want to do. That's why the old black master Aleister Crowley, when he came over to Boston from England, emphasized his slogan: "Do what thou wilt shall be the whole of the law."

Don't be taken by it. It was a permissive idea. The idea caught on. People were told by one formerly connected with the Brotherhood that they could do what they wanted to do. Well, of course we can. I can go out and stick my head in a buzz saw, perish the thought. Maybe my enemies think I should.

But that's not the point. We cannot do what we wish to do with impunity, any of us. We are bound by law—the law of karma. If I do a thing that is not right, it will make me unhappy. If I do what is right, I will be made happy. And sometimes you're not made happy on the instant by the right you do at a given moment, or maybe you immediately stand by for a reward.

People will sow for a million years in discord and the minute they come to God, they think that God is supposed to do an about-face and say, "Here's a million years of your bad sowing. But I'm your heavenly Father and you're my prodigal son, so I love you so much I'm going to take all these million years of prodigal sowing and dump it down the drain. And I'm going to make you king, right now." Instant love.

Well, it doesn't work that way. Because even great avatars [an avatar is an incarnation of God], before they became avatars, served God sometimes for centuries and centuries after they came to the point of their initiations. They were put through the crucial tests that actually gave them their freedom.

Now, the divine opposes the human, and you've got to understand this. I'm not going to try to kid you one little bit. The divine opposes the human because the human is death and the divine is Life, and that is the reason for the opposition.

God cannot perpetuate evil! God cannot take conditions that are wholly unlike himself and say, "You are going to live forever." But God *wants* you to live forever. But you, right now, have conditions in your world (all of us have them) that are not perfect. So we have to understand the need to walk on this pathway with a view to learning the law—to learn the law, to live the law, and to do those things that will bring us our deliverance.

Many people are looking for the simple formula; this formula actually exists. But you only get it after you've gotten to a certain point on the Path. And when you get it, of course, you don't need it because you've already mastered enough of life to be able to use it anyway. It's just like the banker. He'll make you a loan if you can show him that you don't need the money. That's exactly the way it is.

God's formula for eternal Life is written in our inward parts—our cells and atoms—but when we finally unlock it, we don't need the formula because we've become it. God self-realized in us is the grand formula of being—and we know it. And when we know it, no one can take it from us.

So, we have to understand that the divine opposes the human, not in the sense that God is our enemy. He's not at war with us. It is the nature of Life to oppose death. And everything that we do in this world, from the cradle to the grave, is calculated to bring us to death. And everything that God has done to us, from the beginning when he made us to this hour, is to bring us to Life—and yet we're not alive. Not entirely. Not yet.

Why did I say that? Because God is Life. And if we have the totality of God, we have Life. If we don't have a realization of the totality of God, we still are not yet fully alive. Therefore "quickenings" are happenings that are done in part while we're here in this world.

We understand in part and we know in part. But when we come to the point where we have achieved the measure of that Christ who is our own best Mediator, we will know perfectly. We will know ourselves as the Beloved One knows us—in the beauty and wholeness of our original endowment from the Father. We'll see through the veil. And then, effectively, Christ will have stepped through the veil.

Don't you think that Jesus could see through the veil before he ascended? Do you have the idea that you have to wait till you're dead before you are actually going to live? That's ridiculous! You can have it and be here! People won't even know it—that's the funny part of it. They may have a strange sense of it, but they won't really know it. They'll say, "Well, you're different."

Now, divine motives are law. They are cosmic, universal, immovable law, and they're fixed. But in his search for love, man's motives are often very human.

Love has a formula. And the formula always brings results. It brings good fruit. And you can see the results in your life. But you have to understand yourself. And the best way to understand yourself is to understand that you're two people. One of you is attached to the Presence up here, and the other is down here in the human. And you have to understand that these are at war with each other. Yet there's no war in heaven.

Seems kind of contradictory. What we actually mean by this is that the nature of God is contrary to human nature. Love will bear fruits, but we have to learn how to express love.

Is love attention? Is love attraction? Or is love merely affection for the object of its affection?

I think the best definition of love is: "Do unto others as you would have them do unto you." Because Love worketh no ill to his neighbor.[9] But I'd like to carry it a bit further and say that I think that it means that Love worketh all good to his neighbor. And if we get the sense that the more we give to God and the world and the more we give to humanity, the more we're going to get, we won't even worry about the getting. We'll just go out, pouring out our love as the sun pours out its rays.

The rain falls on the just and the unjust.[10] So whether people like you or not, love them just the same. If you will follow that, you will soon have the fruit of love in your life because you will not be controlled by *them.*

The reason we're bound down here and kept bound is because we react to everything that people do to us, and we can't stop them from doing. People are going to do. The traffic cop will cop and the farmer will farm and the banker will bank. The minister will preach, the chiropractor will punch—and the boxer will punch, too. And everybody will do what they're supposed to do, according to their nature. You've heard the saying, "It's the nature of the beast."

Some people are reactors to everything that people do to them. Now, I don't blame them for that because we're all doing the same thing. None of us would be in this room if we were not reactors. We would have long ago ascended. But we let the other fellow dictate our life for us. I'll prove it to you.

You get on a bus and the bus driver says, "Look, lady, I don't have any change for a $20 bill. For heaven's sake, why don't you come on here with something that I can break?"

So you're standing there fumbling for smaller change. And then you hand him a $5 bill and he says, "I might as well quit my job and pull over to the side and resign. Look, lady, I only have change for a dollar."

So you finally find a dollar—you fish way down deep to give him a dollar. About this time you think he's rude. So then he says, "All right. Everybody step to the back of the bus!

Come on, shove it back, shove it back!" And you say, "Well, I know he's rude."

So you begin to get mad. You got on the bus and you just came from a church meeting, and you were just thinking how lovely everybody in the world was, and you were thinking how good God was. And now this guy is getting under your skin. And about the time you're ready to get off, you've got an umbrella in your hand and it's all you can do to avoid rapping him over the head!

And I think you'd be better off if you hit the guy, because then you'd at least have got it out of your system, even if you went to court afterward. But instead of that, you carry the poison of this resentment with you all day long, because of the bus driver. And who in the world is the bus driver that he should run your life?

Then you get home and you burn your meal and your husband comes in and he decides this is a terrible thing, because the food isn't cooked right—and it's all because of the bus driver. It's like the pig that got over the stile, you know. There are so many chains involved in this law of cause-and-effect. And this is why human beings are here, because they don't understand that they cannot keep on reacting to people and circumstances and get where they're supposed to be going.

We all react and we have to learn to quit it. And this takes self-control, and this takes effort, and this takes honest appraisal of ourselves and what we are.

I took Sean to Denver and we went to Furr's Cafeteria. And there were white stones that the Furr people had put around a tree. And Sean said, "I love those white stones, Daddy. I'm going to take some." And he reached down and he grabbed a handful, and he was going to carry these white stones back for his rock collection. And Daddy said, "Sean, you put those stones back, every one of them." So Sean put them back.

And then I said to Sean, "Mr. Furr had these little white rocks put around this tree, and they have a number. There are just so many rocks around that tree—maybe it's a thousand, maybe it's ten thousand. But," I said, "every day hundreds of little boys go by here. And if each one takes only two or three rocks, in a short time all these rocks will be gone and Mr. Furr will have to spend money and another truck will have to come up and dump out more rocks."

And this is one of the things that is basic to law. A lot of people do not understand the reason for laws and order and common-sense thinking.

Now, you could be Mr. Furr. You could own the cafeteria. And you could think of thousands of ways to make it possible for others to live in greater happiness by simply being thoughtful. And so you would prosper in the free-enterprise system by using your gain to follow the golden rule. And with malice toward none and charity for all, as Abe Lincoln said, you could demonstrate the Law of Love at the business level and use it as a mediator for the Christ to reach out and give a helping hand to your neighbors.

If the businessmen and women of America would use the capitalist system to multiply talents[11] and at the same time give love in self-help projects in the community—instead of amassing more wealth than they need to live comfortably—there would be no need for welfare programs; communism would have no allure and socialism would be out of style; the little people would have a sense of self-worth and a sacred labor and they would still hold in their hearts the American dream of the abundant life which Christ comes to give us by way of our own exercise of free will and ingenuity and love.

We have a world today with a mouth for Jesus Christ and a hand for Lucifer. They talk about the kingdom of God, but when it comes to doing it, they just don't do it at all! They do just the opposite of what they're supposed to do. And you know this is true.

But that's no reason, because it has been true yesterday, that it has to be true tomorrow. People can change and they do. And I've seen them change. There is absolutely a lot of hope for everybody—if they can get it through *their* heads that there's hope.

Now, can men forgive sins? The Lord's Prayer says, "Forgive us our debts"—and here's the secret magic word: *"as we forgive our debtors."* People have gotten the wrong idea about that. They don't quite understand what that means. That's a formula. That means forgive us our debts *as*—in the same way in which—we forgive our debtors. And if you don't forgive people who have wronged you, you aren't going to have your wrongs forgiven either, because that prayer is a true statement of God's law.

So we *can* forgive sins. We can forgive sins that other people sin against us, but we cannot forgive all the sins in their life. I can't take one of these ladies who might come to me and say, "Well, I did something I shouldn't do. I stole a pair of silk stockings"—I can't say, "Well, I'm going to forgive you for it," because I don't have that kind of power. Neither does any man on the face of the planet.

But I can say to the woman, "Well, why don't you send the store a check for the stockings and don't do it again." That's the only kind of forgiveness of sins I could do. I could tell her to make it right to the best of her ability.

We must understand, then, that we have a Mediator that acts in the many realms in which we ourselves are incapable of acting. And this is a terrific point of God's law.

Have you ever looked at the world and the world seemed to be so complex that you didn't even see how your mind could possibly fix it in your mind? And you've looked at this business of forgiveness of sins and your relationship with God and somehow it looked like the little story about the little bushy-tailed squirrel that one of the yogis told.

It seems the bushy-tailed squirrel had a family of babies by the seashore, and the tide came in and it swept all the little babies out to sea. So the squirrel stood on the shore and shook her little foot at the ocean and said, "I will dip my bushy tail in you until I dry you up if you don't give me back my babies!" Well, how long would it take a squirrel dipping in the ocean to dry up the ocean?

Now, sometimes you feel that way about the problems of your relationship with God. You say, "This thing is too big for me. I can't handle it." And this is true. We can't handle it in the human. This is the role, then, of the Mediator. This is the role of the Universal Christ. And this is why we need the Beloved One. Our burdens are too hard to bear without the Son of God.

We've got a Christ—every one of us within ourselves—and that Christ Self, the same Light and Life and Love that also was in Christ Jesus, has all the intelligence and the awareness of the universal Mind of God. He knows every mistake you've ever made, and he knows every good thing you've ever done—and he knows exactly what your karmic balance is. He knows how much good is stored up here in your causal body and how much of inequity is down here in the human.

Don't worry about your debts. Worrying will never pay them. Don't think maybe you were some kind of a brigand or a Robin Hood in some past life or your debts are so terrible you must have been Blackbeard the pirate. Don't feel that way! You don't know and I don't know, and we shouldn't even care what we were. It's what we *are* that counts! Forget all that.

If you really want to find your way back home to God, remember that he that has committed many errors loves even more than the one who has committed a few. Jesus pointed this out concerning Mary Magdalene. He explained to Simon the Pharisee: "Her sins, which are many, are forgiven; for she loved much: but to whom little is forgiven, the same loveth little."[12]

"Though your sins be as scarlet, they shall be as white as snow; though they be red like crimson, they shall be as wool."[13] This is fine, as long as people don't get the idea that they want to be more white by committing more sins. As one man said, "Forgiveness feels so good." That's what Rasputin used to say. He used to seduce the girls at the Czar's court and then he'd say, "It feels so good now to ask forgiveness for this sin that I have committed." And he really repented! Yes, he did—until the next time.

People can become conditioned till they're always the sinner, tearfully getting down at the altar and saying, "O God, forgive me, a miserable sinner." But they never ever reach a point where they overcome the sin or summon the will or the strength to resist the temptation. That point can be reached through the Holy Christ Self. We don't have to be drenched in tears for ourselves all the time. We can forget all that. The way is plain. Christ can act in us if we ask him to.

You've got to learn to turn yourself over in sweet surrender to the Christ. You say, "Here I am. You know all about me, I am aspiring to be like you. Now, whatever is necessary to occur in my world to make me like you are, you bring out the answer in my life. And I'm turning the whole thing over to you; and I, like God, will now rest."

That's when you start to work. Because the answer, after all the wheels have stopped spinning up in your Holy Christ Self, is going to come descending right down through the computer of your self and it's going to tell you just what your role is going to be. God has the answer for your life and for the lives of every one of his children. And you can set it into motion by the simple expedient of turning it over to him.

But don't think you can do this with some kind of a little quiver of "Well, this would be nice." Oh no, you've got to do it with the most firm determination. You've got to want it so bad you can taste it! You've got to make enough of an impression on the Holy Christ Self that you move the Holy Christ Self into action—for you.

Through the years, the Holy Christ Self has watched all of your false signals. He's seen how you've thrown up the white handkerchief. You've said, "Help! I'm drowning!" What happens? He comes to the rescue. You say, "Well, I'll see you later. Thanks." Sometimes the Holy Christ Self doesn't even get a thanks. He just has to assume that you were grateful.

Christ is the Christ of all ages and always will be. Christ is the ageless hierarch of Light, Life, and Love—the Great Mediator. So let us, then, understand that the role of the Great Mediator is one that we must assume, and that the best way to assume it is to identify with the Christ.

Don't put people on pedestals. Let Christ raise you up to the lofty office of being a mediator. Be a peacemaker with your fellowmen. Be a peacemaker with yourself.

NOTES

I THE MYSTERY OF THE CHRIST

1. Daniel 8:16; 9:21; Luke 1:19, 26.
2. Isaiah 7:14; 9:2, 6; Matthew 1:18–25; Luke 2:1–38.
3. John 9:35–37; Romans 8:14–17; Galatians 3:26–4:7.
4. Genesis 1:26; 5:1.
5. John 1:12–14; 3:16, 18; I John 3:1–3; 4:9.
6. Matthew 24; Mark 13; Luke 21:5–36; Matthew 2:2, 9, 10; II Peter 1:19.
7. John 1:14; Romans 10:9; I John 4:2, 3, 15.
8. For essential teaching on the **violet transmuting flame,** see Mark L. Prophet and Elizabeth Clare Prophet, *The Science of the Spoken Word,* pp. 4, 69–70, 96–125, 141–43, 150–80; "Violet Flame: Sacred Fire of Transmutation," *The Coming Revolution: A Magazine for Higher Consciousness* 2 (Fall 1981): 30–40; and Mark L. Prophet, "The Violet Flame for the Achievement of God Realization," on 2-cassette album *Discourses on Cosmic Law,* Album VII (A7961).
9. Ephesians 1:13.
10. The **seven archangels:** Michael, Jophiel, Chamuel, Gabriel, Raphael, Uriel, Zadkiel. See Revelation 8:2, 6–13; 9:1, 13; 10:7; 11:15; 12:7; 15:1, 6, 8; 16:1–4, 8, 10, 12, 17; 17:1; 21:9. Summit University Press publications by the seven archangels: *Vials of the Seven Last Plagues: Prophecies for the 1980s by the Seven Archangels,* in paperback and in *El Morya on Discipleship East and West: The Path of the Darjeeling Master and His Chelas,* Pearls of Wisdom, vol. 18 (1975), pp. 175–262; and "The Class of the Archangels," in *Where the Eagles Gather,* Book I, Pearls of Wisdom, vol. 24 (1981), pp. 43–186.
11. Luke 24:50, 51.
12. Revelation 1:8, 11; 21:6; 22:13.
13. Jeremiah 23:6; 33:16.
14. Revelation 12:5.

15. John 6:32–35, 47–58.
16. Revelation 14:1.
17. Exodus 24:12, 13, 15–18; 34:2, 4; II Samuel 15:32; I Kings 18:42; 19:11, 12; Isaiah 2:2, 3; Micah 4:1, 2; Matthew 14:23; 17:1; Luke 6:12.
18. Exodus 3:14.
19. II Peter 1:10.
20. I John 3:2.
21. Acts 17:28.
22. I Corinthians 15:52–54.
23. Galatians 6:7.
24. John 14:2, 3.
25. Daniel 7:9, 13, 22.

II THE MYSTERY OF SALVATION

1. Luke 1:35.
2. Luke 2:13, 14.
3. Revelation 21:1.
4. Proverbs 14:12; 16:25.
5. Matthew 16:18.
6. Revelation 12:1, 2, 5.
7. On November 18, 1978, 913 members of the Peoples Temple at Jonestown, a quasi-religious/socialist commune in Guyana, South America, committed a mass suicide-murder at the direction of leader **Jim Jones.** California Congressman Leo J. Ryan, accompanied by several relatives of temple members and eight newsmen, had arrived in Jonestown the day before to investigate alleged abuses. As Ryan's party and 14 defectors were preparing to board two airplanes at a nearby airstrip to return to Guyana's capital, Jones' aides opened fire on the group—killing Ryan, a defector, and three newsmen. The others, including 11 wounded, escaped. According to a survivor of the suicide-murders at the commune, when Jones discovered that not all the visitors had been killed, he ordered his followers and their children to take their own lives by drinking cyanide-laced Kool-Aid—a ritual they had rehearsed before in middle-of-the-night emergency meetings as a loyalty test. Those who did not drink the poison voluntarily were compelled to do so by armed guards; a few managed to flee into the jungle. Jones, who was found with a bullet wound in the head, apparently committed suicide. In the aftermath of the Guyana tragedy, many religious organizations were forced to defend not only their beliefs but their right to exist. Self-proclaimed "experts" on one or a number of new religions took up the so-called "cult menace" as

their cause, gestapo-type organizations began to collect files of information on groups they labelled "cults," and the number of illegal deprogramming attempts was on the rise. As a result, a growing suspicion—based on the underlying fear that all "cults" used brainwashing and therefore any one of them could become "another Jonestown"—spread across the country, setting brother against brother and family member against family member. With increased pressure for government regulation of "cults," a number of investigations and hearings were held by committees in Congress and state legislatures. The anti-cult movement has backed proposals in several states to redefine or expand guardianship laws to apply to members of religious "cults." In some cases, parents have been able to carry out what is, in effect, tantamount to legalized kidnapping—using existing statutes to obtain a temporary conservatorship or guardianship (and thus an opportunity for deprogramming) by declaring their adult child incompetent or incapable of managing his or her own property or affairs. The attack on unorthodox sects has also taken the form of anti-religious regulations of administrative agencies (such as the IRS) and widespread selective enforcement of existing laws (e.g., municipal zoning ordinances). Both the persecutors and the persecuted have pointed to Matthew 24 as prophetic of this ugly phenomenon: "Take heed that no man deceive you. For many shall come in my name, saying, I am Christ, and shall deceive many. . . . Then shall they deliver you up to be afflicted and shall kill you; and ye shall be hated of all nations for my name's sake. And then shall many be offended, and shall betray one another, and shall hate one another. And many false prophets shall rise and shall deceive many. And because iniquity shall abound, the love of many shall wax cold"—whereas Matthew 10 depicts the bitterness experienced by families divided by the karma of religious controversy: "Think not that I am come to send peace on earth: I came not to send peace but a sword. For I am come to set a man at variance against his father, and the daughter against her mother, and the daughter-in-law against her mother-in-law. And a man's foes shall be they of his own household."

8. Romans 3:8.
9. Exodus 20:3.
10. John 21:15–17.
11. Matthew 7:15–20.
12. I Corinthians 12:10.
13. Matthew 5:8.
14. See Elizabeth Clare Prophet, "Ignorance, the First Habit to Conquer," on 8-cassette album *On the Mother,* Album 1

(A8260); and Kuthumi's teaching on the habit of **ignorance** in *Corona Class Lessons: A Manual for Ministering Servants* by the World Teachers, recorded by Mark L. Prophet, Elizabeth Clare Prophet.
15. Matthew 24:24.
16. Revelation 12:12.
17. Matthew 10:28.
18. Revelation 4:4, 10; 5:5, 6, 8, 11, 14; 7:11, 13; 11:16; 14:3; 19:4.
19. Genesis 11:1–9.
20. Revelation 16:16.
21. Matthew 12:37.
22. Matthew 15:14.
23. John 14:6.

III THE MYSTERY OF CONSCIOUSNESS

1. I John 2:18, 22; 4:3; II John 7.

IV THE MYSTERY OF ARMAGEDDON

1. Psalms 37:28; Matthew 13:38.
2. Matthew 7:15; 24:24; II Corinthians 11:13–15.
3. Revelation 9:3, 7.
4. Daniel 10:13, 21; 12:1; Jude 9; Revelation 12.
5. The **Blue Army** of Our Lady of Fátima is a worldwide movement which claims over 22 million members in 100 countries dedicated to fulfilling the requests made by the Blessed Mother in 1917 at Fátima, Portugal, where she promised, "If my wishes are fulfilled, Russia will be converted,. . . and the world will enjoy a period of peace." During her six appearances to three shepherd children at Fátima, Mother Mary asked them to "say the rosary every day to bring peace to the world and an end to war. . . . Jesus wishes you to make me known and loved on earth. He wishes also for you to establish devotion in the world to my Immaculate Heart. . . . Make sacrifices for sinners and say often, especially while making a sacrifice: O Jesus, this is for the love of Thee, for the conversion of sinners and in reparation for sins committed against the Immaculate Heart of Mary." Following a frightening vision of hell revealed to the children, the Blessed Mother warned, "You have seen hell, where the souls of sinners go. It is to save them that God wants to establish in the world devotion to my Immaculate Heart. If you do what I tell you, many souls will be saved, and there will be peace. . . . When you see a night that is lit by a strange and an unknown light, you will know it is the sign that God gives you that He is about to punish the world with another war and with hunger,

and by the persecution of the Church and the Holy Father. To prevent this, I shall come to the world to ask that Russia be consecrated to my Immaculate Heart, and I shall ask that on the First Saturday of every month communion of reparation be made in atonement for the sins of the world." Blue Army members pledge to offer reparation (sacrifices demanded by daily duty), to pray part of the rosary (five decades) daily while meditating on the mysteries, and to wear the Scapular of Mount Carmel as an act of consecration to Our Lady. On June 27, 1972, the Ascended Master El Morya called the Messenger Elizabeth Clare Prophet to begin giving the rosary and to walk the fourteen stations of the cross in fourteen-day cycles for the balancing of personal and planetary karma. Mother Mary has since dictated through the messenger the Scriptural Rosary for the New Age (thirteen mysteries focusing the power of the eight rays and the five secret rays); the Fourteenth Rosary, the Mystery of Surrender; and the Child's Rosary (see n. 20, p. 347). In fulfillment of the Blessed Mother's requirements outlined at Fátima, Keepers of the Flame worldwide give the rosary daily, followed by the consecration of Russia, China, America, and the world to the Immaculate Heart of Mary, and partake of communion on the first Saturday of each month. In a dictation given March 22, 1978, Mother Mary came to "fulfill the message of Fátima and the command of God" for the public consecration of Russia as well as all nations under World Communism and Socialism to her Immaculate Heart. See "The Consecration of Russia to the Immaculate Heart" on 6-cassette album *Second Coming of Christ,* Album I (A7836).

6. Revelation 12:10.
7. Matthew 26:3, 4; 27:20–23; Mark 15:6–14; Luke 23:18–23; John 11:49–53; 18:39, 40; Acts 7:54–60 (Caiaphas was the high priest in Acts 7:1).
8. Matthew 5:11, 12; Luke 21:12–18; John 15:18–21.
9. Genesis 2:9; 3:24; Revelation 2:7; 22:2, 14.
10. Isaiah 62:6, 7; Ezekiel 3:17; 33:7.
11. The **decree** is the most powerful of all applications to the Godhead. It is the command of the son or daughter of God made in the name of the I AM Presence and the Christ for the will of the Almighty to come into manifestation as Above, so below. It is the means whereby the kingdom of God becomes a reality here and now through the power of the spoken Word. It may be short or long and usually is marked by a formal preamble and a closing, or acceptance. See Mark L. Prophet and Elizabeth Clare Prophet, *The Science of the Spoken Word; Prayers, Meditations, Dynamic Decrees for the Coming Revolution in Higher*

Consciousness I, looseleaf; Jesus and Kuthumi, *Prayer and Meditation;* 4-cassette album *The Science of the Spoken Word: Why and How to Decree Effectively* (A7736); and 2-cassette albums *Decrees and Songs by the Messenger Mark L. Prophet* (A8202) and *Rainbow Rays: Out of the Mouth of the Messenger* by Elizabeth Clare Prophet (A83018).

12. Deuteronomy 32:35, 36; Romans 12:19; Hebrews 10:30.
13. 1968 marked the start of the most recent wave of world **terrorism** as extremists turned increasingly to violence as an instrument of political coercion. Terrorists began to use more sophisticated methods of operation, equipment, and weapons, and took advantage of improved means of mass communication to maximize the impact of their violence. Small, politically weak groups with little or no popular support were able to rivet worldwide attention as satellite television carried news of terrorist attacks instantly around the globe. Terrorist activities, recorded in 48 countries in 1970, had spread to 91 nations by 1981. In July 1983, terrorism expert Brian Jenkins of Rand Corporation reported that in the first three years of the eighties, world terrorism increased about 30% per year, double the rate of increase in the previous decade. The largest number of incidents have occurred in Western Europe, Latin America, the Middle East/North Africa, and North America respectively—directed at diplomats, corporate officials, military personnel, tourists, and missionaries, in that order. Noting that over half of the attacks since 1968 were made in the industrialized democracies of North America and Western Europe, American foreign correspondent Claire Sterling reported in *The Terror Network* (New York: Holt, Rinehart and Winston, 1981), "There is nothing random in this concentrated assault on the shrinking area of the world still under democratic rule. . . . The Italian Red Brigades, who like to think that they speak for many or most of their kind, have made it plain that theirs is a war for the destruction of Western democracy. They have even published a terror timetable." Sterling claims that there is indeed "an international terrorist circuit, or network, or fraternity. . . . A multitude of disparate terrorist groups have been helping one another out and getting help from not altogether disinterested outsiders." In the 1970s, emerging terrorist bands "were indebted to the Cubans and their Russian patrons for that honeycomb of camps around Havana," says Sterling. Among those trained in Havana were members of the Tupamaros, who early on set the example for urban guerrilla strategy and who effectively caused the downfall of Uruguay's democratic republic. Starting out in 1963 as middle-class political revolu-

tionaries who literally robbed from the rich and gave the money, supermarket goods, etc. to the poor, they later turned to violence—bombing homes, occupying police stations, raiding military arsenals, kidnapping for ransom, and murdering. Their Movimiento de Liberación Nacional (MLN) so terrorized Uruguay—which had the most democratic government and one of the highest living standards in South America—that the left-wing government was forced to ask the military to take a more active role. With strong repressive measures, the army quelled the terrorists, then in 1976 took over the government in a military coup. Political rights of all existing party leaders were suspended for 15 years with the promise of a gradual return to representative democracy. In November 1983, at least 200,000 Uruguayans gathered at the capital in one of the largest demonstrations in their history to pressure leaders of the military regime to hold elections in 1984 as promised. The Irish Republican Army (IRA), fighting their terrorist war for over 10 years, has been responsible for numerous bombings and assassinations. Since 1969, more than 2,500 people have died in rioting, sniping, and terrorism. Fellow terrorists from the Red Brigades have called the IRA an "unrenounceable point of reference for generalized guerrilla warfare on the European Continent." Their goal is to unify Northern Ireland (now part of the United Kingdom) with the predominantly Catholic Republic of Ireland, although the government of the Republic of Ireland has outlawed the organization. But the real aim of the IRA, as they once stated, is to "destabilize capitalism in the whole of Ireland through armed struggle." They attack Irish police, officials, British soldiers, and civilians. In March 1979, the IRA planted a car bomb that killed Airey Neave, a leading Conservative Party member of Parliament, as he was leaving the House of Commons. Later that year they murdered Lord Mountbatten, World War II hero and cousin of the queen, by rigging his fishing boat with explosives. The work of the Baader-Meinhof gang, which operates principally in West Germany, has been characterized by the kidnapping and murder of prominent leaders. Most notably, they killed German industrialist Hanns-Martin Schleyer in 1977 after the West German government rejected demands from the kidnappers and from hijackers of a West German jet to release imprisoned terrorists, including three leaders of the Baader-Meinhof group. The Red Brigades, most of whom are now in prison, are known for their kidnappings and knee shootings, designed to permanently cripple victims. They engineered the 1978 kidnapping-murder of former Italian Premier Aldo Moro and the 1981 kidnapping of U.S. Army

General James Dozier, rescued by Italian police 42 days later. It was reported that Dozier's captors were, for one thing, seeking information on U.S. nuclear storage sites in Europe. The Palestinian Liberation Organization (PLO) is a complex organization spread across several Middle Eastern countries that operates, in effect, as a government in exile. The various factions of its military arm have a long and bloody history of international terrorist activity. Their long-range goal is to create a homeland for Arab Palestinians on land currently controlled by Israel; Israeli officials and citizens are their chief targets. On September 5, 1972, a Palestinian commando squad murdered 11 members of the Israeli Olympic team in Munich, West Germany. The Palestinian guerrilla group Black September, apparently affiliated with or an extension of the PLO, took credit for the attack. In 1978, in what was considered at the time the worst terrorist attack in Israel's history, a Palestinian death squad hijacked two buses of tourists and sightseers, shooting at passengers and passing traffic. They forced everyone onto the first bus and when the vehicle was finally stopped outside of Tel Aviv, the terrorists set fire to it with explosives while the hostages were still inside. A commando group within the PLO claimed responsibility for this Sabbath massacre which left 34 Israelis dead and 78 wounded. Armenian nationalists, in a vendetta against the Turks for the alleged 1915 massacre of 1.5 million Armenians exterminated or deported during World War I, have been responsible for a growing number of attacks on Turkish installations and diplomats in the last decade. From 1973–83 they killed 36 Turkish envoys, four of them in the U.S. In Los Angeles, which has the largest Armenian community in the U.S., Turkish Consul General Kemal Arikan was shot near his home on January 28, 1982, by two young men while his car was stopped for a red light. The Justice Commandos of the Armenian Genocide (JCAG)—a Beirut-based group that seeks to restore the Armenian homeland along the Turkish-Soviet border which they claim was seized by the Turks—took responsibility for the murder. Nine years earlier to the day, Arikan's predecessor as consul general had been murdered by a prominent Armenian land developer in Santa Barbara. Within two weeks in July 1983, Armenian terrorists planted a bomb near the Turkish Airlines counter at Orly Airport, Paris, killing seven and wounding 60; shot and killed a Turkish official in Brussels; and, in a suicide mission, blew up the ambassador's residence at the Turkish Embassy in Lisbon, Portugal, killing seven. Armenian terrorist organizations range from pro-Western to pro-Communist. One of the most active groups is the Marxist

Armenian Secret Army for the Liberation of Armenia (ASALA) which, according to some reports, may be backed by Moscow.

14. On November 27, 1978, former San Francisco supervisor **Dan White,** 32, who had two weeks earlier resigned his post, shot and killed **Mayor George Moscone** in the mayor's City Hall office suite, then walked to the opposite side of the building and fired five shots which mortally wounded **Supervisor Harvey Milk.** White had left his post saying he could not support his wife and son on a supervisor's salary. When White later tried to get back the position, Moscone denied his request. The two murders took place less than an hour before the mayor was to name White's successor. Many speculated that the murders were prompted by White's anti-liberal, anti-gay sentiments. A former police officer and fireman, described by those who knew him as clean-cut and all-American, White reportedly viewed both Moscone and Milk (the city's first acknowledged homosexual supervisor) as nonconformists who were lenient toward criminals. During his trial, defense lawyers argued in what was dubbed the "Twinkie defense" that White suffered from "diminished capacity"—partly caused by gorging himself on junk foods during periods of severe depression. They claimed the former supervisor was thus incapable of malice, premeditation, and deliberation (requirements for a first-degree murder conviction) and could only be charged with killing in the heat of passion. On May 21, 1979, the jury returned with a verdict of voluntary manslaughter rather than murder; White, who once faced the possibility of the death penalty, was sentenced to a prison term of only seven years and eight months. The announcement of the verdict set off an explosion of violence that left scores of people injured and an estimated $1 million in damage as a crowd of about 5,000 marched from San Francisco's gay community, rioting, smashing windows at City Hall, and setting fire to police cars. For years after, there were numerous threats on Dan White's life. Learning that he would be eligible for parole from Soledad prison on January 6, 1984 (with time off for good behavior after serving two-thirds of his sentence), concerned state and city leaders urged that White be prosecuted on charges of violating a 1968 federal civil rights statute. That law states that a person who fatally injures a candidate for public office could receive a life sentence. On November 21, 1983, the Justice Department announced that although "there is little doubt that the criminal justice system in California failed to hold Dan White adequately responsible for his actions," they would not prosecute him under the federal law because Moscone and Milk were not

actively campaigning for office at the time of the shootings (though both had filed declarations of intent to run for reelection) and there was no evidence that White had committed the murders to prevent them from seeking reelection. Amid extreme security precautions and secrecy as to his exact location, White was paroled as planned January 6 in Los Angeles County—a decision which evoked righteous indignation from many quarters. It was reported that White's request to return to San Francisco had been denied due to safety reasons. On the day of his release, San Francisco's gay community protested in angry but nonviolent demonstrations. Prompted partly by this controversial case, the California state legislature eliminated the diminished capacity defense in criminal actions in September 1981.

15. The funneling of **taxpayers' money and citizen contributions to guerrilla and terrorist groups** has been reported by several sources. According to a British intelligence report, Americans have given more money to the terrorist Provisional wing of the Irish Republican Army (IRA) than citizens of any other nation, most of it through the New York-based Northern Aid Committee (Noraid) which solicits contributions from Irish-Americans. Purportedly the money aids families of imprisoned Provisionals, but government officials have charged that most of it goes to finance IRA terrorist activities. The Palestinian Liberation Army (PLO) and Southwest African People's Organization (SWAPO), two communist-oriented terrorist groups that have been granted "permanent observer" status at the U.N., have allegedly been using U.N. refugee camps to recruit and train guerrillas. A 1982 Heritage Foundation report claimed that American taxpayers shouldered 25% of the $116 million spent or budgeted since 1975 to support U.N.-sanctioned terrorist groups. The World Council of Churches has been criticized for giving large amounts of money in support of Marxist and Soviet-backed guerrillas in South Africa. See Bernard Weinraub, "Split Among Irish-Americans Said to Cut Funds to I.R.A.," *New York Times,* 7 September 1979; "Passing the Hat for the Provos," *Time,* 26 November 1979, p. 92; David Reed, "Terror in Northern Ireland: The American Connection," *Reader's Digest,* April 1983, pp. 163–70; Thomas G. Gulick, *How the U.N. Aids Marxist Guerrilla Groups,* Heritage Foundation Backgrounder, no. 177 (Washington, D.C.: Heritage Foundation, 1982); "Church Group's Aid to Rhodesian Rebels Widely Assailed," *Washington Post,* 18 August 1978, p. A21; Joseph A. Harriss, "Which Master Is the World Council of Churches Serving . . . Karl Marx or Jesus Christ?" *Reader's Digest,* August

1982, pp. 130–34; "CBS Hits the Councils of Churches," *AIM Report*, February-B 1983; Joshua Muravchik, "Pliant Protestants," *New Republic*, 13 June 1983; and Raël Jean Isaac, "Do You Know Where Your Church Offerings Go?" *Reader's Digest*, January 1983, pp. 120–25.

16. Matthew 5:35; Isaiah 66:1; Acts 7:49.
17. Romans 8:6, 7.
18. Read Ezekiel 33. See also 8-cassette album *The Conversion of the Holy Spirit in the New Jerusalem: Sermons by Jesus Christ Delivered through His Messenger Elizabeth Clare Prophet* (A7758).
19. **Khmer Rouge** ("Red Cambodians"): Marxist insurgents who overturned the Western-backed Lon Nol government in April 1975 after nearly five years of fighting. Although there is no way of accurately counting, it is estimated that as many as three to four million Cambodians out of a population of some seven million were murdered or died from disease, malnutrition, or forced labor during the four-year Khmer Rouge regime. Within hours of their take-over, the new leaders, calling themselves *Angka Loeu*, or "Organization on High," began to implement a preplanned program of social change. Every man, woman, and child in Phnom Penh, Cambodia's capital, was ordered at gunpoint to immediately leave the city (doctors were even stopped mid-operation) and head for the countryside. Survivors of the march later reported that those who could not keep pace were clubbed or shot. As the days passed, the young children and elderly, the sick, wounded, and pregnant were left on jungle trails to die. Soldiers of the former regime as well as professionals of any kind were slaughtered, often in barbaric ways, in an effort to "purify" the new society. All vestiges of modern society—from TV sets to radios, books, and money in the banks—were destroyed, and the country was virtually cut off from the outside world except for contact with the Chinese, who provided some aid in the form of technical advisors and supplies. *Angka Loeu* was intent on eradicating traditional concepts and patterns of family life as well. Parents were stripped of their right to discipline children, and children were encouraged to report on elders. Love was forbidden; even simple flirtation was punishable by execution. The Cambodian population, relocated in rural communes supervised by armed guards, was forced to work long hours planting rice and building irrigation systems. In the wake of these brutal social and political upheavals, Democratic Kampuchea, as Cambodia was renamed in 1976, was ravaged by starvation and disease. It had become what one refugee called "a country of walking dead." "Within a few days *Angka Loeu* had turned Cambodian

society upside down," explain authors John Barron and Anthony Paul in *Murder of a Gentle Land* (New York: Reader's Digest Press, 1977). "The 'Organization on High' had advanced faster and further than any other revolutionaries of modern times toward the complete obliteration of an entire society." Among the handful of revolutionaries behind *Angka Loeu* were: Khieu Samphan, Hou Yuon, Hu Nim, Son Sen, Ieng Sary, Ieng Thirith, Koy Thuon, and Saloth Sar (Pol Pot), who emerged as prime minister and leading figure in the government. Border clashes between Vietnam and the Kampuchean government during 1977 turned into a full-scale war, and by January 1979 Phnom Penh fell to Vietnamese forces and Kampuchean rebels (see chapter XI, n. 6, p. 365). The Khmer Rouge guerrilla army, reportedly still under Pol Pot's command, has continued to mount strong resistance against the Hanoi-backed government. **Soviet Concentration Camps:** A CIA report released in November 1982 estimated that there were at least four million prisoners in forced-labor camps in the Soviet Union, 10,000 of whom were political inmates. *The First Guidebook to Prisons and Concentration Camps of the Soviet Union* (Seewis, Switzerland: Stephanus Edition, 1980) by dissident Avraham Shifrin, who spent 10 years in Soviet camps, describes over 2,000 penal institutions dotted throughout the USSR (a partial list including only those for which the author had an exact address): 1,976 camps (among them 119 women's and children's camps where, for instance, children are forcibly separated from the "bad influence" of religious parents); 273 prisons, where political prisoners are mixed with ordinary criminals; and 85 psychiatric prisons. Some of the crimes for imprisonment are reading banned philosophical and political books, applying for exit visas to emigrate to the free world, participating in anti-Soviet conversations, and posting notices. In psychiatric prisons, where dissidents and those held for practicing their religion are imprisoned alongside the insane, treatments can range from electric shocks to neuroleptic drugs to being bound in a wet straitjacket which, as it dries, compresses the body with tremendous force. An eyewitness at a children's camp reported to Shifrin that "clubcarrying supervisors (officially called 'educators') roaming about the camp grounds subject the young prisoners (aged 10 to 18) to merciless beatings. . . . Children are assigned backbreaking duties, despite prevalence of hunger in the camp. Those who fall ill and request transfer to a hospital are beaten." At the Novosibirsk women's camp, says Shifrin, "1500 prisoners, including nursing mothers, are given physically exhausting duties in a plant in which reinforced concrete plates are manufactured." Testifying on the hazardous working conditions which prisoners are subjected to, former Gulag inmate Mikhail Makarenko told the U.S. Senate in 1982 that "people are working in a temperature 50 degrees below zero without any safety [precautions] on higher elevations, on walls and so on." In some camps, says Shifrin, prisoners are virtually assured disability or death, working at high-risk jobs in uranium mines or military nuclear plants. Dmitry Mikheyev, a Ph.D. in theoretical physics who served six years in hard-labor camps for political opponents, claims that "contrary to widespread opinion, labor in political camps at the present time has only an 'educative' function. Its goal is to help form the Internal Dynamic Stereotype, not to extract profit from free prison labor." Behavioral training methods for political prisoners, such as highly mechanical jobs reduced to a few movements or carried out to a set of commands, "have been borrowed from the army, which has accumulated rich experience in the production of living semi-automatons under Soviet rule," says Mikheyev. See "A New Report: Soviets' Record on Slave Labor," *U.S. News & World Report,* 22 November 1982, p. 31; and Dmitry Mikheyev, "The Great Soviet Art of Intimidation," *National Review,* 5 February 1982, pp. 101–5. **Idi Amin:** Ugandan army commander who ousted President Milton Obote in 1971, abolishing parliament and declaring himself president for life. As many as 300,000 Ugandans are said to have died during his eight-year reign, another 250,000 fled to Kenya, and many others lived in exile in Britain. "Big Daddy," as he liked to call himself, a 270-pound former military boxing champion, drew worldwide attention by his flamboyant eccentricity in foreign policy, outspoken belligerence toward other nations and their leaders (particularly Israel and neighboring Tanzania), and his ruthless purges. These included the periodic liquidation of prominent Ugandans and several thousand Lango and Acholi tribesmen who had supported Obote. "On any given day it was not unusual for 100 to 150 Ugandans to be killed," *Reader's Digest* reported in January 1980. "Entire villages were wiped out. Bodies floated down the Nile by the hundreds." Described as a man who could turn in a moment from gentle and charming to demonic, Amin's bizarre conduct led to persistent rumors about his mental stability. In a blatant show of racialism, Amin expelled the 50,000 Asians living in Uganda in 1972, only to strip the country of the trained personnel vital to its economy. When Britain cut off all aid following renewed reports of torture and brutality, Amin confiscated British businesses in Uganda without compensation—later claiming that relations with Britain went awry because he would not marry an Englishwoman. In 1977, Anglican archbishop of Uganda Janani Luwum and two of Amin's cabinet ministers were killed, beginning the persecution and slaughter of many Christians and non-Muslims (Amin was a convert to Islam). Amin's downfall came when he invaded Tanzania in October 1978 in an attempt to draw attention away from internal problems. In April 1979 Tanzanian troops with Ugandan exiles and rebels took the capital of Kampala, welcomed by its residents. Amin reportedly fled to Libya, leaving the nation once dubbed the "pearl of Africa" with bitter tribal divisions, a bankrupt economy, and a population demoralized by his reign of terror. As of this writing he is believed to be living in Saudi Arabia. **The Hillside Strangler** murders involved the strangulation of 10 young women and girls whose nude bodies were discovered on hillsides in California's Los Angeles-Glendale area between October 1977 and February 1978. The case was finally broken a year later when Kenneth A. Bianchi, a 28-year-old security guard arrested in Bellingham, Washington, for the strangulation murder of two university students, made a surprise confession in court. In a deal with prosecutors, Bianchi admitted to five of the Hillside Strangler slayings and agreed to testify against his cousin Angelo Buono, Jr., 44, a Glendale auto upholsterer whom he implicated as his partner in the crimes. In return, prosecutors agreed not to seek the death penalty against Bianchi. During 80 days of testimony at Buono's trial, Bianchi changed his story, denied his involvement in the murders, pleaded a loss of memory, then reaffirmed his confession. A frustrated Los Angeles district attorney's office tried to drop the case against Buono in 1981, saying it couldn't be successfully prosecuted. The judge, however, refused to dismiss the case. In what became the longest criminal trial in U.S. history, lasting two years and two days, the jury was presented with 55,000 pages of testimony and 2,000 exhibits. In November 1983, Buono was convicted of nine of the murders and received nine concurrent life terms without possibility of parole, though he was eligible for the death penalty. The jurors did not publicly state why they spared Buono from the gas chamber, but the judge and prosecutors in the case speculated that jurors were reluctant to give Buono the death penalty when Bianchi, equally culpable, did not receive it. For the five Los Angeles stranglings and the two Washington murders to which Bianchi pleaded guilty, he was sentenced to seven concurrent life terms with the possibility of parole. **The Skid Row Stabber** stabbed to death 10 men in the Skid Row area of downtown Los Angeles between October 1978 and January 1979. All but one of the victims were described as transients. Twenty-nine-year-old Bobby Joe Maxwell was arrested and charged with the murders in April 1979 and brought to trial November 1983. Most of the delay came as defense attorneys fought for Maxwell's right to sell his life story to pay legal fees—a right which the California State Supreme Court granted to Maxwell and all criminal defendants in 1982. At this writing, the case is still being heard.

20. See **Mary's Scriptural Rosary for the New Age,** in *My Soul Doth Magnify the Lord! New Age Rosary and New Age Teachings of Mother Mary;* **The Fourteenth Rosary: The Mystery of Surrender,** booklet and 2-cassette album (V7538); and **A Child's Rosary to Mother Mary,** for the little Child within you—15-minute scriptural rosaries for children and adults for meditation on the words and works of the apostles and for the adoration of God the Father, the Son, and the Holy Spirit, and God the Mother, on 3-cassette albums: Album 1 (A7864): John, James, Jude; Album 2 (A7905): Paul to the Hebrews; Album 3 (A7934): Paul to the Galatians; Album 4 (A8045): Paul to the Corinthians.

V THE MYSTERY OF BEING

1. Luke 4:5–8.
2. John 8:37–47.
3. Genesis 4:3–5.
4. Genesis 11:5. See Archeia Charity, "The Fire of Love Descending to Implement the Judgment," in *El Morya on Discipleship East and West: The Path of the Darjeeling Master and His Chelas,* Pearls of Wisdom, vol. 18 (1975), pp. 207–8, and in *Vials of the Seven Last Plagues: Prophecies for the 1980s by the Seven Archangels,* pp. 39–40.
5. Psalms 1:2.
6. Matthew 6:33.
7. John 10:7, 9; Revelation 3:8.
8. Psalms 139:9.
9. Romans 8:21, 22.
10. Luke 4:1; John 10:30; 17:11, 21, 22.
11. **The Great White Brotherhood** is a spiritual order of Western "saints" and Eastern "masters" who have transcended the cycles of karma and rebirth and ascended (accelerated) into that higher reality which is the eternal abode of the soul. The 'ascended' masters of the Great White Brotherhood, united for the highest purposes of the brotherhood of man under the Fatherhood of God, have risen from every culture and religion to inspire creative achievement in education, the arts and sciences, government and the economy. The word "white"

refers not to race but to the aura (halo) of white light surrounding their forms. The Brotherhood also includes in its ranks certain unascended chelas of the ascended masters. See Revelation 3:4, 5; 6:9–11; 7:9, 13, 14; 19:14; Elizabeth Clare Prophet, *The Great White Brotherhood in the Culture, History, and Religion of America.*

12. Matthew 6:24; Luke 16:13.
13. Matthew 7:15.
14. Joshua 24:15.

VI THE MYSTERY OF SELFHOOD

1. Psalms 51:10–13.
2. Jeremiah 31:33; Hebrews 10:16.
3. Philippians 2:5.
4. I Corinthians 15:47.
5. In the United States Supreme Court's first case on **prayer in public schools,** *Engel* v. *Vitale* (1962), the Court outlawed the recitation of a nondenominational prayer, even voluntarily, that had been composed by the New York State Board of Regents in consultation with a wide range of religious leaders. It read: "Almighty God, we acknowledge our dependence upon Thee, and we beg Thy blessings upon us, our parents, our teachers and our country." The case was brought by the parents of 10 students who said the prayer was contrary to the religious practices and beliefs of themselves and their children. The Court held, 6–1, that even though participation was not compulsory, recitation of the prayer was opposed to the principle of separation of church and state and violated the First Amendment's establishment clause ("Congress shall make no law respecting an establishment of religion"), which was made applicable to the states through the Fourteenth Amendment in a series of Supreme Court decisions this century. The Court explained that "the constitutional prohibition against laws respecting an establishment of religion must at least mean that in this country it is no part of the business of government to compose official prayers for any group of the American people to recite as a part of a religious program carried on by government." Justice William O. Douglas in his concurring opinion stated that "no matter how briefly the prayer is said" the teacher who leads it "is a public official on the public payroll, performing a religious exercise in a governmental institution." The only justice to dissent, Justice Potter Stewart, disagreed: "I do not believe that this court, or the Congress, or the President has by these actions and practices established an 'official reli-

gion' in violation of the Constitution. And I do not believe the state of New York has done so in this case. . . . To deny the wish of these school children to join in reciting this prayer is to deny them the opportunity of sharing in the spiritual heritage of our nation." The following year, the Supreme Court heard two cases combined for decision—*Abington School District* v. *Schempp*, dealing with a state law that required the reading of 10 Bible verses at the opening of each day, and *Murray* v. *Curlett* (brought by avowed atheist Madalyn Murray O'Hair), challenging a school board rule that required "reading, without comment, a chapter in the Holy Bible and/or use of the Lord's prayer" each day. In each instance, the students could be excused from the exercise. The Supreme Court ruled, 8–1, that both cases violated "the command of the First Amendment that the government maintain strict neutrality, neither aiding nor opposing religion." In the decades following these landmark decisions, the Supreme Court has been faced with a variety of cases testing the constitutionality of religious activities in public schools. One such case was *DeSpain* v. *DeKalb County School District* (1968) in which the parents of one pupil filed suit to stop the recitation of this verse by kindergarten children prior to their morning snacks, claiming it was a prayer: "We thank you for the flowers so sweet;/We thank you for the food we eat;/We thank you for the birds that sing;/We thank you for everything." The teacher testified that she used the poem to promote good citizenship and social manners; the federal district court, agreeing that the verse was not a prayer, dismissed the complaint. When the case was appealed, however, the decision was reversed and the school was not allowed to use the prayer. The Supreme Court let this decision stand by declining to review the case. The Justices also refused to review a lower court decision in *State Board of Education* v. *Board of Education of Netcong, New Jersey* (1971) denying a daily "period for the free exercise of religion." In this case, the New Jersey Supreme Court struck down a school board policy allowing students to meet in the gymnasium prior to the start of school to hear a volunteer read the "remarks" of the chaplain of the Senate or House of Representatives from the *Congressional Record*. In *Johnson* v. *Huntington Beach Union High School District* (1977), the trial court and California Court of Appeal refused to permit students to form a Bible Study group to meet during the school day. The court ruled that recognition of the club would advance religion by providing financial aid to a religious group (in the form of free use of facilities) and said that the students could use other public forums for religious activity. The Supreme

Court also chose not to review that case. In *Stone* v. *Graham* (1980), the Supreme Court ruled, 5–4, that a 1978 Kentucky state law requiring the posting of a copy of the Ten Commandments in every classroom, to be paid for with voluntary contributions and not tax money, violated the First Amendment. The Court stated that the purpose for posting the commandments was "plainly religious" and might "induce the school children to read, meditate upon, perhaps to venerate and obey the Ten Commandments." Even the singing of Christmas carols in public schools became a matter of legal dispute. In November 1980, the Supreme Court declined to review a decision by the lower court in *Florey* v. *Sioux Falls School District* that did allow the celebration of religious holidays with hymns and religious plays. Parents challenging the school board's policy and guidelines for the celebrations said the programs were unconstitutional because they established and advanced religion. However, the district and appellate courts both held that the art, literature, and music connected with holidays such as Christmas had a cultural significance and that they advanced "a secular program of education and not of religion." Many religious leaders—from Buddhist and American Indian to Jew and Christian—have, in fact, supported the Supreme Court's decision banning prayer in public schools. During hearings on the subject by the House Judiciary Committee in 1964, many mainline religious organizations came out in support of the decision—including the National Council of Churches, the United Presbyterian Church, the American Baptist Convention, the Methodist Church, the Episcopal Church, the Synagogue Council of America, and the Union of American Hebrew Congregations. Even so, public fervor over the issue has not subsided and opinion polls have shown that a majority of the public clearly favors prayer in schools. In addition to legislative proposals to deny Supreme Court jurisdiction in the matter and thus give state supreme courts the final say, hundreds of constitutional amendments have been proposed to overturn the Supreme Court decision, though none have yet been successful. President Reagan became the first president to make a proposal to put prayer back in public schools with the following recommended constitutional amendment, sent to Congress May 17, 1982, but not yet voted on as of this writing: "Nothing in this Constitution shall be construed to prohibit individual or group prayer in public schools or other public institutions. No person shall be required by the United States or by any State to participate in prayer." On January 25, 1983, in the State of the Union address, President Reagan said, "Each day, your

[Congress's] members observe a 200-year-old tradition meant to signify America is one nation under God. I must ask: If you can begin your day with a member of the clergy standing right here to lead you in prayer, then why can't freedom to acknowledge God be enjoyed again by children in every schoolroom across this land? America was founded by people who believed that God was their rock of safety. He is ours. I recognize we must be cautious in claiming that God is on our side. But I think it's all right to keep asking if we are on his side." See Thomas R. Ascik, *Congress and the Supreme Court: Court Jurisdiction and School Prayer,* Heritage Foundation Backgrounder, no. 123 (Washington, D.C.: Heritage Foundation, 1980); and David M. Ackerman, *Religious Activities in the Public Schools and the First Amendment: Judicial Decisions and the Congressional Response,* Congressional Research Service, Report No. 82-188A 769/248 (Washington, D.C.: The Library of Congress, 1982).

6. Hosea 8:7.
7. Matthew 19:26; Mark 10:27; 14:36; Luke 1:37; 18:27.
8. The **black magician Adolf Hitler:** A black magician is one who misuses God's light to manipulate individuals against their free will. Some who have studied the Führer's past and the roots of his Third Reich claim that key figures in the Nazi Party actually practiced black magic. Ex-Nazi leader Hermann Rauschning, who defected to the Allies in 1940, said of Hitler, "One cannot help thinking of him as a medium. . . . Hitler was possessed by forces outside himself—almost demoniacal forces of which the individual named Hitler was only the temporary vehicle." In addition, others have theorized that the talismanic power behind the Spear of Longinus (the sacred spear which pierced the side of Jesus) was the inspiration of Hitler's life and the key to his rise to power. Hitler first saw the relic traditionally thought to be the famed Spear when visiting the Hapsburg Treasure House as a young man. He tells of hearing from the tour guide "the words which were to change my whole life: 'There is a legend associated with this Spear that whoever claims it, and solves its secrets, holds the destiny of the world in his hands for good or evil.' . . . I knew with immediacy that this was an important moment in my life." Nearly thirty years later, in 1938, Hitler invaded and annexed Austria, took possession of the relic, and moved it from the Treasure House in Vienna to Nuremburg. The theory that Hitler himself or those who used the Führer as a tool were involved in black magic may explain, in part, why millions of the German people became caught up in the Nazi cause. Aside from the above theories, it is the thesis of the messenger that entities of darkness functioning at astral

planes of existence—a false hierarchy organizing malevolent forces of anti-Light against the purposes of the Great White Brotherhood—worked through Hitler and those at the international level who cooperated with him in the crimes committed in World War II against not only the Jews and Slavic peoples, but also the Germanic peoples. See Louis Pauwels and Jacques Bergier, *The Morning of the Magicians,* trans. Rollo Myers (New York: Stein and Day, 1964; Scarborough House, 1977); Trevor Ravenscroft, *The Spear of Destiny: The Occult Power behind the Spear Which Pierced the Side of Christ* (New York: G. P. Putnam's Sons, 1973); and Jean-Michel Angebert, *The Occult and the Third Reich: The Mystical Origins of Nazism and the Search for the Holy Grail,* trans. Lewis A. M. Sumberg (New York: Macmillan Publishing Co., 1974; McGraw-Hill Paperbacks, 1975).

9. Mark 14:58; II Corinthians 5:1; Hebrews 9:11.
10. John 8:44.
11. I John 4:18.
12. Philippians 4:7.
13. Ecclesiastes 1:2; 11:8.
14. John 5:39.
15. Luke 17:21.
16. Matthew 12:31.
17. I Corinthians 12:3, 10.
18. I Corinthians 10:4.

VII THE MYSTERY OF THE INCARNATE WORD

1. Psalms 46:6.
2. Isaiah 55:11.
3. Ibid.
4. Ibid.
5. John 5:22.
6. Isaiah 55:11.
7. I Peter 3:4.
8. Isaiah 55:12, 13.
9. Isaiah 9:6.
10. I Corinthians 3:16; 6:19; II Corinthians 6:16.
11. Matthew 5:18.
12. John 6:28, 29.
13. John 14:2, 3.
14. John 1:12; Romans 8:14–17.
15. Jeremiah 23:1.
16. Jeremiah 23:4.
17. Hebrews 12:2; John 1:9.
18. Psalms 2:7.

19. Isaiah 65:9.
20. The term **'Son of man'** (with a capital *S*), which Jesus used in reference to his own mission, defines the soul who has descended from the I AM Presence as the Son of God. Integrated with the Christ Self, this soul is now archetypically the presence of the Universal Soul of humanity. As in the life of Jesus, the Christ(Light) of the one becomes the Christ(Light) for all. And the Son of man is perpetually one with and representing the Holy Christ Self of all souls evolving on earth. The term **'son of man'** (with a lowercase *s*) is applied to all souls who embody with the mission of bearing the Light, balancing their karma, fulfilling their divine plan, and returning to God in the ritual of the ascension. The term 'son of man' indicates that the potential exists for Divine Sonship through the path of personal Christhood—putting on day by day the garment of one's LORD, 'eating his flesh and drinking his blood'. See chapters XIX and XX, pp. 280–302, also in *Heart: For the Coming Revolution in Higher Consciousness* 3 (Autumn 1983): 70–71, 80–85.
21. Psalms 2:6.
22. Psalms 19:14.
23. I John 3:4.
24. Romans 3:23.
25. I Samuel 16:13.

VIII THE MYSTERY OF THE TRANSLATION

1. **U.S. recognition of Red China:** On December 15, 1978, President Carter announced simultaneously with officials in Peking that after 30 years of nonrecognition, diplomatic relations between the People's Republic of China (PRC) and the U.S. would be formally established as of January 1, 1979. The U.S. also agreed to sever diplomatic relations with the Republic of China (Taiwan), which it had previously recognized as the sole legal government of China, and to terminate the 1954 Mutual Defense Treaty with Taiwan at the end of 1979. In his nationally televised speech, Carter said that by recognizing the PRC as the single government of China, "we are recognizing simple reality." He added that the U.S. would continue to maintain "cultural, commercial, and other unofficial relations with the people of Taiwan." The first major step in publicly acknowledging the legitimacy of the Communist regime had come in 1972 with the signing of the Shanghai Communiqué by the U.S. and Peking at the conclusion of President Nixon's trip to China. In that communiqué the U.S. pledged to reduce its forces and

military installations on Taiwan as "tension in the area diminishes." But even though efforts toward normalization of relations had been underway for some time, Carter's announcement still came as a surprise to many. It drew angry responses from members of Congress who complained that the president had not informed them of his actions—despite the fact that Congress had earlier adopted a resolution specifically instructing the president to consult them before abrogating the Taiwan defense treaty. Senator Barry Goldwater and 25 other legislators actually contested the constitutionality of the president's unilateral move in a legal suit, but their complaint was dismissed by the Supreme Court on December 13, 1979. In addition, many were concerned that Carter had not properly provided for the security of Taiwan. China, in fact, never pledged in the 1978 joint communiqué to refrain from using force against Taiwan. The PRC's long-standing position that the "liberation" of Taiwan by peaceful or nonpeaceful means did not involve the U.S. was reiterated by the Chinese in their normalization statement: "As for the way of bringing Taiwan back to the embrace of the motherland and reunifying the country, it is entirely China's internal affair." The Nationalist government on Taiwan remained firm in its response to the agreement, declaring that "the United States, by extending diplomatic recognition to the Chinese Communist regime, which owes its very existence to terror and suppression, is not in conformity with its professed position of safeguarding human rights and strengthening the capability of democratic nations to resist the totalitarian dictatorship. The move is tantamount to denying the hundreds of millions of enslaved peoples on the Chinese mainland of their hope for an early restoration of freedom. Viewed from whatever aspect, the move by the United States constitutes a great setback to human freedom and democratic institutions. . . . Under whatever circumstances, the Republic of China shall neither negotiate with the Communist Chinese regime, nor compromise with Communism, and it shall never give up its sacred task of recovering the mainland and delivering the compatriots there." To offset what was considered by some to be a betrayal of Taiwan in the 1978 communiqué, Congress passed the Taiwan Relations Act, signed into law on April 10, 1979. It said that "it is the policy of the United States to consider any effort to determine the future of Taiwan by other than peaceful means, including boycotts or embargoes, a threat to the peace and security of the Western Pacific area and of grave concern to the United States." In addition, it promised to provide the defensive arms necessary for Taiwan to "maintain a sufficient self-defense capability" and stated that the U.S. would "maintain the capacity" to, in effect, resist any use of force by the PRC to gain control of Taiwan. After 1978, the PRC began to issue a series of proposals aimed at peaceful "reunification of the motherland." The Nine-Point Proposal of September 30, 1981, for instance, offered Taiwan a "high degree of autonomy as a special administrative region" that would retain its armed forces and further promised that "the central government will not interfere with local affairs on Taiwan"—an offer flatly rejected by the Republic of China. In a significant development intended to ease U.S.-Peking disagreements over the arming of Taiwan, the U.S. signed a joint communiqué with Peking on August 17, 1982, pledging to gradually reduce arms sales to Taiwan "leading over a period of time to a final resolution." The U.S. also stated that arms sales would not exceed, qualitatively or quantitatively, the level supplied in recent years since normalization of relations. Taiwan charged that the communiqué violated both the spirit and the letter of the Taiwan Relations Act—and according to some political observers, this could indeed be the case. As the military threat posed by modernization and improvement of the PRC's defense capabilities increases, the quantity and quality of arms necessary to maintain Taiwan's self-defense (a level which the U.S. promised to provide in the 1979 Taiwan Relations Act) will probably exceed the limits on arms sales set by a literal reading of the 1982 communiqué. (See Jeffrey B. Gayner, *The China Decision and the Future of Taiwan,* Heritage Foundation Backgrounder, no. 70 [Washington, D.C.: Heritage Foundation, 1978]; John Tierney, Jr., ed., *About Face: The China Decision and Its Consequences* [New Rochelle, N.Y.: Arlington House, 1979]; Robert G. Sutter, *China-U.S. Relations,* Congressional Research Service, Issue Brief No. IB76053 [Washington, D.C.: The Library of Congress, 1982]; Luella S. Christopher, *The August 17, 1982 U.S.-China Communique on Taiwan: A Summary of Its Terms and Possible Implications,* Congressional Research Service, F/A IP 21 [Washington, D.C.: The Library of Congress, 1982]; Martin L. Lasater, *Taiwan: Facing Mounting Threats* [Washington, D.C.: Heritage Foundation, 1984].) The course of events that led to the fall of Nationalist China in 1949, the take-over by the Chinese Communist Party, and normalization of relations in later years has been carefully studied by scholars. One school of thought holds that there was nothing the U.S. could have done to prevent the downfall of Chiang Kai-shek. Others take the view that the establishment of diplomatic relations with the PRC in 1979 was the logical extension of a "hidden" policy undertaken by some members of the American diplomatic corps in the pre-World War II period and possibly earlier. They argue that Foreign Service officers and individuals in prominent positions in the Department of State actively worked to undermine Chiang Kai-shek and to promote the Chinese Communist Party—some working as Communist agents to carry out Moscow's plans and others, such as members of the influential policy-making group called the Institute of Pacific Relations, representing the interests of the international financial coterie. Thus the question, according to these analysts, was never whether the U.S. should recognize the government of Communist China but when. For further reading on this subject, see Anthony Kubek, *How the Far East Was Lost: American Policy and the Creation of Communist China, 1941–1949* (1963; reprint ed., New York: Twin Circle Publishing Co., 1972); and Carroll Quigley, *Tragedy and Hope: A History of the World in Our Time* (New York: Macmillan Co., 1966), pp. 818–19, 904–9, 945–56, 1000–1001.

2. Ezekiel 38:2; Revelation 20:8.
3. Revelation 21:16.
4. Revelation 19:11–16.
5. Matthew 24:35.
6. Revelation 3:12.
7. Revelation 6:15.
8. Revelation 6:16, 17.
9. Revelation 6:9–11.
10. Revelation 2:11; 20:6, 14; 21:8.
11. Matthew 3:11; John 1:33.
12. Revelation 1:18; 20:14; Isaiah 25:8; I Corinthians 15:54.
13. Revelation 11:15.

IX THE MYSTERY OF EVIL

1. The asteroid belt between Mars and Jupiter is what remains today of the planet **Maldek,** destroyed when its lifewaves waged a war ending in nuclear annihilation. A group of asteroids closer to the sun is the record and remains of the destroyed planet **Hedron,** overtaken by the pleasure cult of its lifewaves who, when reincarnated on earth, became known for their cult of hedonism. The existence of a planet between Mars and Jupiter was predicted by Johann Titius and restated in 1772 by German astronomer Johann Bode based on the numerical progression of the distances of the then-known planets from the sun. Following the discovery in 1781 of Uranus, whose location conformed to Bode's law, astronomers began to search for the

missing planet, finding instead the asteroid belt. About 95% of the thousands of asteroids, or minor planets as they are called, that have since been discovered in our solar system are part of this main asteroid belt between Mars and Jupiter. Astronomers have also discovered a group of asteroids whose highly elliptical orbits take them at times among the inner planets (Mercury, Venus, Earth, Mars) that are nearer to the sun. There is still much speculation among scientists over the origin of these minor planets; the two main hypotheses are that asteroids are either fragments of a planet that exploded or was destroyed, or they are particles that never condensed to form a planet.

2. Matthew 13:24–30, 36–43.
3. **Mao Tse-tung** (Mao Zedong): 1893–1976, one of the 12 founders of the Chinese Communist Party in 1921 and leader of Chinese Communists from 1935 to his death. So great was his influence that even after his death, Mao remained a key figure in Chinese politics. Summarizing Mao's early years as chief of state of the Communist People's Republic of China, Dr. Richard L. Walker notes in *The Human Cost of Communism in China:* "Millions were executed in the immediate post-power seizure period in Communist China. Many of the executions took place after mass public trials, in which the assembled crowds, whipped up to a frenzy by planted agitators, called invariably for the death penalty and for no mercy for the accused. During this early period, Mao and his colleagues made no effort to conceal the violent course being followed. On the contrary, the most gruesome and detailed accounts were printed in the Communist press and broadcast over the official radio for the purpose of amplifying the condition of mass terror the trials were clearly intended to induce." As Mao himself had foretold in 1927 in one of his earliest works, "to put it bluntly, it is necessary to create terror for a while in every rural area." There is a broad range of estimates as to the exact number of Chinese who have died at the hand of the Communists; Dr. Walker estimates that the figure was probably close to 50 million. Some of the most brutal campaigns waged by the Communists under Chairman Mao were: the Agrarian Reform (1949–52) resulting in the execution of several million landlords; invasion and take-over of Tibet (1950), promising Tibetan autonomy but eventually establishing a Chinese military dictatorship that killed hundreds of thousands of Tibetans, confiscated or destroyed monasteries and religious scriptures, stripped the people of their private property, and reorganized the country into peasant associations; campaign against counterrevolutionaries (1951–52, 1955), leaving one and a half

million dead in the first 12 months; purges in business, finance, and industrial circles leading to many executions and suicides (1951–53); a vehement liquidation campaign to silence rightist critics following Mao's "Hundred Flowers" speech inviting intellectuals and others to voice their criticism (1957–58); the Great Leap Forward (1958–60), a disastrous attempt to rapidly increase economic development through the formation of large rural communes, in some cases separating families and forcing peasants to adopt a militarized lifestyle; the Great Proletarian Cultural Revolution (1966–69), used by Mao to strike back at pragmatic leaders who had risen to power after his economic failures and to secure a group of successors devoted to his revolutionary ideals—included uncontrolled and violent attacks by radical youth organizations, called the Red Guards, against those who were "taking the capitalist road," purges of intellectuals who were forced to work in labor camps or were executed, and relocation to the countryside of an estimated 25 million youth, many of whom were assigned to work the land for life; the tearing down of traditional Chinese culture, customs, and religious practices with systematic destruction of libraries, shrines, and art works. **Hua Kuo-feng** (Hua Guofeng): born 1920, succeeded Mao after his death in 1976 as Communist Party chairman. According to the research of leading Hong Kong journalist Ting Wang, Hua was notorious for his brutality and ruthlessness during his early political career. As the man in charge of land reform in Chiaotung and Yangchu counties, he reportedly arrested, beat, tortured, and killed people at random, suppressing landlords and peasants who did not support the Communists—often under the guise of a program to root out "local bandits and bullies." During the anti-rightist campaigns starting in 1957, Hua reportedly supervised the purging of dissidents in the province of Hunan. He fanatically supported Mao's programs and went out of his way to show that Mao's theories could be implemented successfully, no doubt facilitating Hua's rapid rise to power. After 1971, Hua worked in Peking directly under Premier Chou En-lai in agriculture and forestry and perhaps as a troubleshooter. He was elected to the Politburo in 1973 and was appointed minister of public security and sixth-ranking vice-premier in 1975. Following Chou's death in January 1976, Hua was named premier. In April he was also named first vice-chairman of the party and thus second in command under Mao, who is said to have remarked of Hua: "With you in charge, I am at ease." During the power struggle that followed Mao's death, Hua moved quickly to arrest the top radical leaders known as the "Gang of Four," who were blamed for the excesses of the Cultural Revolution. Hua then became the first man to fill all three positions of premier, chairman of the Central Committee of the Communist Party, and chairman of the Military Commission. After Teng Hsiao-p'ing's comeback (see below), Hua's power was reduced, though he continued to hold top positions. In 1980 Hua lost his position as premier, was succeeded by Teng Hsiao-p'ing as head of the Military Commission the following year, and in 1982 was ousted from the Politburo. **Teng Hsiao-p'ing** (Deng Xiaoping): born 1904, Communist leader noted for his pragmatic departure from Mao's radical ideology and for his effort to modernize China through economic reform and contact with the West. Teng rose through the Communist Party ranks to become China's vice-premier from 1952–66. In 1956, when he was elected to the powerful standing committee of the Politburo and was given the responsibility for party administration as Communist Party general secretary, Teng ranked among the four or five most powerful men in China. It is said that Teng, working alongside Chou En-lai, was the chief organizer of the ruthless purges that followed the "Hundred Flowers" speech. Twice during his political career, Teng was stripped of his posts—once from 1966–73 during the Cultural Revolution and again in 1976 for a little over a year—and was twice reinstated. In 1977, following the death of Mao, he regained his former positions and began to reestablish his strong power base. Though Teng officially holds no government office today, he is nevertheless the leading power in China. In October 1983, *Time* magazine reported that a new campaign to reevaluate and confirm Chinese Communist Party membership was underway and that "in everything but name. . . it will be a purge, an attempt by China's Deng Xiaoping, 79, to secure his own authority and that of his chosen successors. . . . No personality cult has developed, but it is clear that Deng is being placed on a pedestal almost as high as the one once reserved for Mao Tse-tung." See Richard L. Walker, *The Human Cost of Communism in China* (Washington, D.C.: U.S. Government Printing Office, 1971); Ting Wang, *Chairman Hua: Leader of the Chinese Communists* (Montreal: McGill-Queen's University Press, 1980); U.S., Congress, House, Representative Robert J. Lagomarsino citing "The Defacto Warden," an article by John P. Roche, *Congressional Record,* 96th Cong., 1st sess., 1979, pt. 3: 3803; and "New Purges," *Time,* 31 October 1983, p. 50.

4. **Chiang Kai-shek:** 1887–1975, soldier and statesman who ruled China from 1928–49 and headed the Chinese Nationalist government on Taiwan. Chiang Kai-shek was trained for a military

career and took part in revolutionary activities against the Manchus and President Yuan Shih-k'ai. In 1918 he joined Sun Yat-sen (leader of the Kuomintang, or revolutionary Nationalist Party) in his attempt to unify China and overthrow the warlords. He served as chief of staff of a Cantonese army and was later named as commandant of the Whampoa Military Academy. After Sun's death in 1925, Chiang Kai-shek, who had previously followed Sun's policy of cooperating with the Communists, became the central figure of the growing anti-Communist movement. In 1927, he broke with the Communists in a bloody coup that marked the beginning of the long civil war between the Kuomintang and the Communist Party. As commander in chief of the Nationalist army, he waged a campaign against the warlords from 1926–28 and in 1928 became head of the central government in Nanking and generalissimo of Chinese Nationalist forces. Chiang Kai-shek's reign was fraught with intermittent fighting with the Communists and full-scale war with the Japanese. After a Kuomintang-Communist alliance to fight Japanese aggression, hostilities between the two groups continued. A major Communist campaign against Chiang Kai-shek finally drove him off the mainland to Taiwan in 1949. There he established and headed the Nationalist government in exile, promising to retake the mainland. **Madame Chiang** (Soong Mayling): born 1897, belonged to the prominent, westernized Soong family. She was the sister of Soong Ch'ing-ling (wife of Sun Yat-sen) and T. V. Soong, famous industrialist and statesman. Mayling spent nine years in America as a young girl and was educated in the U.S., an honor graduate of Wellesley College. She married Chiang Kai-shek in 1927 after he first agreed to become a Christian like herself. Madame Chiang did social service work in her homeland, was commander of the airforce during the Second Sino-Japanese War, and became a member of the central executive committee of the Kuomintang in 1945. She was the first Chinese woman to be decorated by the Nationalist government of China, receiving the highest military and civil decorations. She did much to promote her husband's cause in the West and wrote articles on China published in U.S. journals. In 1943 she became the second woman and the first Chinese to address Congress. So great was her popularity with the American public that from 1943–67 she was listed among the 10 most admired women of the world. Madame Chiang joined her husband in Taiwan in 1950 and organized the Chinese Women's Anti-Aggression League. As of this writing, Madame Chiang is residing in New York. **Chiang Ching-kuo:** born 1910, the oldest son of Chiang

Kai-shek by his first wife and current leader of the Nationalist government on Taiwan. He held various administrative and military offices in the Kuomintang government while his father was in power on the mainland and he accompanied Chiang Kai-shek to Taiwan after the Communist take-over. On Taiwan, Chiang Ching-kuo became his father's personal aide and took command of the military intelligence and security agencies. In 1965 he was named minister of national defense in command of the army, served as vice-premier 1969–72, and was appointed prime minister by his father on June 1, 1972. After Chiang Kai-shek fell ill in October 1973, Chiang Ching-kuo acted as the effective ruler. He became chairman of the Kuomintang in 1976 and in March 1978 was elected, unopposed, to the office of president.

5. A **root race** is a group of souls, or a lifewave, who embody together and have a unique archetypal pattern, divine plan, and mission to fulfill. They are sponsored by Manus, who ensoul the Christic image for the root race. According to esoteric tradition, there are seven primary groups of souls, i.e., the first to seventh root races. See Mark L. Prophet and Elizabeth Clare Prophet, *Climb the Highest Mountain: The Path of the Higher Self,* pp. 68, 411; and H.P. Blavatsky, *The Secret Doctrine* (Pasadena: Theosophical University Press, 1977), 1:42; 2:171–72, 248–51, 300–303, 433–36, 614–15, 768–70.
6. Ephesians 3:16.
7. **Thermopylae,** in ancient times a narrow pass between mountain and sea along the east coast of Greece, is celebrated in history and literature as the site of a heroic battle in the face of overwhelming odds. There, in 480 B.C., 300 Spartans led by King Leonidas temporarily halted the invasion of Greece by the Persians under Xerxes. Instead of fleeing the much larger Persian army, the Spartans put up a valorous fight for three days, dying almost to the last man, while the Persians lost 20,000 according to Greek historians. Although the Greeks were not victorious at Thermopylae, they soon turned the tide of the war by defeating the Persian fleet at Salamis—where but a few Greeks were lost—thus forcing Xerxes and half his army to retreat to Asia.
8. John 16:2.
9. The **Illuminati** ("Enlightened Ones"): a secret order founded in Bavaria May 1, 1776, by Adam Weishaupt (1748–1830), a professor of canon law at Ingolstadt University, Germany, and a former Jesuit. This order, originally called the Society of Perfectibilists, was divided into an intricate system of graded classes and degrees of initiation. Members observed strict oaths

of secrecy and obedience to superiors, with secret confessions and mutual surveillance. At its height, the Illuminati operated throughout a wide area of Europe. It is said that Weishaupt's real aim—hidden from novices at the outer rings of his group—was to replace Christianity with the worship of reason and to establish a world government through which the Illuminati would rule the world. The group was outlawed by edict of the Bavarian government in 1785, though some claim that the order and/or its ideals and methods have lived on. See John Robison, *Proofs of a Conspiracy* (1798; reprint ed., Los Angeles: Western Islands, 1967); and G. Edward Griffin, *The Capitalist Conspiracy* (Thousand Oaks, Calif.: American Media, 1971).

10. Revelation 10:2, 8–10.
11. Revelation 14:6.

X THE MYSTERY OF ALPHA AND OMEGA

1. Proverbs 3:11, 12; 13:24; Hebrews 12:6; Revelation 3:19.
2. **Helios and Vesta** are twin flames who sponsor the evolutions of this solar system from the spiritual Sun behind the sun. They receive and step down the light of Alpha and Omega, Elohim and cosmic beings, making it accessible to the various lifewaves of the planets in our solar system.
3. Psalms 121:5, 7, 8.
4. Matthew 5:13, 14.
5. Matthew 5:13.
6. Matthew 5:15.
7. Nineteenth-century nursery rhyme.
8. Matthew 5:16.
9. James 4:7.
10. The term **"international capitalist/communist conspiracy"** (ICCC) is used by Elizabeth Clare Prophet to describe the transactions of international bankers, financial institutions, and multinational corporations based in the U.S. and the free world that have built and sustained the economies and military machines of Communist nations to their mutual benefit. For documentation see the following books by Antony C. Sutton: *Western Technology and Soviet Economic Development 1917 to 1930* (Stanford: Hoover Institution Publications, 1968); *Western Technology and Soviet Economic Development 1930–1945* (Stanford: Hoover Institution Publications, 1971); *Western Technology and Soviet Economic Development 1945–1965* (Stanford: Hoover Institution Publications, 1973); *National Suicide: Military Aid to the Soviet Union* (New Rochelle, N.Y.: Arlington House Publishers, 1973); *The War on Gold* (Seal Beach, Calif.: '76 Press, 1977); *Wall*

Street and the Bolshevik Revolution (New Rochelle, N.Y.: Arlington House Publishers, 1981); *An Introduction to the Order* (Phoenix: Research Publications, 1983). See also Carroll Quigley, *Tragedy and Hope: A History of the World in Our Time* (New York: Macmillan Co., 1966); Charles Levinson, *Vodka-Cola* (London: Gordon & Cremonesi, n.d.); and Joseph Finder, *Red Carpet* (New York: Holt, Rinehart and Winston, 1983). Exposés by Elizabeth Clare Prophet revealing the strategies and influence of the ICCC at all levels: 4-cassette album *The Religious Philosophy of Karl Marx, The Economic Philosophy of Jesus Christ* (A7896); 3-cassette album *Mother's Manifesto on the Manipulators of Capitalism and Communism* (A7938); *Prophecy for the 1980s: The Handwriting on the Wall,* in paperback and on 2-cassette album (A8020); 16-cassette album *Life Begets Life* (A83035); and 4-cassette album *Freedom 1984: Factors of Control* (A83111).

11. James 1:8.
12. Matthew 7:13, 14.

XI THE MYSTERY OF THE SACRED EUCHARIST

1. Matthew 19:16, 17.
2. Matthew 23:34–36; Luke 11:49–51; Revelation 16:6; 17:6; 18:24; 19:2.
3. **Saint Clare** of Assisi's special devotion to the Holy Eucharist saved her convent at San Damiano from a group of Saracens in the army of Frederick II who were on their way to plunder nearby Assisi c. 1240. As the soldiers scaled the convent walls, Clare rose from her sick bed and, according to one account, had the Blessed Sacrament set up in view of the enemy—prostrating herself before it and calmly praying aloud (other versions of the story state that Clare herself held up the Sacrament while facing the infidels). At the sight of this, the advancing soldiers were suddenly seized with terror and took flight. Not long after, a larger group led by one of Frederick's generals returned to attack the town. Clare and the nuns prayed fervently through the day and night that Assisi might be spared. At dawn, a furious storm broke over the army's camp, scattering their tents and forcing them to flee in panic.
4. Revelation 14:1, 3.
5. Isaiah 14:12. Before the Great Rebellion, **Lucifer** (Latin, "lightbearer") had attained to the level of archangel; but through his ambition, pride of the ego, and defiance of the laws of God, he fell from grace and lost his title and office. On April 16, 1975, Lucifer was bound by Archangel Michael and taken to the Court of the Sacred Fire on the etheric plane of the God Star

Sirius, where he stood trial before the Four and Twenty Elders over a period of ten days. The testimony of many souls of light in embodiment on Terra and other planets and systems were heard, together with that of the ascended masters, archangels, and Elohim. On April 26, 1975, he was found guilty of total rebellion against Almighty God by the unanimous vote of the Twenty Four and sentenced to the second death. As he stood on the disc of the sacred fire before the court, the flame of Alpha and Omega rose as a spiral of intense white light, canceling out an identity and a consciousness that had influenced the fall of one third of the angels of the galaxies and countless lifewaves evolving in this and other systems of worlds. Many who followed the Fallen One in the Great Rebellion have also been brought to trial. The ascended masters teach that prior to the final judgment at the Court of the Sacred Fire and the second death, there is a daily **judgment** weighing each individual's actions, words, deeds, and integrity. It is a sifting process activated by the chastening love of the LORD whereby the individual learns to choose between right and wrong. For further instruction by the ascended masters and the messengers on the judgment, see: Mark L. Prophet, "The Alchemy of Judgment," on 8-cassette album *Sine Wave to the Sun* (A8165); Saint Germain, "The Opening of the Temple Doors VI," in *The Seven Chohans on the Path of the Ascension,* Pearls of Wisdom, vol. 16 (1973), pp. 63–64; Alpha, "The Judgment: The Sealing of the Lifewaves throughout the Galaxy," and Elizabeth Clare Prophet, "Antichrist: The Dragon, the Beast, the False Prophet, and the Great Whore," in *The Great White Brotherhood in the Culture, History, and Religion of America,* pp. 234–37, 239–49, and on 8-cassette album *Shasta 1975: A Conference for Spiritual Freedom* (A7524); *Vials of the Seven Last Plagues* by the Seven Archangels, in paperback and in *El Morya on Discipleship East and West: The Path of the Darjeeling Master and His Chelas,* Pearls of Wisdom, vol. 18 (1975), pp. 177–262; Elizabeth Clare Prophet, "Admonishments of the Seven Archangels on the Judgment of the LORD," on 8-cassette album *New Age Discipleship* (A7662); Elizabeth Clare Prophet, "Idolatry and the Fiery Trial," on 8-cassette album *Feast of the Resurrection Flame Album 1* (A8116); Jesus Christ, "The Final Judgment of Satan," in *Kuan Yin Opens the Door to the Golden Age: The Path of the Mystics East and West,* Book I, Pearls of Wisdom, vol. 25 (1982), pp. 187–96, and on 8-cassette album *The Class of Elohim* (A8204); Elizabeth Clare Prophet, "The Acceptance and the Rejection of the Living Christ," and the Maha Chohan, "The Fiery Trial," in Pearls of Wisdom, vol. 26 (1983), pp. 393–428, and on 16-cassette album

Conclave of the Friends of Christ (A83063); Jesus Christ, "The Second Advent: 'The Day of Vengeance of Our God,'" in Pearls of Wisdom, vol. 26 (1983), pp. 511–19, 521–34; and Elizabeth Clare Prophet, *Forbidden Mysteries of Enoch: The Untold Story of Men and Angels.* For an understanding of the science of the Judgment Call, see Elizabeth Clare Prophet, "Disciples Empowered with the Energy of the Word," on 8-cassette album *Energy Is God* (A7700); Jesus Christ, "They Shall Not Pass!" in *Spoken by Elohim: For Contact with the Inner God,* Pearls of Wisdom, vol. 21 (1978), pp. 165–67; Archangel Raphael, "The Archangels Stand Up for the Deliverance of the People," on 6-cassette album *The Second Coming of Christ,* Album II (A7842); Elizabeth Clare Prophet, "Sanat Kumara's Teaching on the LORD's Ritual of Exorcism," on 8-cassette album *A Retreat on the Ascension—An Experience with God* (A7953); Elizabeth Clare Prophet, "The Prophecy of Malachi: The Holy Spirit as the Messenger of the LORD Who Sounds the Judgment in the Temples of the Sons of God," on 8-cassette album *The Call of Camelot* (A8037); Saint Germain, "The Watchman of the Night," in *A Prophecy of Karma to Earth and Her Evolutions: From the Last Days of Atlantis to the Present Era,* Pearls of Wisdom, vol. 23 (1980), p. 332; Archangel Gabriel and Hope, "Sendings of the Sacred Fire," in *Where the Eagles Gather,* Book I, Pearls of Wisdom, vol. 24 (1981), pp. 104–9, and on 8-cassette album *The Class of the Archangels* (A8100); Cyclopea, "The Personal Path of Christhood" and "Unto the Watchman of the House of Israel," in *Kuan Yin Opens the Door to the Golden Age,* Book II, Pearls of Wisdom, vol. 25 (1982), pp. 394–414, and on 8-cassette album *Freedom 1982* (A8284); Jesus Christ, "The Awakening of the Dweller on the Threshold," in Pearls of Wisdom, vol. 26 (1983), pp. 383–91, and on 16-cassette album *Conclave of the Friends of Christ* (A83063); and Elizabeth Clare Prophet, "Christ and the Dweller," in Pearls of Wisdom, vol. 26 (1983), pp. 429–54.

6. Frequent border conflicts in 1977 and 1978 between Cambodia and Vietnam, enemies for centuries, escalated when the Vietnamese and a small group of Khmer Rouge rebels invaded Cambodia in December 1978. In early January 1979 it was reported that five columns of Vietnamese troops with thousands of guns and tanks were moving deeper into the country threatening to topple the regime of Cambodia's Prime Minister Pol Pot, who declared in a January 5 radio broadcast, **"We pledge to fight them to the end** to keep our national prestige." By January 7, the Vietnamese had taken Cambodia's capital, Phnom Penh, replacing Pol Pot with the Hanoi-backed People's Revolutionary Council (see chapter IV, n. 19, pp. 343–44).

7. Differences between President Carter's **secretary of state** Cyrus R. Vance and White House **national security affairs adviser** Zbigniew Brzezinski grew into a visible power struggle during 1978 over who would have the upper hand in directing the nation's foreign policy. For the most part, the feud centered around the best approach to Soviet-American relations. See Rowland Evans and Robert Novak, "Brzezinski Calls the Foreign-Policy Shots," *Washington Post,* 7 June 1978; Tad Szulc, "The Vance-Brzezinski Squabble," *Saturday Review,* 8 July 1978, pp. 18–19; Jack Anderson, "Brzezinski-Vance Feud Bubbles," *Washington Post,* 25 July 1978; Martin Schram, "The Ascendancy of Cyrus Vance," *Washington Post,* 6 August 1978; Norman Birnbaum, "Vance, Brzezinski and Kojak," *The Nation,* 3 February 1979, cover page, pp. 99–100; and Jack Anderson, "Brzezinski Tactic on Cuba Irks Vance," *Washington Post,* 13 December 1979.
8. Ephesians 6:12.

XII THE MYSTERY OF THE JUDGMENT

1. Amos 3:8.
2. Amos 8:11–14. **"They that swear by the sin of Samaria,"** also rendered "They who swear by the guilt of Samaria" and "Those who swear by Ashimah of Samaria": "Samaria" may refer to the city in Israel that was the capital of the northern kingdom or to the northern kingdom as a whole. During Amos' time (c. 750 B.C.) the city of Samaria was at the height of its prosperity and cultural achievement; the materialism and oppression of the poor that took place there were often rebuked by the prophet (see Amos 3:9, 10; 4:1; 6:1–6). The "sin of Samaria" has also been interpreted as the worship of Baal, the Canaanite god of fertility, still entrenched among the Israelites at that time. Many scholars believe that the original text read "Ashimah," the name of a Syrian goddess worshipped in the northern kingdom (see II Kings 17:30). *Ashimah* is only slightly different from *ashmah* 'guilt', and thus the substitution of *ashmah* for *Ashimah* may have been a play on words with an intended double meaning: "In swearing by Ashimah they are not aiding their souls but incurring further guilt" (Donald Guthrie and Alec Motyer, eds., *The New Bible Commentary,* 3d ed., rev. [Grand Rapids: Wm. B. Eerdmans Publishing Co., 1970], p. 739). **"Thy god, O Dan, liveth,"** also "As thy god lives, O Dan": Following the secession of the northern tribes, Dan was one of two cities in the northern kingdom where Jeroboam I erected a shrine with a golden calf to discourage the people from traveling to the

Temple at Jerusalem in the southern kingdom of Judah. These calves were probably intended as symbols of Yahweh's presence, but their worship degenerated into an idolatry which the LORD rebuked through his prophets (see also Amos' contemporary, Hosea, chapters 8:4–6; 13:2). **"The manner of Beer-sheba liveth,"** also "As the way of Beer-sheba lives" and "As thy patron deity lives, O Beer-sheba": Scholars are not certain of the meaning of this passage. Since it is known that pilgrimages were made to the sanctuary in Beer-sheba, it may refer to an oath like that taken by Moslems on the way to Mecca. The phrase "as [name] lives . . ." expresses an oath to a particular god; some scholars regard the gods cited in Amos 8:14 as strange gods, while others believe they refer to appellations for Yahweh favored at those particular shrines. Thus, the explanation of Amos 8:12–14 could be: Though the people will seek Yahweh in all parts of the land and will appeal to or swear oaths by the names of God, or the gods, worshipped from Dan to Beer-sheba, it shall be to no avail. In Amos 8:14, the prophet names the two shrines in the far north (Dan) and far south (Beer-sheba) by way of encompassing the whole nation. See James Luther Mays, *Amos: A Commentary* (Philadelphia: Westminster Press, 1969), pp. 148–50; and *The Interpreter's Bible*, 12 vols. (New York: Abington Press, 1956), 6:844.

3. Matthew 5:6.
4. John 2:1–11; Jude 12, 13.
5. Amos 9:1.
6. Revelation 11:3; 14:6.
7. Hebrews 9:27; John 5:29.
8. Amos 9:9, 10.
9. Psalms 62:12; Matthew 12:36, 37; 16:27; Revelation 2:23; 20:12, 13; 22:12.
10. Ecclesiastes 11:1.
11. Amos 9:2, 3.
12. Psalms 19:1.
13. The **Dark Cycle** of the return of mankind's karma began April 23, 1969. It is a period when mankind's misqualified energy (i.e., their returning negative karma), held in abeyance for centuries under the great mercy of the Law, is released for balance according to the cycles of the initiations of the solar hierarchies (charted on the cosmic clock) in this time of transition into the Aquarian age. As of April 23, 1984, the Dark Cycle will be on the 3 o'clock line, signifying the return of mankind's karma through their misuse of God's light and their failure of Christic initiations under the hierarchy of Aries. For further background on the Dark Cycle, see *Kuthumi on Selfhood—Consciousness: The*

Doorway to Reality, Pearls of Wisdom, vol. 12 (1969), pp. xi, 10, 30, 263–66.

14. Ephesians 6:17, 18; Hebrews 4:12; Revelation 1:16; 19:15.
15. John 14:16, 17, 26; 15:26; 16:7.
16. John 5:22.
17. I John 2:1; Hebrews 4:16.
18. Amos 7:3.
19. II Chronicles 20:7; Isaiah 41:8; James 2:23.
20. James 5:16.
21. Amos 7:7–9.
22. John 12:35, 36.
23. John 9:4.
24. In both the **dark night of the soul**, in which the soul's light is eclipsed chiefly by personal karma, and the **dark night of the Spirit,** in which the light of the I AM Presence is eclipsed by planetary karma as well as Christic initiation, the individual must deal with the tests unique to his lifestream and those common to all on the path of the ascension. In the dark night of the soul, "the darkness that covers the land" is the weight of each individual's own returning karma as he is also learning to come to grips with world karma. Both types of karma eclipse for certain cycles the light of the soul and therefore its discipleship under the Son of God. When that personal karma is balanced by the soul, it must forge the Christ-identity, pass through the alchemical marriage (of the soul's union with the Christ Self), and be in a position, if required, to hold the balance for some weight of planetary karma. The latter occurs as the initiation of the dark night of the Spirit which each initiate must face as the supreme trial of his Christhood. The dark night of the soul, karmically created by individual free will, is the test of the soul's confrontation with its own karma of relative good and evil (the sin that can be forgiven); the dark night of the Spirit is the initiation of the soul's encounter with the Great God, Absolute Good, and, by that Good which he has become, of the vanquishing of Absolute Evil, its antithesis. This is experienced as the presence and the absence of Light, as Christ and Antichrist, as well as the active and passive participation of the Son of man in the cycles of Armageddon within and without. This initiation deals with the sin against the Holy Ghost which is unforgivable (Matthew 12:31)—the deification of Absolute Evil and the nonsurrender of the 'dweller on the threshold' in the very face of the living God. The dark night of the soul is the tolerance of the Law, a period of grace for the soul to separate out from error and to transmute it; it is the prerequisite for the dark night of the Spirit. Those who have been given the cycles

necessary to pass through the dark night of the soul, but have not done so, must move on, regardless, to the initiation of the dark night of the Spirit. This is the initiation of the I AM Presence. It is the Self-limiting principle of the Law which does not tolerate the abuse of Christ by Antichrist. The latter initiation, given to saint and sinner alike, signifies that opportunity has run out for the individual to choose to be God. After hundreds of thousands and even millions of years of cycling through the wheel of rebirth, the soul-identity that denies the Presence of the Godhead dwelling in him bodily—His Word and His Work—is cancelled out by his own final decree ratified by the judgment before the 24 elders at the Court of the Sacred Fire and the second death (Revelation 2:11; 20:6, 11–15; 21:8). The system of the Godhead for grace, mercy, and opportunity afforded to all for a season assures that all souls are given many lifetimes to repent of their evil works and be saved. It also assures that though mercy endures forever, Evil does not. The only hope for the perpetuation of holy innocence is that the evil word and the evil work (including that of the Evil One and his agents) can be and is terminated at the conclusion of abundant cycles of God's justice extended to all. See also St. John of the Cross, "The Ascent of Mount Carmel" and "The Dark Night," in *The Collected Works of St. John of the Cross,* trans. Kieran Kavanaugh and Otilio Rodriguez (Washington, D.C.: ICS Publications, 1979), pp. 66–389; Jesus Christ, "The Awakening of the Dweller on the Threshold," in Pearls of Wisdom, vol. 26 (1983), pp. 383–91, and on 16-cassette album *Conclave of the Friends of Christ* (A83063); and Elizabeth Clare Prophet, "Christ and the Dweller," in Pearls of Wisdom, vol. 26 (1983), pp. 429–54.

25. Matthew 27:46.
26. Jesus explained the office of the avatar (the Person of the Son, God-incarnate) in these words: "As long as I am in the world, I am the Light of the world" (John 9:5), which is to say: "As long as the I AM Presence is in the world through my physical incarnation, that Logos, that I AM THAT I AM, is the Light of the physical universe." Conversely, he prophesied **the coming night** (John 9:4) as the period when the Son of man would no longer be in physical embodiment, his I AM Presence no longer physically anchored in flesh and blood. This is the night "when no man can work" out his karma or his Christhood because the Son of man is no longer the Light of the physical world of the person or the planet to hold the balance of Light in the face of karma or Antichrist. The Dark Ages of the Piscean age are a witness of the absence of his physical presence on earth and the world karma for nonacceptance of the Saviour. This night

foretold by Jesus is also evidence that the dispensation of the coming of The LORD Our Righteousness in the descent of the Christ Self into the temple in the hour of the Second Advent had not yet taken place. Jesus made it clear that in his absence, the disciples of the LORD are the Light of the world as extensions of Jesus' Light (the Son-Light of the I AM THAT I AM) manifest in them. This he affirmed thusly: "Ye are the Light of the world. . ." (Matthew 5:14).

27. Amos 9:11, 12.
28. Amos 9:14.
29. Amos 9:14, 15.

XIII THE MYSTERY OF THE ANTICHRISTS

1. Luke 11:52.
2. Matthew 15:1–9.
3. Luke 11:46.
4. Matthew 16:11, 12.
5. The **Babylonian captivity** of the Jews began in 597 B.C. when Nebuchadnezzar, king of Babylon, crushed the rebellious Judah by besieging Jerusalem and deporting the Hebrew king and leading men of Judah—"all the princes and all the mighty men of valor. . . all the craftsmen and smiths. . . all that were strong and apt for war." Nine years later Zedekiah, the appointed regent over Judah, also rebelled, and after a siege of one and a half years the Babylonians destroyed Jerusalem (587 B.C.)—looting, burning every building including the Temple, and deporting all but a few inhabitants. A third deportation occurred in 582 B.C., probably as punishment for the assassination of Gedaliah (II Kings 24–25; Jeremiah 39:1–10; 41:2; 52). Though they had been taken from their homeland, the conditions for the exiles were not unfavorable. For one, the rich soil in Babylonia was far superior to the rocky fields of Judea and the farmers prospered. Later some Jews became merchants, traders, soldiers, even government officials, some rising to positions of wealth. When the Persian king Cyrus, conqueror of Babylonia, issued a decree in 538 B.C. permitting the Jews to return to Jerusalem and rebuild the Temple, only a small remnant of approximately 42,000–50,000 led by Joshua, the high priest, and Zerubbabel, appointed governor of Judah, made the journey back, carrying the Temple vessels that had been stripped from them in 587 B.C. (II Chronicles 36:22, 23; Ezra 1–2). The **Chasidim,** or Hasidim (meaning "pious ones" or "saints"), also called Hasideans or Assideans, were a sect of devout Jews that developed between 300 B.C. and 175 B.C. during

the Hellenistic era, centuries after the return of the exiles to Jerusalem. They lived mostly in the rural areas, were dedicated to the strict observance of Jewish ritual and law, and strongly resisted the influence of Greek culture that had been introduced to the Jews following the conquest of the Persian Empire by Alexander the Great. Because of their firm loyalty to the tradition of their fathers, the Chasidim were among the first to suffer under the persecutions of the Syrian ruler Antiochus IV. Claiming to be "god manifest," Antiochus forbade the Jews to practice their religion and desecrated the Temple by erecting a statue of Zeus in the inner court and sacrificing pig's flesh on the altar. The Chasidim broke their silence to fight alongside Judas Maccabeus in the early phases of the Jewish revolt that ensued (I Maccabees 2:42; II Maccabees 14:6). In 164 B.C., the Maccabean revolt succeeded, and the Temple was cleansed and rededicated. Some scholars say the unknown writer of the Book of Daniel was one of the Chasidim, and it is now widely accepted that the book was written during the time of Antiochus IV, whose career is described (Daniel 11:21–35) as well as his polluting of the sanctuary—the "abomination that maketh desolate" (11:31; 12:11). In fact, the Book of Daniel—in which the angel Gabriel himself figures as the interpreter of the visions of the prophet—has been called the "Manifesto of the Chasidim." The Chasidim are believed to be the spiritual forerunners of the later sect of Pharisees (see chapter XIV, n. 1, pp. 376–77).

6. Luke 11:47, 48.
7. II Chronicles 24:19, 20; Luke 11:49.
8. Matthew 3:7; II Chronicles 24:21.
9. I John 4:3; II John 7.
10. Revelation 13:8.
11. II Chronicles 24:22; Luke 12:51.
12. Exodus 22:22; Deuteronomy 24:17, 19–21; Psalms 82:3, 4; Isaiah 1:17, 23; Zechariah 7:10.
13. Matthew 9:6; John 1:17; Romans 6:14; Ephesians 1:7; Colossians 1:14.
14. Titus 3:5.
15. Matthew 23:23–28.
16. Deuteronomy 25:4; I Corinthians 9:9; I Timothy 5:18.
17. Revelation 17–18.
18. Following the desert wanderings of the Israelites, Joshua set up a tribal confederacy—a community bound by common laws and obligations and based on a mutual devotion to Yahweh. Though they acted autonomously, the tribes united in times of emergency as well as for religious festivals and were guided by

judges—charismatic military leaders who also served as arbiters (c. 1200–1030 B.C.). With the people's wish to have "a king to judge us like all the nations" (I Samuel 8:4, 5), Samuel anointed Saul (c. 1020 B.C.) and a monarchy was created. The kings ruled a united kingdom until 922 B.C., when the ten northern tribes seceded to form an independent state, Israel, separate from the southern state of Judah. **"The Spiritual Confederation of Israel and Judah"** in the text refers to the inner matrix of the unity of the once-united kingdoms.

19. Matthew 7:15.
20. Matthew 7:21–23.
21. Acts 7:57.
22. II Peter 2:19.
23. Psalms 1:1.
24. John 8:44.
25. Matthew 18:6, 7.
26. Luke 11:50.
27. In the 1973 *Roe* v. *Wade* and *Doe* v. *Bolton* decisions, the Supreme Court **legalized abortion** nationwide based on an implied constitutional right of privacy and declared that the unborn child is not included in the definition of a "person" as protected under the Constitution. The basic guidelines set by the Court were: (1) during the first three months (first trimester) the decision for an abortion is between a woman and her doctor only, (2) after the first trimester the state may regulate abortion procedures in the interest of the mother's health, and (3) during the third trimester (when the fetus could be considered viable, i.e., able to live outside the mother's womb) the state may prohibit abortions unless they are necessary to preserve the mother's life or "health"—a term that in practice is broadly interpreted to include mental health. On June 15, 1983, the Supreme Court, in its most sweeping abortion decision in a decade, reaffirmed the *Roe* decision and struck down restrictions on abortion procedures in Akron, Ohio, which the Justices said infringed upon a woman's constitutional right to have an abortion. The Court ruled, 6-3, that abortions after the first three months do not have to be performed in a hospital but can take place in a licensed clinic, physicians do not have to inform patients of birth-giving alternatives or potential dangers of the abortion procedure, and a woman does not have to wait 24 hours after she signs an "informed consent" form to have her abortion. In a companion case the Court did, however, uphold a Missouri requirement that unemancipated minors obtain parental or judicial consent for an abortion and that two doctors be on hand when the fetus has a chance of living

outside the womb to care for both the mother and child. In 1972, the year before the *Roe* v. *Wade* decision, there were about 600,000 legal abortions in the U.S. In the 10 years since that decision, an average of 1.5 million abortions have taken place per year—ending one out of every three pregnancies. The *Akron* decision is likely to increase the number of abortions even more. For further reading on abortion laws, see Cyril Means, Jr., "The Phoenix of Abortional Freedom: Is a Penumbral or Ninth-Amendment Right About to Arise from the Nineteenth-Century Legislative Ashes of a Fourteenth-Century Common-Law Liberty?" *New York Law Forum* 17 (1971):335–410; Thomas W. Hilgers and Dennis J. Horan, *Abortion and Social Justice* (New York: Sheed & Ward, 1972); Robert M. Byrn, "An American Tragedy: The Supreme Court on Abortion," *Fordham Law Review* 41 (May 1973):807–62; Bob Woodward and Scott Armstrong, *The Brethren: Inside the Supreme Court* (New York: Simon & Schuster, 1979), pp. 193–209, 215–23, 271–84, 491–94; Elder Witt, "Supreme Court Reaffirms Abortion Rights," *Congressional Quarterly Weekly Report*, 18 June 1983, pp. 1247–49; Ted Gest, "Anti-Abortion Groups Have a Bad Day in Court," *U.S. News & World Report*, 27 June 1983, p. 31. See also Elizabeth Clare Prophet's detailed analyses of the abortion issue on 16-cassette album *Life Begets Life* (A83034), with supplemental 4-cassette album *Life Begets Life: Prayers, Invocations, Dynamic Decrees, and Songs of Praise unto Life* (A83079); and 8-cassette album *Abortion Update—Exposé: The Controllers and the Destroyers of the Human Race* (A83135). In addition to the abortion issue, the Supreme Court and the judicial system as a whole have come under attack for a runaway **leniency** which many claim protects the criminal far more than the victim of the crime or the public. Some major areas of concern are the widespread practice of plea bargaining, the insanity defense, leniency toward child molesters and drunk drivers, and the death penalty. Approximately 80% of all cases are settled by negotiating a plea bargain. Prosecutors enter into a deal with defendants who agree to plead guilty to a lesser charge for a promise of a lighter sentence. While this greatly reduces the number of cases that go to trial, saving both time and money in courtroom proceedings, opponents argue that a lighter sentence shortchanges the true cause of justice in many instances. Public fervor over the insanity defense came to a head when a Washington, D.C., court found John Hinkley, Jr., not guilty by reason of insanity in the attempted assassination of President Ronald Reagan on March 30, 1981. The insanity defense is based on the belief that a person who is mentally ill, and thus incapable of controlling his conduct, should not be punished. In particular, critics of the insanity plea object to the practice of relying on psychiatrists' speculations and opinions as expert testimony. The problem of leniency and the insanity plea was also underscored in the Dan White case (see chapter IV, n. 14, pp. 341–42). Using the "diminished capacity" defense, a variation of the insanity defense, White received a light sentence for manslaughter rather than first-degree murder and was subsequently paroled within four years. As a result of well-publicized cases like these, a few states have abolished the insanity plea altogether; others have passed laws allowing a "guilty but mentally ill" verdict instead. These new laws stipulate that a convict who begins his term in a mental institution must complete his prison sentence after treatment. Until recently, treatment of convicted child molesters has also been based on the theory that offenders should be hospitalized and cured rather than imprisoned and punished. During 1977–79, it was reported that only about 10% of convicted molesters in California were imprisoned. The *Frank* case is a prime example of how the system failed. Theodore Frank, with a long record of sex crimes against children, pleaded guilty to a charge of child molestation and in 1974 was sent to a state hospital as a mentally disordered sex offender. In January 1978, he was released as a model patient. Four months later, he was arrested for abducting, molesting, and brutalizing an eight-year-old girl. In 1980, he was sentenced to death in the murder of a two-year-old girl who had been found dead just six weeks after his release from the hospital. Following Frank's sentencing, concerned citizens formed SLAM (Concerned Citizens for Stronger Legislation Against Child Molesters). The group gained widespread support and succeeded in convincing the California legislature to impose tougher penalties on convicted child molesters, such as mandatory imprisonment for serious offenders and recidivists. Staggering statistics of the number of deaths due to drunk driving have made leniency toward drunk drivers an issue close to home to many Americans. *Newsweek* reported in 1982 that a quarter of a million Americans died at the hand of drunk drivers over the past decade, and in just two years—from 1980–1982—drunk drivers killed more Americans than were killed in Vietnam. Fed up with the legal system's soft treatment of drunk drivers, citizens have formed groups like MADD (Mothers Against Drunk Drivers) and RID (Remove Intoxicated Drivers-USA) to fight for stricter laws. One of the most controversial leniency issues that has faced the Supreme Court in the last decade is the death penalty. In the 1972 *Furman* v. *Georgia* case, the Court struck down in a 5-4 vote all state death penalty statutes. The Justices ruled that the practice of capital punishment at that time amounted to "cruel and unusual punishment" because of the arbitrary nature of sentencing. The Court reinstated capital punishment in 1976 after a review of revised state laws, but the issue is still far from clear-cut. In 1983, *U.S. News & World Report* summarized the problem: "The justices have made numerous attempts in recent years to clarify how the death penalty can be imposed. But each time they dispose of one issue, defense lawyers raise a new one. Result: Only eight death-row inmates have been executed since 1967." One important question before the Court that blocked the imposition of the death penalty in California and other states was settled by the Justices on January 23, 1983, in their review of California's *Pulley* v. *Harris* case. The Court ruled that states do not have to study each death sentence to make sure it is proportional to other sentences imposed for similar offenses. For more information on these topics, see Aric Press et al., "The Insanity Plea on Trial" and "The Case for the Victim," *Newsweek,* 24 May 1982, pp. 56–61; Walter Isaacson, "Insane on All Counts," and John Leo, "Is the System Guilty?" *Time,* 5 July 1982, pp. 22, 25–27; "American Justice: ABC's of How It Really Works," *U.S. News & World Report,* 1 November 1982, pp. 35–58; William J. Winslade and Judith Wilson Ross, *The Insanity Plea* (New York: Charles Scribner's Sons, 1983); Irving Prager, "'Sexual Psychopathy' and Child Molesters: The Experiment Fails," *Journal of Juvenile Law* 6 (1982): 49–79; Mark Starr et al., "The War against Drunk Drivers," *Newsweek,* 13 September 1982, pp. 34–39; "Why So Few Drunk Drivers Go to Jail," *U.S. News & World Report,* 12 September 1983, p. 14; Raoul Berger, *Death Penalties: The Supreme Court's Obstacle Course* (Cambridge, Mass.: Harvard University Press, 1982); "Supreme Court's Death-Row Dilemma," *U.S. News & World Report,* 17 October 1983, p. 17; Aric Press et al., "To Die or Not to Die," *Newsweek,* 17 October 1983, pp. 43–45; Philip Hager, "Ruling Leaves Other Major Questions on Law," and Jim Mann, "Supreme Court Reverses State Executions Ban," *Los Angeles Times,* 24 January 1984, pp. 1, 12.

28. Matthew 10:33.
29. Revelation 2:11; 20:6, 11–15; 21:8.
30. Daniel 9:27; 11:31; 12:11; Matthew 24:15.
31. Psalms 11:4; Habakkuk 2:20.
32. Malachi 3:2, 3.
33. I John 1:7, 9.
34. Mark 3:2; 12:13; Luke 11:54; John 8:6.
35. Matthew 22:46; Luke 14:6.

36. Revelation 10:7; 11:3; 14:6.
37. Matthew 23:31.
38. II Chronicles 24:15–21.
39. Luke 21:15.
40. Matthew 27:34.
41. Matthew 25:32, 33.
42. Isaiah 55:1; Revelation 21:6; 22:1, 17.
43. Exodus 33:11; Numbers 14:14; Deuteronomy 5:4; 34:10.
44. Jude 19. *Pharisees* means literally "separated ones" or "separatists."
45. Jude 13.
46. Matthew 23:15.
47. I John 4:18.
48. Jude 12.
49. John 10:11, 15, 17, 18.
50. John 13:1, 34; 15:9, 12, 13; 17:26.
51. John 3:16; I John 4:9.

XIV THE MYSTERY OF THE WICKED ONE

1. Matthew 3:7. The **Pharisees** were one of the chief Jewish religious sects during the last two centuries B.C. and the first two centuries A.D. Their name means "separated ones," probably indicating their desire to remain apart from all that was "unclean" and from those who did not follow them in the strict observance of the Law. During Jesus' time, the priests, laity, and almost all the scribes (scholars devoted to the preservation, transcription, and exposition of the Law, often serving as teachers and lawyers) were Pharisees. As the chief interpreters of the Torah (Law), the Pharisees were greatly respected by the people. They led an austere life dedicated to obeying every detail of the Law as spelled out in the "tradition of the elders." This extensive oral tradition, developed over the centuries by the rabbis to explain the written Law of Moses, governed everything from Sabbath regulations to diet, fasting, and the minutest facets of ritual worship. The Pharisees did not view this growing body of religious interpretation as a departure from the Law but as the unfolding of the full revelation of God through an unwritten tradition they claimed had existed since Moses' time. Eventually, however, their legalistic interpretations became more important than the Law itself, and they looked with scorn upon those who did not measure up to the standards set by the rabbis. Thus Jesus denounced the worst of the Pharisees for their self-righteous hypocrisy and attachment to petty tradition. Some of the Pharisees, however, were

sincerely devoted men; Nicodemus, Gamaliel, and the Apostle Paul are prominent New Testament figures who were Pharisees (John 3:1; 7:50; 19:39; Acts 5:34; 23:6; 26:5; Philippians 3:5). The Pharisees believed in a coming Messiah, the existence of angels and demons, resurrection after death for the righteous, and eternal punishment for the wicked. Some scholars feel that the Pharisees' ability to adapt the written Law to changing needs and conditions is what kept Judaism a living religion. Unlike the Sadducees, whose power centered around the Temple, the Pharisees survived the fall of Jerusalem and the destruction of the temple in 70 A.D. Their ideas and methods, later codified in the Talmud, have influenced Judaism to the present day. The **Sadducees** were the chief opponents of the Pharisees. Their name is probably derived from "Zadokites," the priestly descendants of Zadok (high priest of Solomon). The Sadducees belonged to the aristocratic, wealthy class and held the highest offices in church and state. They controlled the temple priesthood and were influential in the highest judicial and religious council, the Sanhedrin, along with the Pharisees. Caiaphas, the high priest who played a key role in Jesus' crucifixion, belonged to this sect. As conservatives who wished to preserve the status quo, the Sadducees had a common-sense outlook based on political realities. Their cooperation with the Roman authorities (who appointed the high priest) gained them political influence but made them unpopular with the people. The Sadducees accepted only the authority of the written Mosaic Law and rejected the vast body of oral tradition espoused by the Pharisees. They also rejected the Pharisees' belief in angels as well as their doctrines of the resurrection and final judgment, claiming they were not based on the Pentateuch.

2. Matthew 16:27; 24:27–51.
3. Isaiah 40:3; Malachi 3:1; Matthew 3:3; 19:28; Luke 22:30.
4. Matthew 3:5, 6.
5. Matthew 11:14; 17:10–13.
6. Psalms 104:4; Hebrews 1:7.
7. Revelation 12:8, 9; John 12:31.
8. Matthew 3:7; Colossians 2:9.
9. Matthew 3:8.
10. Genesis 2:6.
11. Matthew 3:11.
12. Matthew 3:9.
13. John 8:39–44.
14. Matthew 3:9.
15. Matthew 3:10.

16. Matthew 7:15–20; 12:33–37.
17. Matthew 26:3, 4; Matthew 17:12.
18. Matthew 3:12.
19. Luke 12:9.
20. James 2:10.
21. Matthew 12:38; 16:1; Luke 11:16; Matthew 27:40.
22. I Kings 17; II Kings 1–8:15.
23. II Kings 2:11–14.
24. Exodus 7–12:36; 14:13–31; 17:5, 6; 32:15, 16; 34:1, 4, 5, 28–35.
25. Acts 1:3.
26. Matthew 10:8; 15:14; Luke 6:39.
27. Matthew 4:3.
28. Exodus 17:1–7.
29. Numbers 20:7–13; 27:12–14.
30. Matthew 10:16.
31. Genesis 14:18; Psalms 110:4; Hebrews 5:6, 10; 6:20; 7:1–4.
32. Revelation 2:9; 3:9.
33. Matthew 23:2.
34. Jude 12.
35. Jude 11; Numbers 16:1–35.

XV THE MYSTERY OF THE MESSENGERS

1. Matthew 22:36.
2. Acts 2:3.
3. Mark 12:29–31.
4. Matthew 21:23.
5. Deuteronomy 6:4, 5.
6. Leviticus 19:18.
7. Matthew 5:17.
8. Acts 7:51–53.
9. Romans 13:10.
10. John 14:17.
11. Jeremiah 31:33; Hebrews 10:16.
12. Matthew 22:32.
13. Matthew 22:42–45.
14. John 15:1–8.
15. This union is the alchemical marriage, whereby the soul becomes the Anointed One—endued and identified with the Christic light and consciousness.
16. Mark 12:36.
17. I Samuel 16:13. The **prophet Samuel** reincarnated as Joseph to fulfill both Person and Principle of the Father side by side with

Mary who fulfilled the role of both Person and Principle of Mother.

18. Matthew 7:21.
19. Luke 9:20.
20. Job 1:6.
21. "God standeth in the **congregation of the mighty;** he judgeth among the **gods**" (Psalms 82:1): In the congregation of the mighty, God also judges the infamous Watchers—angels who left off from their service with this august body, abandoned their God-estate (consciousness), and fell to earth through lust. In Psalms 82:6, 7, the LORD pronounces the judgment: "I once said, 'You too are gods, sons of the Most High [you once had the divine spark], all of you,' but all the same, because of your sin you shall die like other men; as one man, princes, you shall fall" (see *Jerusalem Bible*). For Hebrew scholar Julian Morgenstern's analysis of this passage as Yahweh's denunciation of the fallen angels, see *Hebrew Union College Annual* 14 (1939): 114–16, 122–23, excerpted in Elizabeth Clare Prophet, *Forbidden Mysteries of Enoch: The Untold Story of Men and Angels,* pp. 285–86, n. 4.
22. Psalms 89:7.
23. I Kings 22:19.
24. Matthew 28:18.
25. **Chakras:** centers of spiritual energy anchored along the spinal column in the etheric body that govern the flow of energy to man's four lower bodies (physical, emotional, mental, and etheric). For the ascended masters' teaching on chakras, with color illustrations, visualizations, and meditations, see Djwal Kul, *Intermediate Studies of the Human Aura;* "Integration: The Missing Dimension in Physical Fitness—An Exercise in the Toning of the Chakras" and "The 'Spinning Wheels' of the Yogi," *Heart: For the Coming Revolution in Higher Consciousness* 3 (Autumn 1983): 52–68; Elizabeth Clare Prophet, 8-cassette album *Mother's Chakra Meditations and the Science of the Spoken Word* (A82162); and Gautama Buddha, "The Prayer Wheel of the Crown Chakra," in *Kuan Yin Opens the Door to the Golden Age: The Path of the Mystics East and West,* Book II, Pearls of Wisdom, vol. 25 (1982), pp. 327–30, and on 2-cassette album *The Seventh Commandment: Thou Shalt Not Commit Adultery* (A8239).
26. Matthew 28:19, 20.
27. **Guru:** the One who is the remover of Darkness; the one Light incarnate who transmutes all Darkness into Light by the Person and the Energy of Brahma, Vishnu, Shiva, which he has become.
28. Matthew 1:23.
29. Matthew 25:21.

XVI THE MYSTERY OF THE RELENTLESS WAVE

1. Matthew 23:13.
2. Matthew 23:27, 28. *Iniquity:* literally "lawlessness."
3. Uppercased **Tree of Life** refers to the individual I AM Presence and causal body of man and woman (upper figure in the Chart, facing p. 278) and the momentum of their good words and works recorded therein. When the I AM Presence is activated by the Guru, as it was in many through the preaching of John the Baptist and Jesus Christ, it brings to the outer mind the awareness of the Christ consciousness and releases the fruit of good deeds stored in the causal body. Such preaching by the Holy Spirit also forces the individual's encounter with his lower self and its untransmuted momentums. Lowercased **tree of life** refers to the lower personality (lower figure in the Chart), self-awareness in the four lower bodies, and the tree of selfhood rooted in karma and recorded in the electronic belt. (The electronic belt is formed of the individual's misqualification of God's energy as it collects and intensifies in the subconscious to form a negative spiral shaped like a kettledrum surrounding the chakras below the heart.) This energy veil, or darkness, is activated by the light of the Guru in order that the soul may choose to cast those subconscious momentums into the sacred fire and seek only the Absolute Good of the I AM Presence and causal body focused in the Garden of Eden as the Tree of Life. "Tree of life" in the text refers to both the upper and lower storehouses of life's experiences, each bearing fruit after its kind.
4. Matthew 19:28.
5. Revelation 16:7; 19:2.
6. John 20:22, 23.

XVII THE MYSTERY OF HIERARCHY

Salutation: John 15:16.

1. William Wordsworth, "Ode: Intimations of Immortality from Recollections of Early Childhood," stanza 5.
2. John 17:16.
3. Oliver Wendell Holmes, "The Chambered Nautilus," stanza 5.
4. Genesis 3:19, 21.
5. For further teaching on the science of **alchemy,** see Saint Germain, *Studies in Alchemy: The Science of Self-Transformation* and *Intermediate Studies in Alchemy: Alchemical Formulas for Self-Mastery;* 2-cassette album *The Creation of the Cloud by Saint Germain and Meditations on the Alchemy of Constructive Change and the Control of the Aura by Elizabeth Clare Prophet* (A8063); and the

Sacred Ritual for the Creation of the Cloud, booklet and cassette (B83050).

6. Isaiah 55:8, 9.
7. **Pearls of Wisdom** are weekly letters from the ascended masters sent to their students throughout the world. Since 1958, the Darjeeling Council of the Great White Brotherhood has sponsored the release of their teachings in this format through the messengers Mark and Elizabeth Prophet. These letters are the intimate contact, heart to heart, between the Guru and the chela. They contain both fundamental and advanced teachings that illumine the path of the mystics East and West with practical application of spiritual truths to personal and planetary problems. Write for thirty-week introductory series "A Study in Christhood by the Great Initiator," $15.00; annual subscription rate, $33.00. Get your name on the list today!
8. Genesis 1:22, 28.
9. Luke 1:19; 2:10.
10. See the Great Divine Director, "Law," "Man," and "Non-Man," in *The Mechanization Concept: The Mysteries of God on the Creation of Mechanized Man,* Pearls of Wisdom, vol. 8 (1965), pp. 70–71, 79–81, 83–87.
11. A growing body of evidence indicates that the Soviet Union has developed and may already be using advanced techniques of psychic warfare that have the power to manipulate or harm populations. The term **"psychotronics"** has been used to describe the machine-age application of telepathy, hypnosis, and telekinesis as well as novel uses of low-frequency radio waves, microwaves, and other technologies. A 1981 U.S. Army study referred to psychotronics as the "projection or transmission of mental energy by individual or collective mental discipline and control, or by an energy-emitting device—a kind of mind jammer." Using electronic generators to broadcast energy over long or short distances, psychotronic weapons can alter the mind, emotions, and physical state of an individual. Some experts claim that these weapons can generate earthquakes, control the weather, modify behavior patterns, and even induce disease or death. See Elizabeth Clare Prophet, 2-cassette album *Psychotronics: "The Only Way to Go Is Up!"* (A7890); Sheila Ostrander and Lynn Schroeder, *Psychic Discoveries behind the Iron Curtain* (Englewood Cliffs, N.J.: Prentice-Hall, 1970); Paul Brodeur, *The Zapping of America: Microwaves, Their Deadly Risk, and the Cover-Up* (New York: W. W. Norton & Co., 1977); John B. Alexander, "The New Mental Battlefield: 'Beam Me Up, Spock,'" *Military Review* 12 (1980): 47–54; Thomas E. Bearden, *Excalibur Briefing* (San Francisco: Strawberry Hill Press,

1980); "Psychotronic Warfare in the 80s: Rising above the Crossfire," *The Coming Revolution: A Magazine for Higher Consciousness* 2 (Spring 1981): 55–56; and Martin Ebon, *Psychic Warfare: Threat or Illusion?* (New York: McGraw-Hill Book Co., 1983).

12. Matthew 24:22.

XVIII THE MYSTERY OF THE SPOKEN WORD

Salutation: John 16:25.

1. John 12:44, 45.
2. John 12:46.
3. John 12:47, 48.
4. John 9:39.
5. John 1:5.
6. Hebrews 6:20.
7. John 12:49, 50.
8. "Do you not know what you are seeing? Will you not believe what you are seeing? The **I AM** of me (my own state and action of being) is **in the Father and** the I AM of **the Father** (his own state and action of being) **is in me**—by the figure-eight flow."
9. John 14:10.
10. John 14:11.
11. John 14:12–14.
12. John 14:18.
13. John 12:32.
14. Revelation 11:5.
15. Even Jesus said: "The kingdom of heaven is likened unto a man which sowed good seed in his field; but while men slept, his enemy came and sowed tares among the wheat, and went his way" (Matthew 13:24, 25).
16. Those serving with the hosts of the Lord on the inner planes during the hours of sleep usually return to the physical plane on or before the hour of 4:00 a.m. The ascended masters recommend that their chelas begin their dynamic decrees and their rosary to the Blessed Mother at dawn or before. This is a recommendation for those who are able. Those whose schedules and responsibilities do not allow them to follow the cycles of the day and the night should find a workable solution, setting the ritual of the day as karma and dharma dictate, nevertheless endeavoring to seek ye first the consciousness of God. The **setting of the blueprint of the day** which begins at 4:00 a.m. is the converging of the inner Christ matrix with the outer soul awareness. This takes place even during sleep and may be summoned to full conscious awareness upon awakening at the chela's regular morning schedule. The ascended

masters have often recommended that their chelas retire by 11:00 p.m. to be at their places in the etheric retreats on schedule. Those desiring to maintain a schedule of early rising will seize the opportunity of this further explanation given by Archangel Gabriel to also be in bed early, services to the sacred fire and to all life permitting.

17. The **retreat of Archangel Michael** is located in the etheric octave over Banff and Lake Louise in the Canadian Rockies. The **retreat of Archangel Gabriel and Hope,** his divine complement, is located in the etheric plane between Sacramento and Mount Shasta, California. As Archangel and Archeia of the Fourth Ray of Purity and the Ascension, they also serve with Jesus and Mother Mary at the Temple of the Resurrection over the Holy Land and with Serapis Bey, Chohan of the Fourth Ray, at the etheric retreat of the Ascension Temple at Luxor, Egypt.
18. John 3:19–21.
19. John 9:4, 5.

XIX THE MYSTERY OF YOUR DIVINE SELF

1. Matthew 3:16, 17; 12:18; 17:5; II Peter 1:17.
2. I Thessalonians 4:17.
3. John 6:53.
4. Philippians 2:5, 6.
5. Colossians 1:12, 27.
6. Galatians 2:20.
7. John 12:44–50.
8. John 3:13.
9. John 8:23; Matthew 3:7; 12:34; 23:33; John 8:42, 44.
10. Revelation 17:14.

XX THE MYSTERY OF JESUS CHRIST

1. John 1:17.
2. John 1:46, 49.
3. John 14:12.
4. Hebrews 1:3.
5. John 1:3, 14.
6. John 1:16.
7. John 1:9.
8. John 3:16.
9. Luke 17:21.
10. John 18:37.
11. John 1:12.
12. Philippians 2:5; John 2:1–11; Mark 11:15, 16; Matthew 5:48.
13. John 3:14, 15.

14. Merle Severy, ed., *Great Religions of the World* (Washington, D.C.: National Geographic Society, 1971), front flap.
15. John 12:26.
16. Hebrews 12:1.
17. Matthew 7:21; 12:50; John 5:30, 36; 10:25; 14:12; Matthew 10:8.
18. Saint Germain, *Studies in Alchemy: The Science of Self-Transformation,* pp. 9, 10.
19. John 10:10.
20. Job 19:26.
21. Genesis 15:5; 22:17; Hebrews 11:12.
22. **Archangel Zadkiel** is the angel of the seventh ray of the violet flame and Aquarius. **Holy Amethyst** is his divine complement, a beautiful Mother figure of great light and devotion to the souls of humanity.
23. John 10:30.
24. Philippians 2:8.
25. Revelation 3:8.
26. Revelation 3:11; 22:7, 12.
27. Revelation 1:4; 3:1; 4:5; 5:6.
28. Revelation 7:9, 14.
29. Revelation 3:4.
30. Revelation 5:11.
31. Revelation 14:3.
32. Revelation 19:13, 14.
33. Revelation 19:10.
34. Revelation 12:11.
35. Revelation 3:20, 21.

XXI THE MYSTERY OF THE GREAT MEDIATOR

1. Revelation 1:16.
2. Matthew 25:40.
3. I Corinthians 13:9, 12.
4. Edward FitzGerald, trans., *Rubáiyát of Omar Khayyám,* quatrain 66.
5. Hebrews 6:6.
6. Henry Wadsworth Longfellow, "The Ladder of St. Augustine," stanza 10.
7. Revelation 16:15; 22:12.
8. Matthew 24:40, 41; Luke 17:34–36.
9. Matthew 7:12; Luke 6:31; Romans 13:10.
10. Matthew 5:45.
11. Matthew 25:14–30.
12. Luke 7:47.
13. Isaiah 1:18.

INDEX OF SCRIPTURE

Mark

INDEX

In every age there have been some, the few, who have pursued an understanding of God and of selfhood that transcends the current traditions of doctrine and dogma. Compelled by a faith that knows the freedom of love, they have sought to expand their awareness of God by probing and proving the infinite expressions of his law. Through the true science of religion, they have penetrated the 'mysteries' of both Spirit and Matter and come to experience God as the All-in-all.

Having discovered the key to reality, these sons and daughters of God have drawn about them disciples who would pursue the disciplines of the law of the universe and the inner teachings of the 'mystery schools'. Thus Jesus chose his apostles, Bodhidharma his monks, and Pythagoras his initiates at Crotona, Gautama Buddha called his disciples to form the *sangha* (community), and King Arthur summoned his knights to the quest for the Holy Grail at the Table Round.

Summit University is a mystery school for men and women of the twentieth century who would pursue the great synthesis of the teachings of the ascended masters—the few who have overcome in every age, the many who now stand as our elder brothers and sisters on the Path. Together Gautama Buddha and Lord Maitreya sponsor Summit University with the World Teachers Jesus and Kuthumi, El Morya, Lanello, and Saint Germain, Confucius, Mother Mary, Moses and the Apostle Paul, the Archangels Michael and Gabriel, and the "numberless numbers" of "saints robed in white"—the Great 'White' Brotherhood. To this university of the Spirit they lend their flame, their counsel, the momentum of their attainment, and the living teaching for us who would follow in their footsteps to the source of that reality they have become.

Founded in 1971 under the direction of the Messengers Mark L. Prophet and Elizabeth Clare Prophet, Summit University currently holds three twelve-week retreats each year—fall, winter, and spring quarters—as well as summer sessions. All of the courses are based on the unfoldment of the inner potential of the Christ, the Buddha, and the Mother flame. Through the teachings of the ascended masters given through their messengers, students at Summit University pursue the disciplines on the path of the ascension for the soul's ultimate reunion with the Spirit of the living God.

This includes the study of the sacred scriptures of East and West taught by Jesus and Gautama; exercises in the self-mastery of the energies of the chakras and the aura under Kuthumi and Djwal Kul; beginning and intermediate studies in alchemy under the Ascended Master Saint Germain; the Cosmic Clock—a new-age astrology for charting the cycles of karma and dharma given by Mother Mary; the science of the spoken Word in conjunction with prayer, meditation, and visualization—the key to soul liberation in the Aquarian age; weekly healing services, "Be Thou Made Whole!" at the Chapel of the Holy Grail at Camelot in which the messenger gives personal and planetary healing invocations; the psychology of the family, the marriage ritual and meditations for the conception of new-age children; counseling for community service through the sacred labor; the teachings and meditations of the Buddha taught by Gautama Buddha, Lord Maitreya, Lanello, and the bodhisattvas of East and West; and individual initiations transferred to each student from the ascended masters through the messengers.

Summit University is a twelve-week spiral that begins with you as self-awareness and ends with you as God Self-awareness. As you traverse the spiral, light intensifies, darkness is transmuted. You experience the rebirth day by day as the old man is put off and the new man is put on. Energies are aligned, chakras are cleared, and the soul is poised for the victorious fulfillment of the individual divine plan.

In addition to preparing the student to enter into the Guru/chela relationship with the ascended masters and the path of initiation outlined in their retreats, the academic standards of Summit University, with emphasis on the basic skills of both oral and written communication, prepare students to enroll in top-level undergraduate and graduate programs and to become constructive members of the national and international community. A high school diploma (or its equivalent) is required and a willingness to become the disciplined one—the disciple of the Great God Self of all.

Summit University is a way of life that is an integral part of Camelot—an Aquarian-age community secluded on a beautiful 218-acre campus in the Santa Monica Mountains west of Los Angeles near the beaches of Malibu. Here ancient truths become the law of everyday living to hundreds of kindred souls brought together again for the fulfillment of the mission of the Christ through the oneness of the Holy Spirit.

Montessori International is the place prepared at Camelot for the tutoring of the souls of younger seekers on the path. A private school for infants through twelfth grade, Montessori International was founded in 1970 by Mark and Elizabeth Prophet as an alternative to the public schools for their children. Dedicated to the spirit of the principles set forth by Dr. Maria Montessori earlier in this century, Montessori International strives not only for academic excellence, but for the standard of the Christ and the true education of the heart.

For those aspiring to become teachers of these little ones, Summit University Level II offers a special in-depth study of the methods taught by Maria Montessori, as well as her life and work. Those completing the initial phase of this course may then elect to pursue a nine-month internship at Montessori International.

For information write or call Camelot, Box A, Malibu, CA 90265 (818) 880-5300.

Summit University does not discriminate on the basis of race, color, sex, national or ethnic origin in its admission policies, programs, and activities.

BOOKS IN PRINT

Paperback

STUDIES OF THE HUMAN AURA
by Kuthumi $3.95

INTERMEDIATE STUDIES OF THE HUMAN AURA
by Djwal Kul $5.95

STUDIES IN ALCHEMY
The Science of Self-Transformation
by Saint Germain $3.95

INTERMEDIATE STUDIES IN ALCHEMY
Alchemical Formulas for Self-Mastery
by Saint Germain $3.95

FORBIDDEN MYSTERIES OF ENOCH
The Untold Story of Men and Angels
by Elizabeth Clare Prophet $9.95

THE LOST YEARS OF JESUS
by Elizabeth Clare Prophet $14.95

PRAYER AND MEDITATION
by Jesus and Kuthumi (Saint Francis) $6.95

THE SCIENCE OF THE SPOKEN WORD
Mark L. Prophet/Elizabeth Clare Prophet $4.95

MYSTERIES OF THE HOLY GRAIL
by Archangel Gabriel $9.95

UNDERSTANDING YOURSELF
Doorway to the Superconscious
by Kuthumi, Lanto, and Meru $4.95

CORONA CLASS LESSONS
A Manual for Ministering Servants
For Those Who Would Teach Men the Way
by Jesus and Kuthumi (Saint Francis) $9.95

QUIETLY COMES THE BUDDHA
by Gautama Buddha $3.95

DOSSIER ON THE ASCENSION
The Story of the Soul's Acceleration into Higher Consciousness on the Path of Initiation
by Serapis Bey $4.95

THE CHELA AND THE PATH
Meeting the Challenge of Life in the Twentieth Century
by El Morya $3.95

VIALS OF THE SEVEN LAST PLAGUES
The Judgments of Almighty God
Delivered by The Seven Archangels $4.95

COSMIC CONSCIOUSNESS
as the highest expression of Heart
by Lanello $5.95

THE GREAT WHITE BROTHERHOOD
in the Culture, History, and Religion of America
by Elizabeth Clare Prophet $8.95

CLIMB THE HIGHEST MOUNTAIN
The Path of the Higher Self
by Mark and Elizabeth Prophet $14.95

MORYA
The Darjeeling Master speaks to his chelas
On the Quest for the Holy Grail
by El Morya $9.95

MY SOUL DOTH MAGNIFY THE LORD!
New Age Rosary and New Age Teachings of Mother Mary $4.95

PROPHECY FOR THE 1980s
The Handwriting on the Wall
by Elizabeth Clare Prophet $1.95

Hardback

CLIMB THE HIGHEST MOUNTAIN
by Mark and Elizabeth Prophet $19.95

THE SACRED ADVENTURE
by El Morya $4.95

Pearls of Wisdom—An Anthology of Teachings of the Ascended Masters for Discipleship in the New Age
Mark L. Prophet • Elizabeth Clare Prophet

THE MECHANIZATION CONCEPT
Mysteries of God on the Creation of Mechanized Man Vol. 8 $9.95

THE MASTERS' PRESENCE
On Consciousness
Spiritual Education for the New Age Vol. 11 $9.95

KUTHUMI
On Selfhood
Consciousness: The Doorway to Reality Vol. 12 $10.95

SAINT GERMAIN
On the Freedom to Create
Secrets of Alchemy for the Path of Transmutation Vol. 13 $9.95

MASTERS OF THE FAR EAST
On the Pillars of Eternity
Mysteries of the Eternal Christ Vol. 14 $9.95

MARY THE MOTHER
On the Temple of Understanding
A Challenge to the Christian World Vol. 15 $9.95

THE SEVEN CHOHANS
On the Path of the Ascension
The Opening of the Temple Doors Vol. 16 $9.95

DJWAL KUL
On the Aura and the Chakras
Meditation and Mastery in the Sacred Fire of the Heart Vol. 17 $10.95

EL MORYA
On Discipleship East and West
The Path of the Darjeeling Master and His Chelas Vol. 18 $10.95

SAINT GERMAIN
On Freedom
A Prophecy of America's Destiny Vol. 20 $9.95

SPOKEN BY ELOHIM
For Contact with the Inner God Vol. 21 $11.95

A PROPHECY OF KARMA TO EARTH AND HER EVOLUTIONS
From the Last Days of Atlantis to the Present Era Vol. 23 $11.95

WHERE THE EAGLES GATHER
The Story of the Western Shamballa and the Journey to the Heart of the Inner Retreat (2-volume set) Vol. 24 $33.00

Available through your local bookstore. When ordering from the publisher add $1.00 postage and handling.

For more information on this summer's Summit University Retreat at the Royal Teton Ranch—survival seminars, wilderness treks, teachings of Saint Germain, dictations from the ascended masters, dynamic decrees, prophecy on political and social issues, personal initiation through the messenger of the Great White Brotherhood, meditation, yoga, the science of the spoken Word, seminars on personal and planetary astrology, children's program, Glastonbury, a self-sufficient spiritual community, summer camping and RV accommodations—call 406/848-7381 or write Royal Teton Ranch, Box A, Corwin Springs, Montana 59021 U.S.A.

For information on Summit University, Montessori International, retreats, conferences, and seminars conducted by Elizabeth Clare Prophet, and Pearls of Wisdom, write Summit University Press, Box A, Malibu, California, 90265 or Box A, Livingston, Montana, 59047 U.S.A. (406) 222-8300. Our International Headquarters is located at Camelot, 26800 West Mulholland Highway (corner of Mulholland Highway and Las Virgenes Road), Calabasas, California, 91302 U.S.A., phone: (818) 880-5300. For further information write for the address of the Community Teaching Center nearest you.